Marketing Island Destinations

Marketing Island Destinations
Concepts and Cases

Edited by

Acolla Lewis-Cameron
Sherma Roberts

ELSEVIER

AMSTERDAM • BOSTON • HEIDELBERG • LONDON • NEW YORK • OXFORD • PARIS • SAN DIEGO
SAN FRANCISCO • SINGAPORE • SYDNEY • TOKYO

Elsevier
32 Jamestown Road London NW1 7BY
30 Corporate Drive, Suite 400, Burlington, MA 01803, USA

First published 2010

Notices
Knowledge and best practice in this field are constantly changing. As new research
and experience broaden our understanding, changes in research methods, professional
practices, or medical treatment may become necessary.

Practitioners and researchers must always rely on their own experience and knowledge in
evaluating and using any information, methods, compounds, or experiments described herein.
In using such information or methods they should be mindful of their own safety and the
safety of others, including parties for whom they have a professional responsibility.

To the fullest extent of the law, neither the Publisher nor the authors, contributors, or editors,
assume any liability for any injury and/or damage to persons or property as a matter of
products liability, negligence or otherwise, or from any use or operation of any methods,
products, instructions, or ideas contained in the material herein.

British Library Cataloguing in Publication Data
A catalogue record for this book is available from the British Library

Library of Congress Cataloging-in-Publication Data
A catalog record for this book is available from the Library of Congress

ISBN: 978-0-12-384909-0

For information on all Elsevier publications
visit our website at www.elsevierdirect.com

This book has been manufactured using Print On Demand technology. Each copy is
produced to order and is limited to black ink. The online version of this book will show
colour figures where appropriate.

Working together to grow
libraries in developing countries

www.elsevier.com | www.bookaid.org | www.sabre.org

ELSEVIER   BOOK AID International   Sabre Foundation

Transferred to Digital Printing in 2011

Table of Contents

Preface

Over the past three decades, tourism has emerged as a major force in the global economy, with most countries, whether developed or developing, having increasing opportunities to participate, as both host and guest, in this socio-economic phenomenon. Competition for a share of the tourism market has intensified as rapid tourism developments have been undertaken by various destinations in an attempt to reap those economic benefits from one of the world's leading industries. The growth in tourism has propelled significant changes in the way in which destinations are managed and marketed. The challenge for many small island destinations is how to become or remain competitive. It is against this background that destination marketing has assumed the critical role of ensuring that the destination life cycle does not enter into a stage of saturation and decline, and the destination is able to adapt to the changing marketplace, seize opportunities and sustain its vitality.

The editors of this book are both Caribbean nationals and tourism academicians. Based on our research and experience in the industry in the region, we have recognized that there is a dearth of information available in the area of destination marketing in the Caribbean and by extension, other Small Island Developing States (SIDS). Tourism has been the mainstay of many island economies for several decades and therefore these islands are well positioned to share their marketing successes and challenges. To date, there has been much literature published in the areas of Tourism Marketing and Marketing in Travel and Tourism where the emphasis is on applying the four Ps of marketing to tourism. The focus of the content of the majority of the texts in these areas is the marketing of the tourism product, i.e. accommodation and transport. This book takes a holistic approach and considers marketing from a macro perspective, from the view of the destination.

The book makes a unique contribution to the literature on destination marketing in three noteworthy ways. First, it takes a multi-dimensional approach to the area by addressing the amalgam of issues involved in the marketing of a destination. This is distinct from the one-dimensional approach adopted by the more recent publications. Second, it seeks to capture the practice of destination marketing and its concomitant challenges at the ground level. By prefacing the case study discussions with the conceptual framework of destination marketing, it provides a rich balance of theory and practice in action. Third, it adopts an SIDS perspective of destination marketing, which adds tremendous value to the literature. The majority of the destinations under study are tourism-dependent islands and therefore destination marketing takes on a different meaning in this context, as it is a means to economic survival.

Contributions for this book have been received from both academics and practitioners in the Caribbean, the Mediterranean and the South Pacific, thus providing a rich balance in terms of contexts and perspectives. The core areas of branding, image development and management, niche marketing and crisis marketing have been well developed in the case studies. The inclusion of discussion questions at the end of chapter gives users of this book an opportunity to engage with the key issues and to apply the suggested frameworks to their specific contexts. The research findings presented in this book are timely and, we believe, will be relevant to academics, practitioners and students of island destinations and strategic destination marketing.

We want to take this opportunity to firstly thank all our contributors for their invaluable input into this text and for their patience in staying the course and seeing the process through to completion in the midst of the various setbacks. It has certainly been a pleasure working with you all and we trust that we can do this again. We thank the publisher, Elsevier, for willingly accepting this project and for their support and guidance throughout the publishing process. Thanks to our family and friends who have been pillars of support in so many ways. Last, but NOT least, thanks to the **Lord Jesus Christ** for His love, grace and patience.

Foreword

One of the notable features of the development of tourism studies over recent years has been a de-centring of tourism knowledge and research. This has enabled two important developments to take place. The first of these is that the issues and problems of tourism have widened out from the narrow and somewhat self-centred concerns of the well-established metropolitan centres of tourism and tourism research. The second related development is a growth in academic capacity in tourism studies that is now more widely distributed throughout the world. These two factors mean that we can look forward to an era of the surfacing and analysis of regional issues by regionally based academics.

The editors of this book, Dr. Acolla Lewis-Cameron and Dr. Sherma Roberts, are both nationals of the Caribbean, now based at the University of the West Indies, but both have been educated in the Caribbean and in the United Kingdom. They therefore bring a nuanced, hybrid view to the issues of importance to Island States and contribute to the ability of Island States to understand, analyse and solve problems with a deep and sensitive contextual knowledge and on their own terms. Thus, the cases represented in this text provide deep regional insights on how islands, many of which are very tourism-dependent, are grappling with the rapid changes taking place in their sources markets, among their consumers, and within their own national and regional spaces. How these 'global' transformations are impacting upon the marketing of island destinations are therefore worthy of analytical consideration and have been addressed by many of the authors in this volume.

The editors together with other academic colleagues have already put down a marker of regional academic self-sufficiency by their recent (2009) organization of the First International Caribbean Tourism Conference, held at the University of the West Indies, Barbados. This book – *Marketing Island Destinations: Concepts and Cases* – is an important further milestone in this journey.

John Tribe
Professor of Tourism
University of Surrey, 2010

Contributors

Jennifer V. Barrow
The University of the West Indies,
Cave Hill, Barbados,
West Indies

Anne Campbell
University of Canberra,
Canberra,
Australia

Erdogan H. Ekiz
Taylor's University College,
Malaysia

Kashif Hussain
Taylor's University College,
Malaysia

Stanislav Ivanov
International University College,
Bulgaria

Carolyn James
St Kitts Tourism Authority,
Toronto,
Canada

Acolla Lewis-Cameron
The University of the West Indies,
St Augustine, Trinidad and Tobago,
West Indies

Devon Liburd
Nevis Tourism Authority,
Nevis,
West Indies

Novelette Morton
St Kitts Tourism Authority,
Toronto,
Canada

Barney G. Pacheco
The University of the West Indies,
St Augustine, Trinidad and Tobago,
West Indies

Girish Prayag
SKEMA Business School,
France

Bruce Prideaux
James Cook University,
Queensland,
Australia

Sherma Roberts
The University of the West Indies,
Cave Hill, Barbados,
West Indies

Julie Tate-Libby
University of Otago,
Dunedin,
New Zealand

Terry Watson
James Cook University,
Queensland,
Australia

1 Small Island Developing States: Issues and Prospects

Acolla Lewis-Cameron* and Sherma Roberts[§]

*The University of the West Indies, St Augustine, Trinidad and Tobago, West Indies; [§]The University of the West Indies, Cave Hill, Barbados, West Indies

Introduction

Often referred to as the Barbados Programme of Action (BPOA), The United Nations Global Conference on the Sustainable Development of Small Island Developing States (SIDS) hosted in Bridgetown Barbados in 1994 affirmed the commitment of over 40 SIDS to improving the quality of life of all their residents, building and strengthening institutional capacities and reiterating their sovereign rights over ownership of their resources (www.sidsnet.org). The states also acknowledged their economic, social and environmental constraints and vulnerabilities, and declared that these could be mitigated, and the long-term goal of sustainable livelihoods achieved through joint action and the formation of sustained, equitable and working partnerships with inter-governmental, non-governmental and other agencies. The BPOA, rooted in Chapter 17 of Agenda 21, identified a number of activities that each small state should pursue, including distance education, environmental education, global sea-level monitoring, natural hazards and disaster management, preservation of tangible and intangible cultural heritage, and the application of information and communication technologies (ICTs) to mitigate the problems of isolation. The conference also recognized the need to harness tourism potential but also the need to manage its negative environmental and sociocultural impacts.

The foregoing discussion highlights the issues and aspirations of many small island developing states, then and now. In view of the openness of their economies, relative peripherality and costs associated with production and trade, many of these islands have opted to use tourism as a developmental tool, pursuing their comparative advantages. While the rhetoric of constraints and challenges has largely remained, a more positive discourse has been developing (Scheyvens & Momsen, 2008) and has sought to valorize the cultural heritage and norms of SIDS. The latter also highlights the desire of many of these islands to protect their social and cultural heritage, increase their wealth and mitigate their vulnerabilities. This chapter therefore considers the tourism potential of SIDS by examining their vulnerabilities as well as their strengths and the implications of these for strategic marketing and destination competitiveness.

Marketing Island Destinations. DOI: 10.1016/B978-0-12-384909-0.00001-5

Definitions of SIDS

Quantitative definitions of SIDS tend to focus on population size. However, over the last five decades these bands have changed considerably. For example, in 1950–60 a small state was defined as a country with a population size of 10–15 million; in 1970–80 this figure was lowered to 5 million, and in 2000 a small state was seen as a geographic region with fewer than 1.5 million people. Others (Downes, 2001) use 'an upper limit of 5 million people to denote a small country'. Weaver (2001) employs a similar definition, stating that 'small island states are dependencies with less than three million permanent residents and a land area of no more than 28,000 km squared'.

The more widely cited definitions, however, have to do with qualitative descriptors of SIDS. In these definitions, SIDS are described as being environmentally fragile, low-lying coastal countries that share similar sustainable development challenges, including small population, limited resources, remoteness, susceptibility to natural disasters, vulnerability to external shocks and excessive dependence on international trade (UN Department of Economic and Social Affairs, www.un.org/esa/desa). Furthermore, it is argued that the growth and development of these islands is often stymied by high transportation, production, export and communication costs, governance constraints, disproportionately expensive public administration and little opportunity to create economies of scale (Briguglio, 2007).

The Sidsnet website (www.sidsnet.org) lists 51 countries that fall within the definition of SIDS. Most of them have membership in the Commonwealth, 6 belong to the African continent, 23 are from Latin American/Caribbean and 22 are located within the Asia-Pacific region. While graduation from SIDS to newly industrialized country (NIC) or more-developed country (MDC) should be regarded as highly desirable, the reality is that graduation often comes with removal of special concessions and loss of preferential treatment pertaining to financing, aid, trade and access to markets and trade (Kisanga & Mitchell, 2007). Consequently, many of these islands while showing notable improvements on the United Nations Human Development Index (UNHDI) and reflecting relatively well-managed economies prefer to maintain their status rather than jeopardize the gains they have made in the new global economic order. Concomitantly, 'the UN does not penalize countries for demonstrating good economic management by graduating them if this will result in their being worse off after graduation than before' (Kisanga & Mitchell, 2007:281). Botswana has been noted by the authors as a model of graduation as it continues to record outstanding growth.

Traditional Perspectives on SIDS

The challenges and vulnerabilities of SIDS have been well documented. Accordingly this section will address only three – high reliance on foreign resource flows, peripherality and high vulnerabilities to exogenous events. Small island states are usually perceived as being highly donor-dependent whether it is with respect to technical cooperation or capital financing of projects. Within the tourism industry, this dependence has historically led to a high degree of foreign ownership of the tourism superstructure (Brohman, 1996; Freitag, 1994), with locals occupying the base of the pyramid in terms of ownership and employment. The new calls for more sustainable and equitable involvement of locals in the tourism industry have been very much reflected in the tourism master plans of most SIDS. However, the reality remains that the majority of residents do not have the capital required to finance hotel and other sizeable projects, so that equitable involvement may only be at the low end of the entrepreneurial spectrum.

Many SIDS are located more than eight or nine hours away from their main generating markets, which are usually the United States, Canada and Europe. While remoteness has been lauded as a strength (Scheyvens & Momsen, 2008) and has been diminished somewhat as a result of developments in transportation and ICTs, the reality is that peripherality and remoteness impact considerably upon the cost of travel and often the cost of goods and services that go into making the tourist experience. As noted by Craigwell (2007:20), 'the cost of airline travel is found to be negatively related to market share, which indicates that the further the destination from the source market, the less competitive that destination is likely to be'. This insularity is compounded by the new environmental movement, which is referred by some as eco-imperialism (Mowforth & Munt, 1998) and which is being embraced by governments who are championing domestic tourism. For example, former British Prime Minister Gordon Brown called on Britons to 'holiday at home', and Australia in 2009 embarked on a 'no leave no life' campaign aimed at getting its residents to use their holiday entitlements at home. While promoting and protecting national and environmental interests, these campaigns will have an impact upon the competitiveness of many tourism-dependent small states.

Small states are highly susceptible to a number of risks that make them more vulnerable than some of their larger counterparts. The risks range from economic to environmental, and if not well managed these can have a deleterious effect on the socio-economic fabric of many islands. The environmental risks include natural disasters, sea-level rise, tsunamis, earthquakes and poor waste management. The preponderance of coastal tourism in many SIDS has implications for the existence of healthy coastal habitats (wetlands, beaches and dunes, sea grass beds, mangroves, coral reefs, estuaries, etc.). The January 2010 earthquake in Haiti, which killed at least 250 000 persons, bears witness to the devastation that can be wreaked by a natural disaster. It also highlights the lack of capabilities of some SIDS to handle the onslaught of natural disasters. Grenade (2008) also addresses socio-economic vulnerabilities in a discussion on HIV/AIDS in Grenada. She argues that HIV/AIDS poses a real threat to small open economies such as Grenada's and cause a dilemma for the island: on the one hand tourism is a vehicle for economic development but on the other it can facilitate the spread of diseases that can undermine the very development the government is working towards.

The global economic crisis has highlighted the economic vulnerability of many SIDS that are highly dependent on one export – tourism. The massive lay-off in the source countries of the United States and the United Kingdom saw a concomitant decline in tourist arrivals for many of these islands. Consequently, there have been significant declines in government revenues, with many governments opting to go to the International Monetary Fund for loans to fund capital projects, service debts and control recurrent expenditure.

The discussion on the challenges of SIDS cannot be discounted and every effort must be made by these states to counter, mitigate and cope with all of these issues. However, the traditional conceptualizations of SIDS are only but part of the conversation. The other part highlights the strengths of small states and the way in which these strengths have and can be used to position SIDS more competitively.

New Perspectives on Small Island Developing States

In contrast to the traditional perspectives presented above, some authors (Scheyvens & Momsen, 2008; Turnball, 2003) argue that there is another reality of SIDS that is under-represented in the generic development and tourism literature. These authors reason that once we move beyond narrow neo-liberal discourses on development that only privilege notions of economic growth, we might acknowledge that small island states have strengths that can be utilized to gain competitiveness. The following discussion focuses on the strengths of small states, including democracy, improved standard of living and quality of life as evidenced by the UNHDI and the social, cultural, natural and intellectual capital that is resident either locally in many SIDS or through transnational diaspora networks. The discussion makes the point that these strengths are necessary and vital conditions for the development of a competitive and sustainable tourism industry and should therefore be included in the 'development conversation' on islands.

One of the often overlooked strengths of many SIDS is that many have 'emerged into statehood through the tried and tested procedure of tutelary devolution of responsibility and the adoption and adaptation of the Westminster–Whitehall system of government and administration' (Sutton, 2007:202). In other words, transitioning from colonial rule to independence for many was achieved through a peaceful democratic system of free, fair and competitive elections. In its 2010 survey of states, Freedom House (www.freedomhouse.org) confirms that many SIDS (using the 1.5 million population definition) continue to experience a relatively high degree of freedom, with 28 states being classified as free, 14 as partially free and 6 as not free. Similar studies also suggest that SIDS by and large have fairly strong democratic systems as evidenced in political freedom, civil liberties and political rights (Ott, 2000; Hadenius, 1992, cited in Sutton, 2007). Safety and security are critical factors when choosing a tourism destination, and so democracy and certain civil liberties cannot be discounted. In fact, it is this sense of security that visitors have identified as one of the critical brand elements in the Barbados tourism product.

Small states are also able to command resources, aid and some degree of power and respect owing to their historical antecedents (many being former colonies of France, Britain, Spain or Holland) and sovereign rights as states (Campling, 2006). For example, at the United Nations General Assembly small states have utilized the 'politics of scale' to secure equal voting rights with much larger countries and are able to vote as blocs with a major power who offers the most state-specific incentives.

Over recent years, many Caribbean countries have been recipients of generous capacity and infrastructural development initiatives by the People's Republic of China (www.caribbeannetnews.com). In fact, Cuba – a non-free Commonwealth state – also competes with the larger countries through its use of medical and educational diplomacy. While the geographical location of many SIDS makes them vulnerable to natural disasters, the converse of this is that their strategic geo-political location has made many of these islands critical to the United States and Europe.

Many small states have also shown notable improvements in their rankings on the UNHDI (United Nations Human Development Report, 2009) that go beyond income to measure life expectancy, gender equality, adult literacy, access to basic needs, etc. The 2009 Human Development Report reveals that many SIDS are in the high to medium human development ranking, with Barbados occupying 37th place in the very high HDI and Guinea-Bissau 173rd rank in the low HDI (www.hdr.undp.org). Downes (2007) points out that small states in the Commonwealth have performed fairly well in providing universal primary education, although many still lag behind when it comes to universal secondary education. Many small states have also shown improvements in access to basic health care, declining infant mortality rates, regular servicing and preventative education on chronic diseases such as hypertension and diabetes, improvements on physical and technological infrastructure and access to fundamental liberties. In terms of gender equity and female empowerment, Barbados, the Bahamas and Trinidad and Tobago 'outrank Japan, Italy, Portugal, Greece and all of the new Central European countries' in giving women access to participation in civil society (Pulsipher & Holderfield, 2006:301). While women in the Commonwealth small states have been able to outnumber or achieve parity with men in the educational system, they have been noticeably absent in the political arena (Downes, 2007). These combined improvements have created an environment that is conducive to tourism development in many SIDS. In addition, the progress made on the UNHDI has also been reflected in the level of travel and tourism competitiveness for at least two SIDS – Mauritius and Barbados (World Economic Forum, 2009).

Small island developing states possess a rich cultural and natural heritage and in many cases strong intellectual and social capital. The coral reefs, rivers, sea and landscape, biodiversity, intangible and tangible heritage all attest to the high capital resident in many SIDS. These are often the elements that serve as the pull factor for many tourists. The emergence of what has been described by Poon (1993) as the new tourist who is looking for an experience beyond the traditional sun, sea and sand (3S) offerings should find island states very appealing. We have seen recently a concerted attempt by many SIDS to valorize their cultural expressions whether through the food, music, dance, rituals or sportsmanship. The current Jamaican tourism marketing campaign is using sprinter Ussain Bolt as an industry champion. This shift away from the 3Ss also marks a departure from a tourism industry premised upon modernization ideas where only that which is Western is privileged and marketed. Moreover, what is marketed serves to reinforce images and misconceptions of islands as primitive, backward and untouched 'paradises':

> ... some of [the withdrawal by the tourists] is as a result of tourist's ignorance ...
> but island people are also at fault for not adequately and proactively defining and

marketing their islands as modern societies worth visiting. ... The tours they offer are too often bland and nearly devoid of intellectual content, focusing on nothing more than smiling faces, pretty vistas, a few scraps of inaccurate history and trivializing comments about local people.

Pulsipher and Holderfield (2006:299)

Earlier in the discussion, reference was made to the strident gains made by many SIDS in terms of economic growth and other developments. Among them has been at least five Nobel Laureates, one hailing from Mauritius and four 'sons of the Caribbean soil'. The social and intellectual capital of these islands has also been enhanced by the vast diaspora scattered in many metropolitan countries, 'who constitute a huge reservoir of capital, information, information and material resources ... remittance flows from overseas migrant communities are as valued as direct financial aid and assistance' (Potter, Barker, Conway, & Klak, 2004:447). While the diaspora for many SIDS represents remittances, the diaspora potential goes beyond this and remains largely untapped. In countries such as Taiwan, the US-based diaspora was key in facilitating technology transfer and cross-border technological learning (Saxenian, 2001). Given that many small states have emigration rates of between 50% and 90% of their skilled, university-educated labour force (Adams & Page, 2003), the potential is there for many SIDS to build knowledge economies and networks and a more resilient tourism industry through focused diaspora strategies.

The diaspora also represents untapped potential when it comes to tourism. Normally categorized as the VFR (visiting friends and relatives), the value of diasporic tourism is largely underestimated as it is seen as the 'poor cousin' of international tourism (Scheyvens, 2007). Asiedu (2005) points out that Ghanaian nationals returning home spend on average £2769 on international travel, £585 on incidentals and £433 on food and entertainment. A smaller amount of £274 was spent on commercial accommodation. In addition to the financial benefit of spending within the economy, the diaspora through various associations (e.g. the alumni in Guyana) strengthens the social and economic fabric of their communities through donations such as computers, books, school refurbishment projects, equipment and mentorship schemes (Roberts, 2009). Thus, unlike the 'Northerner' who visits the destination to sample its climate, culinary and cultural offerings and leaves with a 'tan, memories and photos', the diaspora visitor invests significant funds to build up the social infrastructure of his homeland (Potter, 2005, cited in Scheyvens, 2007). Moreover, as Scheyvens (2007:311) posits, this group is not vulnerable to changing international tastes, perceived security threats or media representations of their home country.

Even against the challenges that they face, island states have always declared their right to self-determination. While all small states may not be at the same development stage or can attest to achieving all of the gains presented above, the evidence suggests that many across the Caribbean and a few in the Asia-Pacific and Africa region have made positive strides in progressing towards the Millennium Development Goals. These gains should not be underestimated as they form the basis of factors that influence demand in the tourist-generating region. Safety and security, a fairly well-developed tourism superstructure and educated workforce and rich cultural and natural legacies, some of which have incredible marquis value, are all critical demand determinants. These strengths need to be given more attention so that the discourse of powerlessness, non-viability and vulnerability is not taken as a priori and accepted by the next generation of island progeny.

Tourism Flows to SIDS – Implications for Competitiveness and Destination Marketing

Possessing natural comparative advantages such as salubrious climate, pristine coral reefs, compelling architectural heritage, a smorgasbord of culinary offerings, rich and vibrant cultures and friendly and welcoming people, many small island states have explicitly and deliberately chosen tourism as a development option. With the exception of a few of these states, tourism is the main economic driver. The rationale for tourism-induced development is premised upon the belief that it generates much-needed foreign exchange, increases employment numbers, fosters intersectoral linkages and promotes entrepreneurship (Lea, 1993; Lickorish & Jenkins, 2005). The period 1986–2004 shows an increase of almost 10% in tourist arrivals and 11% in visitor expenditure. Growth in foreign exchange earnings was also recorded as three times that of export of goods. Direct tourism employment also doubled over the same period (Craigwell, 2007). With respect to tourism's direct contribution to GDP, Craigwell (2007:3) notes that it has grown from 'US$3.2 billion in 1988 to US$9.2 billion in 2004 and its direct and indirect contribution has also jumped from US$6.9 billion to US$18.8 million'.

The key generating markets for many SIDS are the United States, the United Kingdom and Canada. In the Asia-Pacific region, islands such as Fiji and Guam showed minimal increases in both their arrivals and receipts even though this region's share of tourism market had showed an overall increase of 7.8% in 2000–2007 (World Travel and Tourism Control (WTTC), 2008). In the Americas, international tourism arrivals grew by 3% in 2005–2007. However, this growth was highest in the Central and South American countries of Panama, Honduras, Ecuador and Chile. Growth among SIDS in this region, particularly the Caribbean, was minimal at 1% and has since declined even further, largely as a result of the global economic crisis and the introduction of the Western Hemisphere Travel Initiative (WHTI) and the Airline Passenger Duty imposed by the United Kingdom. For example, Barbados saw a decrease (-0.8%) in US visitors but an increase of 5.3% in Canadian visitors in 2008. Similar trends were recorded in the Bahamas and Bermuda. Cruise passenger arrivals have, however, increased exponentially in many of the Caribbean island destinations between 2007 and 2008 (Caribbean Tourism Organization, 2010). In the African region, SIDS have been making positive strides, with Mauritius and the Seychelles registering a 15% increase in arrivals in 2006–2007 and Mauritius an increase of 4% in tourism receipts (WTTC, 2008).

Craigwell (2007) argues that most of the SIDS have not been able to fully exploit the European market despite its size. The reasons for this may be the price sensitivity of this market, the high number of substitutes, and the costs in terms of airfare and accommodation. These factors raise questions regarding the competitiveness of many SIDS. The Travel and Tourism Competitiveness Index (World Economic Forum, 2009) shows only two SIDS, Barbados (no. 30) and Mauritius (no. 40), coming in the top 50 countries for overall destination competitiveness. The T&T Competitiveness Index is based upon a destination's competitiveness in a number of areas including safety and security, health and hygiene, air transport infrastructure, ICT infrastructure, cultural resources and price competitiveness. A similar study on SIDS' competitiveness found that the overall competitiveness of SIDS is below that of developed countries but slightly higher than the global level. Small island states were found to be uncompetitive in terms of hotel accommodation, technological and social development and air transport (Craigwell, 2007). While the grouping has maintained its 2% share of the global tourism market over the last few years, the current global economic crisis, the threat of climate change, the incentives to 'holiday at home', and the growth of the discerning and price-conscious tourist, among other factors, can potentially threaten this small but critical share.

Increasing competitiveness requires the combined efforts of destination marketing organizations and policy makers. The policy makers are needed to create an environment that is conducive to competitive business practices including the appropriate pricing of non-traded inputs (energy, telecommunications and business services) (Craigwell, 2007). The marketing agencies need to ensure that their marketing efforts and limited budgets are underpinned by current and robust research. Clear identification of target markets, distribution channels and communication strategies are all critical. Even more important is the profiling of the consumer whose needs are changing rapidly but who ultimately is looking for good value for money. Market diversification is another strategy that SIDS should consider. The current financial crisis has underscored the fragility of dependence on one or two source markets. Perhaps SIDS should begin to explore the growing markets of China, Brazil and India whose population and per capita income are increasing.

In the Asia-Pacific and Caribbean regions, cooperative marketing has been made possible through the Pacific Asia Travel Association and the Caribbean Tourism Organization. These organizations are able to represent their membership in key generating markets and lobby on their behalf to governments, principals and other industry players. One of the critical functions of these bodies is the strategic intelligence support which they provide to their membership and which includes inbound and outbound statistics, analyses and forecasts as well as in-depth reports in strategic tourism markets.

Conclusion

Understanding the challenges that face many SIDS is very important. Equally significant is an understanding of the strengths of these islands and the ways in which these strengths can be leveraged to achieve destination competitiveness. Destination marketing organizations are required to search for innovative ways to exploit these strengths, including the use of ICTs, the formation of strategic partnerships, the exploration of new niche and source markets, and destination branding.

The chapters in this book address both challenges and innovations for strategic destination marketing as SIDS strive to become or remain competitive. The first part of the book provides the general context for the case study discussions that follow in part two. This opening chapter succinctly captures the nature of SIDS with specific emphasis on the challenges and strengths that set them apart from mainland destinations. The following chapter examines the role that strategic destination marketing plays in establishing a competitive advantage for SIDS. Some key destination marketing concepts are explored, including image development, destination branding and clarifying the target market. These two chapters lay the foundation for the second part of the book, which explores the specific issues in the respective destinations.

References

Adams, R., & Page, J. (2003). *International migration, remittances and poverty in developing countries*. World Bank Policy Research Working Paper 3179. www.worldbank.org. Accessed 10 March 2010.

Antigua-Barbuda receives further support from China. www.caribbean nettnews.com. Accessed 20 March 2010.

Asiedu, A. (2005). Some benefits of migrants' return visits to Ghana. *Population, Space and Place, 11*, 1–11.

Barbados Programme of Action. *Small Island Developing States Network*, www.sidsnet.org. Accessed 7 February 2010.

Briguglio, L. (2007). Economic vulnerability and resilience: Concepts and measurements. In E. Kisanga & S. Danchie (Eds.), *Commonwealth small states: Issues and prospects* (pp. 99–109). London: Commonwealth Secretariat.

Brohman, J. (1996). New directions in tourism for third world development. *Development and Change, 23*(1), 48–70.

Campling, L. (2006). A critical political economy of the small island developing states concept: South–south cooperation for island citizens? *Journal of Developing Societies, 22*(3), 235–285.

Caribbean Tourism Organisation. *Air and cruise passenger statistics*. www.onecaribbean.org. Accessed 23 February 2010.

Craigwell, R. (2007). *Tourism competitiveness in small island developing states*. United Nations University–World Institute for Development Economics Research. Research Paper No. 2007/19.

Downes, A. (2007). Progress towards achieving the millennium development goals in the small states of the commonwealth. In E. Kisanga & S. Danchie (Eds.), *Commonwealth small states: Issues and prospects* (pp. 301–317). London: Commonwealth Secretariat.

Freedom in the World. (2010). *Table of independent countries*. www. freedomhouse.org. Accessed 26 March 2010.

Freitag, T. (1994). Enclave tourism development: For whom the benefits roll. *Annals of Tourism Research, 21*(3), 538–554.

Grenade, W. (2008). An unwelcome guest: Unpacking the tourism and HIV/AIDS dilemmas in the Caribbean: A case study of Grenada. In M. Daye, D. Chambers, & S. Roberts (Eds.), *New perspectives in Caribbean tourism* (pp. 88–218). New York: Routledge.

Kisanga, E., & Mitchell, C. (2007). Small states and graduation. In E. Kisanga & S. Danchie (Eds.), *Commonwealth small states: Issues and prospects* (pp. 279–300). London: Commonwealth Secretariat.

Lea, J. (1993). *Tourism development in the third world*. London: Routledge.

Lickorish, L., & Jenkins, C. (2005). *Tourism: An introduction*. Boston: Elsevier Butterworth-Heinemann.

Mowforth, M., & Munt, I. (1998). *Tourism and sustainability: New tourism in the third world*. London: Routledge.

Ott, D. (2000). *Small is democratic: An examination of state size and democratic development*. New York: Garland Publishing Inc.

Poon, A. (1993). *Tourism, technology and competitive strategies*. UK: CABI Publishing.

Potter, R., Barker, D., Conway, D., & Klak, T. (2004). *The contemporary Caribbean*. Harlow: Pearson-Prentice Hall.

Pulsipher, L., & Holderfield, L. (2006). Cruise tourism in the eastern Caribbean: An anachronism in the post-colonial era? In R. K. Dowling (Ed.), *Cruise ship tourism* (pp. 299–314). Oxon: CAB International.

Roberts, S. (2009). The socio-economic sustainability potential of diasporic tourism flows between toronto and guyana. *Research proposal presented at an authors' workshop on strategic opportunities in Caribbean migration: Brain circulation and diasporic tourism and investment*. Barbados: Sir Shridath Ramphal Centre, the University of the West Indies.

Saxenian, A. (2001). *Taiwan's Hsinchu Region: Imitator and Partner for Silicon Valley*. Revised Draft, SIEPR Discussion Paper no. 00-44. Stanford Institute for Economic Policy Research.

Scheyvens, R. (2007). Poor cousins no more: Valuing the development potential of domestic and diaspora tourism. *Progress in Development Studies, 7*(4), 307–325.

Scheyvens, R., & Momsen, J. (2008). Tourism in small island states: From vulnerability to strengths. *Journal of Sustainable Tourism, 16*(5), 491–510.

Sutton, P. (2007). Democracy and good governance in small states. In E. Kisanga & S. Danchie (Eds.), *Commonwealth small states: Issues and prospects* (pp. 201–217). London: Commonwealth Secretariat.

Telfer, D., & Sharpley, R. (2008). *Tourism and development in the developing world*. London: Routledge.

Turball, J. (2003). South Pacific agendas in the quest to protect natural areas. *Development and Change, 34*(1), 1–24.

United Nations Department of Economic and Social Affairs. www.un.org.esa/desa. Accessed 19 March 2010.

United Nations Human Development Report (2009). *HDI rankings*. www.hdr.undp.org. Accessed 19 March 2010.

Weaver, D. (2001). Mass tourism and alternative tourism in the Caribbean. In D. Harrison (Ed.), *Tourism and the less developed world: Issues and case studies.*(pp.161–174). Oxon: CABI Publishing.

World Economic Forum. (2009). *The travel and tourism competitiveness index 2009: Measuring sectoral drivers in a downturn*. World Economic Forum.

World Travel and Tourism Council. (2008). *Tourism highlights 2008*. Madrid: United Nations World Tourism Organisation.

2 Strategic Destination Marketing: The Key to a Competitive Advantage

Acolla Lewis-Cameron* and Sherma Roberts[§]

*The University of the West Indies, St Augustine, Trinidad and Tobago, West Indies; [§]The University of the West Indies, Cave Hill, Barbados, West Indies

Introduction

Over the last three decades, tourism has emerged as a major force in the global economy, with most countries, whether developed or developing, having increasing opportunities to participate, as both host and guest, in this socio-economic phenomenon. Competition for a share of the tourism market has intensified as rapid tourism developments have been undertaken by various destinations in an attempt to reap those economic benefits from one of the world's leading industries. Tourism demand has exploded in recent years from 565 million international arrivals in 1995 to an expected 1006 million in 2010 and an anticipated 1.6 billion by 2020 (World Tourism Organization WTO (2009a).

The growth in tourism has propelled significant changes in the way in which destinations are managed and marketed. The challenge for many destinations is how to become or remain competitive. According to Ritchie and Crouch (2003:2),

> what makes a tourism destination truly competitive is its ability to increase tourism expenditure, to increasingly attract visitors while providing them with satisfying, memorable experiences, and to do so in a profitable way, while enhancing the well-being of destination residents and preserving the natural capital of the destination for future generations.

It is against this background that destination marketing has assumed the critical role of ensuring that the destination life cycle does not enter into a stage of saturation and decline (Page & Connell, 2006) and that the destination is able to adapt to the changing marketplace, seize opportunities and sustain its vitality. Herein lies the challenge for Small Island Developing States (SIDS). Many island states have found it comparatively easy to attract tourists, and thus the tourism industry has become the cornerstone of the majority of these island economies. Although tourism has been criticized as a fragile form of development, it is, nevertheless, in an island context, almost universal (Weaver, 1995). It is this almost exclusive dependency on tourism in many cases that places extreme pressure on island states to remain competitive.

Marketing Island Destinations. DOI: 10.1016/B978-0-12-384909-0.00002-7

This chapter examines the role that strategic destination marketing plays in establishing a competitive advantage for SIDS. This is done against the backdrop of a discussion on the volatile global marketplace with emphasis on the key characteristics of the new operating environment. The focus then shifts to the strategic marketing response of SIDS in the face of changing global circumstances. This chapter lays the foundation for the destination cases, which highlight specific marketing strategies adopted by different SIDS in an attempt to become or remain competitive.

A Changing Global Marketplace

The international tourism landscape has changed dramatically over the last decade, with the industry welcoming *new* players, adapting to *new* tourists and responding to *new* crises. In the midst of this changing landscape, one constant over the last three decades has been the resiliency of the industry as an economic sector. According to the WTO (2009b), real per capita income continues to rise alongside international trips per head. The real challenge for SIDS is how to become and remain competitive in this new environment.

New Players

The fall of communism in Eastern Europe has given rise to the emergence of new market economies. This shift in political and economic systems has resulted in gravitation among these economies towards the development of tourism as a tool to facilitate entry into a Western economic system, underpinned by the traditional rationale of increasing foreign exchange and employment, regional and overall economic development. According to EuroMonitor International (2004), Eastern Europe offers the global travel and tourism industry a golden opportunity for growth. In the period 1999–2003, Eastern Europe experienced a growth rate of approximately 17%, which surpassed that of Western Europe and North America.

The growth in this region in particular can be credited to government investment in infrastructure and in the tourism industry. Furthermore, several of these nations were welcomed into the European Union (EU), which has opened doors for trade and investment. Along with this comes the benefit of the EU Structural and Cohesion Funds with a stable macroeconomic environment being a key conditionality. Finally, Eastern Europe has further opened its doors to low-cost airlines such as Sky Europe, which facilitates cheaper travel from Western Europe. This combination of market factors has placed Eastern Europe in a very favourable position vis-à-vis its competition. In terms of comparative advantage, these *new* tourist destinations possess a mystical appeal for the experienced tourist as emerging from behind the 'iron curtain', and they are well able to provide both the psychocentric and allocentric tourists with a product that can rival that of SIDS. Key markets to monitor include Slovakia, Bulgaria, Serbia and Montenegro as these territories continue to benefit from domestic investment in tourism and the appeal and growing availability of low-cost flights (EuroMonitor International, 2004).

'BRIC Countries are the world economy's building blocks'. This was the title of an article in *The Banker* magazine in 2005 (The Banker, 2005). According to the author, the fortunes of the world economy over the next decade would depend on what happens in the BRIC (Brazil, Russia, India and China) countries as these destinations were expected to be major players in the world economy by 2050. In a tourism context, it is estimated that China, for example, has great potential to be the top visitor destination within the next two decades. The WTO further predicted that China will generate 100 million arrivals worldwide by 2020, making it the fourth largest market in the world WTO (2009b). Similarly, India's tourism industry is experiencing a strong period of growth, driven by the burgeoning Indian middle-class, growth in high-spending foreign tourists, and coordinated government campaigns to promote 'Incredible India' (Economy Watch, 2009).

New Tourists

According to Poon (1993), the maturing of the tourist market is creating what she refers to as a *new* tourist. A clear demarcation is made between the 'old' or 'mass' tourist and this *new* tourist, who is characterized as more knowledgeable, experienced, sophisticated, discerning and flexible. There is a shift in the motivations for travel from passive sun-lust to educational and curiosity motives. Quality and value for money are a premium. For these tourists leisure and tourism have become part of their lifestyle. No longer is tourism seen as an escape, but rather viewed as a source of fulfilment.

There is also a shift in attitude as the mindset is 'see and enjoy but do not destroy', which points to greater environmental consciousness and stewardship. Holiday booking patterns have changed to a great extent, particularly in the United States, from travel agent dependency to the individual packaging of tailor-made vacations online.

A combination of factors is highlighted as the driving force behind this apparent shift from 'old' to 'new', including airline deregulation, environmental pressures, consumer protection and action by host countries to arrest the detrimental impacts of tourism development. Fundamentally, Poon's (1993) thesis is that the demand determinants and motivations of these new tourists are different from the 'old' and are framed in large part by changes in the global environment. These different motivations and interests have led to the development of new products, e.g. dark tourism (cemetery tourism), in an attempt to satisfy the interests of this market.

Arguably, there is insufficient evidence to suggest a complete shift away from mass or old tourism but rather an embracing of the new alternative forms of tourism. The frame conditions delineated earlier allow for the emergence of this *new* tourism, which is defined as 'a phenomenon of large-scale packaging of non-standardised leisure services at competitive prices to suit the demands of tourists as well as the economic & socio-environmental needs of destinations' (Poon, 1993:85). This new tourism landscape depicts both the 'old' and the 'new' tourist co-existing in the tourist-generating regions of the world.

New Crises

'Tourism Sector Looking Shaky' and 'Bleak Outlook for Tourism' are two of the many headlines in Latin America Monitor (2009) that point to the instability in the financial outlook for SIDS in the Caribbean. In the Bahamas, a *USA Today* report noted 'a year ago, tourists lined up to eat at Conch Fritters, a downtown restaurant there known for its blackened grouper, conch chowder and other local specialties. Yet, on a recent midweek night last month, tourists were scattered among just a few tables' (De Lollis & Hansen, 2009). The global economy faces an unprecedented crisis that has resulted in one of the world's worst recessions in generations. The world's economy is forecast to decline by some 1.3% in 2009, while preliminary figures for tourism in the first few months of 2009 indicated a continuation of a negative growth trend from the latter half of 2008 WTO (2009b). Destinations around the world have suffered from diminished demand in source markets, and many mass market island destinations have been hit hard because of their dependency on a few source markets, notably the Bahamas and the Dominican Republic. This global economic meltdown has forced SIDS in particular to re-examine their marketing strategies, seek to develop and promote new products, and identify new target markets. Moreover, this economic crisis has mandated introspection on the part of SIDS. It is a season of internal analysis and preparation. Those destinations that strategically organize themselves in this season will be the forces to reckon with when the global economy turns around.

Concomitant to the global financial crisis, many SIDS are obliged to cope with the impacts of climate change on their fragile natural environments. Carbon emissions have increased greatly over the last 150 years. The large-scale emissions of industrial gases such as carbon dioxide have contributed in no small measure to global warming and the erosion of the ozone layer. The global changes in climatic conditions have far-reaching implications for the Earth's climate. Notably, agriculture may become unviable over large parts of the world. The water supply for billions may fall to all-time lows. Rising sea levels will affect tourism destinations, particularly in SIDS, such as wetlands and coastal areas. Much of the tourism investment in SIDS is along the coast, and global warming will impact on tourism resources such as flora and fauna and beaches.

The relationship between climate change and tourism is biodirectional, in that tourism activity is both impacted by, as well as being a major contributor to this phenomenon. Thus, on the demand side, some transport modes contribute to climate change and will need to change. The seriousness of the situation has received international attention by the WTO (2003), which issued the *Djerba Declaration on Tourism and Climate Change*, urging governments to:

- adopt the Kyoto Protocol and its approximations on greenhouse gas emissions;
- research and collaborate on climate change;
- move tourism up the agenda in climate change discussions;
- implement sustainable water use practices and the ecological management of sensitive areas;
- raise consumer awareness of the issue.

The new consumers of tourism in particular are more environmentally conscious where they are cognizant of and taking responsibility for their carbon footprint. For example, carbon offsetting has emerged as an effective way to neutralize the greenhouse gases emitted by individual travel. Companies like lastminute.com provide their customers carbon offsetting schemes to help them be 'carbon neutral travellers'.

For SIDS, the implications are twofold. The environmentally conscious tourist is seeking out destinations that are committed to preserving their natural resources and minimizing their contribution to climate change. However, the environmental sustainability of SIDS depends heavily on a commitment to the proper management, responsible marketing and preservation of the destination's resources.

A Strategic Marketing Response

Wahab *et al.* (1976:24), as cited in Page and Connell (2006:320), outlined the scope of destination marketing as

> the management process through which the National Tourist organizations and/or tourist enterprises identify their selected tourist, actual and potential, communicate with them to ascertain and influence their wishes, needs, motivations, likes and dislikes, on local, regional, national and international levels and to formulate and adapt their tourist products accordingly in view of achieving optimal tourist satisfaction thereby fulfilling their objectives.

In operational terms, destination marketing is a strategic process that is built on competitive advantages, targeted markets and mixed marketing techniques, and appeals to actual and potential visitors. This strategic process involves the matching of the resources of a destination to the opportunities existing in the market. In this vein, each destination should seek to differentiate itself by highlighting its unique tangible and intangible products and services in such a way as to induce visitation. Moreover, the highly competitive global market for tourists mandates that destinations go beyond that initial visitation to engendering a degree of loyalty among their visitor base.

Against this backdrop of a changing global marketplace, it is incumbent on destinations to be proactive, resilient and strategic in their approach to marketing their destinations. One of the great challenges facing tourism managers is to understand why individuals choose one particular destination over the wide range of possibilities and how the destination ensures that these individuals keep visiting the destination and telling others about it. Some destinations have been immensely successful at this, notably, France and the United Kingdom in the North and Mexico in the South. A combination of factors is responsible for the success of these destinations, including effective imaging and branding and affordable packages. With the changing global marketplace, there is increasing opportunity for SIDS to gain some level of competitive advantage through the adoption of key strategic positions. The chapter continues with an analysis of the key strategic actions that must be considered by SIDS as they approach destination marketing in this dynamic global industry.

Clarifying My Identity

As destinations navigate this competitive global market, it is those destinations that understand who they are, what they are about and can effectively communicate that message to the 2020 tourists that will be recognized and patronized as they move towards 2020. It has now become an imperative that destinations, particularly SIDS, clarify their identity for the benefit of both the hosts and the guests. This involves considering two questions:

1. What is the destination's appeal?
2. What is the destination's representation of itself in the marketplace?

Destination's Appeal

Destinations are usually defined as 'specific places' or 'the focus of facilities and services designed to meet the needs of tourists' (Cooper *et al.*, 2008). According to the conceptual model of destination competitiveness (Ritchie & Crouch, 2003), it is the core resources and attractors that are the fundamental reasons why prospective tourists choose one destination over another. They note that the core resources and attractors are the primary motivations or pull factors for inbound tourism, and they identify physiography, culture and history, mix of activities, special events, entertainment and superstructure as the core pull factors at the destination.

What is of paramount importance for SIDS as they move forward is a clear determination of the combination of core resources and attractors that best define the destination. For SIDS in the Caribbean in particular, this has been straightforward for the last 40 and more years as emphasis was placed almost exclusively on the 3S (sun, sea and sand) product where the white sandy beaches have been the main drawing card. In this more competitive decade, many destinations are now exploring or considering exploring other attractors, e.g. special events like jazz festivals and physiography focusing on ecotourism. As destinations consider additional attractors, the challenge is to ensure that the combination of attractors is an accurate and effective representation of the destination's appeal. Further to this, as this representation is communicated to the marketplace, there must be no ambiguity in the minds of the tourists as to what the destination is and what it is marketing. In the words of Fan (2006:10), a destination that 'tries to be all things to all people will inevitably fail as it will isolate a significant proportion of its target audience through its vagueness'.

The embracing of new attractors demands the effective development and management of the core resources under consideration in a sustainable manner. The prolonged emphasis on the 3S product in many SIDS has resulted in minimal attention being placed on the development and packaging of the culture and history of these islands, for example. As such, there must be a paradigm shift towards the development and management of tourism products that accurately maintain and represent the true essence of the destination. The communication of the destination's appeal to the marketplace must be captured in the imaging and branding.

Destination's Representation

In clarifying the identity of the destination, it must be made clear that the destination is not just a geographical location with spatial, physical properties. It is a mental concept that is thought to exist in the minds of its tourists and potential tourists. This mental construct is developed by the consumer 'on the basis of a few selected impressions among the flood of total impressions; it comes into being through a creative process in which these selected impressions are elaborated, embellished and ordered' (Reynolds, 1965:69). The traveller's choice of a given destination depends largely on the favourableness of his or her image of that destination (Lee *et al.*, 2002; Leisen, 2001). Some argue that images are more important than the core resources (Gallarza *et al.*, 2002). An alternative argument is that the perceptions of individual destination attributes as well as the holistic impression made by the destination influence destination choice (Echtner & Ritchie, 1991).

As the competition for tourists and their spending dollars continues to increase, a coherent, consistent destination image is integral to be valued as the destination of choice. Two main implications are noteworthy for SIDS. First, SIDS must engage in strategic image management. This involves 'the ongoing process of researching a place's image among its audiences, segmenting and targeting its specific image and its demographic audiences, positioning the place's benefits to support an existing image or create a new image, and communicating those benefits to the target audiences' (Kotler *et al.*, 1993:143). Second, effective marketing of SIDS requires the building of a recognizable brand. 'Effective destination branding provides visitors with an assurance of quality experiences, reduces visitor search costs, and offers a way for destinations to establish a unique selling proposition' (Blain *et al.*, 2005:330).

For the past two decades, SIDS have focused their communications around portrayals of blue seas, endless golden beaches and hospitable local people. The question has often been asked, particularly among Caribbean destinations, as to what differentiates one island destination from another. According to Morgan, Pritchard, and Piggott (2002:336), 'the battle for customers in tomorrow's destination marketplace will be fought not over price but over hearts and minds – in the territory of brands'. One destination that has gained a very positive reputation for the quality and consistency of its brand presence is New Zealand. Based on the New Zealand experience, Morgan Pritchard, and Piggott (2003) propose that successful brand development involves:

- establishing the core values of the destination;
- determining how contemporary the brand is with regard to both consumers and competitors;
- identifying what the destination represents;
- determining the means by which this representation should be translated into a 'brand personality'.

The development of an effective destination brand is certainly a key strategic move for SIDS in this changing marketplace. Moreover, as noted by Morgan, Pritchard, and Pride (2002:21–2), 'the development of an emotional relationship with the consumer through choreographed and focused communications campaigns holds the key to destination differentiation'. As SIDS move towards 2020, this will involve not only the development of a powerful destination brand but the movement towards a lasting emotional connection with the consumer through emotional branding (Gobe, 2001). Understanding people's emotional needs and desires is more than ever the key to success.

Satisfying the 2020 Tourist

The provision of high-quality, creative, relevant and meaningful experiences is another critical challenge facing destinations today. Jayawardena (2002) points out that the future of tourism markets is dependent on the ability of tourism countries to deliver 'a high-quality product that corresponds to the changing tastes, needs, wants and demands of the international traveller'. The core issue is the unpredictable nature of the international tourist and the myriad of external factors that impinge upon his decision-making. At the outset, what is encouraging for SIDS is the emergence of the 'new tourist'. These 'new tourists' are 'consumers who are flexible, independent and experienced travelers, whose values and lifestyles are different from those of the mass tourists' (Poon, 1993:114). This new value system, along with the tourists' search for the real and authentic and the need to confirm individuality presents a new operating environment for SIDS.

This presents both an opportunity and a threat for SIDS. Historically and presently, the majority of SIDS depend heavily on the mass tourists because of the nature of their product, the 3S product. The challenge that faces these SIDS has been well put by Connell (1988), cited in Hall and Page (1996:2):

> for island states that have very few resources, virtually the only resources where there may be some comparative advantage in favour of [island microstates] are clean beaches, unpolluted seas and warm weather and water, and at least vestiges of distinctive cultures.

This new tourism allows SIDS to step out of their mass tourism mould at two points of exit. First, there is the opportunity to expand their market share by developing new products to capture this growing new market. Cuba is already leading the way in medical tourism in the Caribbean region while other islands have been focusing on the events market through the promotion of jazz and music festivals, e.g. St. Lucia and the British Virgin Islands. The WTO (2009a) has identified what they refer to as the top five 'hottest' tourism products/markets to 2020. These include:

* *Adventure Tourism*
  The trend will be for tourists to travel to the world's highest peaks, to underwater sites (Titanic) and places at the 'end of the earth' (Antarctica).
* *Cruises* (Themed Cruises)
* *Eco Tourism*
  Trips containing a nature component will continue to gain in popularity.
* *Cultural Tourism*
  Eastern Europe, the Middle East and Asia are predicted to enjoy especially strong tourism growth.
* *Themes*
  Thematic tourism, where a special interest is the main travel motivator, is expected to see strong growth.

The pressing issue for SIDS is the extent to which they are well positioned to tap into these new forms of tourism by meeting the needs of and exceeding the expectations of the new tourists. A core component of the positioning of these islands is the market segmentation strategy adopted. With increasing emphasis being placed on understanding the consumer's needs and desires, psychographic and behavioural segmentation must be at the forefront. This is necessary to provide detailed customer profiles; to identify motivations, needs and determinants; and to offer an appropriate marketing mix and service delivery strategy (Cooper *et al.*, 2008).

Second, the new consumer of tourism is knowledgeable, discerning and seeks authenticity. For the new tourist, travel is not just about *being at the destination* but *experiencing being there* as travel becomes the medium for personal fulfilment and identity (Cooper *et al.*, 2008). This new paradigm forces SIDS to rethink their approach to mass tourism with a shift in focus from the 3S product to the 3S 'plus' experience, which allows for a better integration of all that the destination has to offer. Integral to this shift is a requirement for high standards of product design, efficiency and safety as the more experienced traveller expects quality and has the wherewithal to compare offerings.

Furthermore, the new tourist is more technologically savvy, as highlighted earlier in the chapter. The increasing demands of the new tourist for personalized, complex, specialized and quality products necessitate the use of information and communication technologies (ICTs), namely the Internet. Worldwide Internet users reached 1.6 billion in March 2009 – Asia leading with 657 million Internet users, followed by Europe with 393 million and North America with 251 million. During the period 2000–08, the main source markets for the majority of SIDS, Europe and North America, recorded a 274% and 133% growth in the number of Internet users, respectively (www.internetworldstats.com). The hard reality for SIDS is that if you are not online you are not on sale.

SIDS must adopt a strategic approach to their use of the Internet. The Internet must be used as a tool to gain a competitive advantage in the marketplace. For many SIDS, ICTs can be used to differentiate the tourism offerings of certain destinations that are in danger of being commodified in the sun, sea and sand category. This allows SIDS to improve their relative position in the international market. Small and medium-sized tourism enterprises that dominate the tourism industry in SIDS can adopt sophisticated technologies through the Internet, and confront their markets with a professional interface that is capable of competing on equal terms with large global corporations. Moreover, the Internet is a tool that can empower local communities in SIDS to engage directly with global tourism markets, thereby bypassing intermediaries so as to retain a larger percentage of tourism receipts.

Armed for the Crisis

The tourism industry in SIDS has been frequently subjected to natural disasters such as hurricanes, tsunamis and earthquakes, e.g. Hurricane Ivan in Grenada in 2004 and the Indian Ocean tsunami in December 2004. SIDS in the Caribbean in particular are located in the hurricane belt and thus are more highly susceptible to storms and hurricanes than other tourist destinations. Until recently, the focus of these destinations has been the development of measures to treat with managing and marketing the destination after a hurricane. However, the events of 9/11 (2001) and the global economic crisis of 2008/09 have signalled to SIDS that a crisis, be it natural or man-made, can strike any destination at any time. The challenge for SIDS is managing a crisis and promoting the destination after a crisis. This would require not only effective collaboration with the national disaster management agency, but a more proactive approach to crises.

SIDS need to adopt a proactive approach to crises. Proper preparation can prevent some crises and minimize the impact of those that cannot be avoided. Although proactive crisis management can be considerably challenging, there is much value in it for destinations. A proactive approach to crisis management for SIDS should entail the development of a national crisis management policy for the tourism sector. Sausmarez (2004) provides some useful guidelines on the establishment of such a policy. She indicated that it should give consideration to the importance of tourism to the economy, identify sources of greatest risk, identify and monitor indicators, address the issue of implementation, develop a crisis plan, and research the potential for regional cooperation. Such an approach can be encumbered with challenges of availability of funding, lack of institutional structures for implementation and moreover the possibility of a varying number of crises that may strike. Nonetheless, this approach would enable governments and tourism sector professionals to address some of the preliminary issues so that time would not be wasted in the event of a crisis.

Conclusion

The global tourism industry continues to be resilient in the face of the continuous external forces that impact upon it. In the midst of a dynamic global marketplace, the overriding challenge for SIDS is to remain competitive as these tourism-dependent destinations seek to accurately position themselves in an increasingly hostile environment. This new environment is characterized by aggressive emerging destinations, demanding consumers and unparalleled crises. SIDS are compelled to engage in strategic destination marketing in order to survive, let alone gain a competitive advantage in this new disposition. Clearly, there is an implicit requirement for constant research into the changing needs and wants of the source market. A warning is sounded that SIDS must keep on the pulse of their market if they are to remain relevant in this dynamic global tourism environment. There must be no ambiguity in the representation of the destination. A proactive approach to crisis management is mandatory in this era of competition.

The destination case studies that follow in this book examine in more detail how island destinations are negotiating this new global marketplace. The cases are drawn from island destinations in the Caribbean, the Pacific and the Mediterranean, and provide valuable insight into the strategic issues with destination marketing. The cases are divided into two core areas, including strategic destination marketing issues and the marketing of niche products. The former cases focus on issues of branding, image development, market positioning and the use of ICTs and destination marketing. The latter cases examine the niche products of village-based tourism and conventions tourism. Each case study is punctuated with discussion questions on issues pertaining to the case. Based on the case studies, the concluding chapter proposes a strategic response to the issues that destination marketers are confronted with in this volatile global tourism environment.

References

Blain, C., Levy, S., & Ritchie, B. (2005). Destination branding: Insights and practices from destination management organizations. *Journal of Travel Research*, *43*, 328–338.

Cooper, C., Fletcher, J., Fyall, A., Gilbert, D., & Wanhill, S. (2008). *Tourism: Principles and practice* (4th ed.). UK: Longman.

De Lollis, B., & Hansen, B. (2009). *Caribbean islands slammed with double financial hit, USA Today*, http://www.usatoday.com/travel/destinations/2009-01-18-caribbean-economic-woes_N.htm Accessed 19 January 2009.

Echtner, C., & Ritchie, B. (1991). The meaning and measurement of destination image. *Journal of Tourism Studies*, *2*(2), 2–12.

Economy Watch. (2009). *India's tourism industry*. http://www.economywatch.com/business-and-economy/tourism-industry.html. Accessed 8 June 2009.

EuroMonitor International. (2004). *Eastern Europe – A key growth market for the global travel and tourism industry*. http://www.euromonitor.com/Eastern_Europe_a_key_growth_market_for_the_global_Travel_and_Tourism_industry Accessed 5 June 2009.

Fan, Y. (2006). Branding the nation: What is being branded? *Journal of Vacation Marketing*, *12*(5), 5–14.

Gallarza, M. G., Saura, I. G., & Garcia, H. C. (2002). Destination image: Towards a conceptual framework. *Annals of Tourism Research*, *29*(1), 56–78.

Gobe, M. (2001). *Emotional branding: The new paradigm for connecting brands to people*. New York: Allworth Press.

Hall, M., & Page, S. (Eds.), (1996). *Tourism in the pacific: Issues and cases*. London: International Thomson Business Press.

Jayawardena, C. (2002). Mastering Caribbean tourism. *International Journal of Contemporary Hospitality Management*, *14*(2), 88–93.

Kotler, P., Haider, D. H., & Rein, I. (1993). *Marketing places: Attracting investment, industry and tourism to cities, states and nations*. New York: Macmillan Inc.

Latin America Monitor. (2009). Key sector outlook. *Latin America Monitor: Caribbean*, *26*(4).

Lee, G., O'Leary, J. T., & Hong, G. S. (2002). Visiting propensity predicted by destination image: German long-haul pleasure travelers to the U.S. *International Journal of Hospitality and Tourism Administration*, *3*(2), 63–92.

Leisen, B. (2001). Image segmentation: The case of a tourism destination. *Journal of Services Marketing*, *15*(1), 49–66.

Morgan, N., Pritchard, A., & Piggott, R. (2002). New Zealand, 100% pure. The creation of a powerful niche brand. *Brand Management*, *9*(4–5), 335–354.

Morgan, N., Pritchard, A., & Pride, R. (Eds.), (2002). *Destination branding: Creating a unique destination proposition*. Oxford: Butterworth-Heinemann.

Morgan, N., Pritchard, A., & Piggott, R. (2003). Destination branding and the role of stakeholders: The case of New Zealand. *Journal of Vacation Marketing*, *9*(3), 285–299.

Page, S., & Connell, J. (2006). *Tourism: A modern synthesis*. London: Thomson Learning.

Poon, A. (1993). *Tourism, technology and competitive strategies*. Oxon: CAB International.

Reynolds, W. H. (1965). The role of the consumer in image building. *California Management Review*, *7*, 69–76.

Ritchie, J. R. B., & Crouch, G. I. (2003). *The competitive destination: A sustainable tourism perspective*. London: CABI.

Sausmarez, N. (2004). Crisis management for the tourism sector: Preliminary considerations in policy development. *Tourism and Hospitality Planning and Development*, *1*(2), 157–172.

The Banker. (2005). BRIC countries are the world economy's building blocks. *The Banker* 2 May.

Wahab, S., Crampon, L., & Rothfield, L. (1976). *Tourism marketing*. London: Tourism International Press.

Weaver, D. B. (1995). Alternative tourism in Montserrat. *Tourism Management*, *16*(8), 593–604.

World Tourism Organization. (2003). *The Djerba declaration on tourism and climate change*. Madrid: WTO.

World Tourism Organization. (2009a). *Tourism 2020 vision*. http://www.unwto.org/facts/menu. html. Accessed 4 June 2009.

World Tourism Organization. (2009b). *UNWTO world tourism barometer: Interim update, April*. http://www.unwto.org/facts/eng/pdf/barometer/UNWTO_Barom09_update_april_en_ excerpt.pdf. Accessed 8 June 2009.

3 Rebranding Norfolk Island – Is it Enough to Rebuild Visitor Numbers?

Bruce Prideaux and Terry Watson

James Cook University, Queensland, Australia

Brands are powerful marketing tools that are used to build consumer awareness of a product. From a destination perspective a unique brand facilitates differentiation from competitors. An important element in the branding process is identifying the psychological push factors that motivate consumer segments to select a particular destination type over other destination types, e.g. selecting an island holiday over a city holiday location. Brands build on destination image and should give an indication of the experiences that are offered and in some cases are targeted at specific market segments. Brands may also give indications of value. Over time the psychological push factors of consumers, described as those internal factors that stimulate an individual's desire for travel, change. This process may be a result of changing lifestyle status, the change from a family with children to empty-nester being a common example, or a change in the level of income of the nature that occurs when a person transitions from employment to retirement. Destinations need to be aware of changes in their target segments and when necessary refresh their brand or even rebrand if the current brand has lost its effectiveness. One of the difficulties of rebranding a destination is that many destination brands are based on location and the images associated with that geographical location. Rebranding may therefore be a difficult task.

Located in the Pacific Ocean two hours flying time from the east coast of Australia, Norfolk Island is a popular holiday destination for Australian and New Zealand seniors. After a sustained period of growth, arrivals began to fall in the mid-2000s, creating alarm in the island's tourism industry and concerns for the island's administration. Research undertaken by Prideaux (2007) found that one of the major reasons for this decline was the failure of the island's tourism industry to recognize that the seniors market, its principal market segment, was undergoing generational change. The types of products and experiences and the quality of infrastructure that attracted the seniors market during the 1980s and 1990s are of marginal interest to the baby-boomer seniors of the 2000s. Recognizing that significant changes were required in both its products and services and the manner in which the island is promoted a number of change strategies were implemented during the late 2000s. These changes included the adoption of a new five-year tourism development strategy, market research into the island's shopping sector and more recently the introduction of a new destination brand titled 'The World of Norfolk'. The aim of this chapter is to examine the process leading to the development of the new brand and comment on its likely

Marketing Island Destinations. DOI: 10.1016/B978-0-12-384909-0.00003-9

effectiveness. The methodology used for this research was based on face-to-face interviews with staff of the island's DMO (destination management organization), tourism operators and government officers.

Previous Research

The push–pull model of tourism behaviour provides a useful platform for analysing the factors that have led to the current situation on Norfolk Island where visitor numbers are declining despite strong marketing and significant growth in the number of Australians travelling overseas. The following discussion will first briefly examine the push–pull model as it applies to Norfolk Island and then examine how the development of a consumer gap of the nature postulated by Glover and Prideaux (2009) has occurred. This is followed by a discussion on aspects of the destination's recent rebranding campaign.

Destination success is a complex issue that involves a range of interrelated factors, which include the consumer, the destination's tourism sector, the host population, the public sector and the distribution system. In its simplest form the long-term success of a destination relies on four related factors:

1. *A realistic understanding of the 'pull' factor that the destination is able to offer to potential visitors.* Pull factors (Uysal & Jurowski, 1994) are those aspects of a destination that attract tourists and include attractions, culture, low cost, the environment, ability to rest and relax and, importantly, ease of access. Collectively, pull factors constitute the resources that the destination is able to offer potential visitors. Pull factors include tourism-specific experiences as outlined above as well as the infrastructure that supports tourism and the various processes of government and the private sector that collectively underpin the tourism sector. In some cases, the type of resources available will determine the type of visitor who may be interested in visiting a destination. Norfolk Island's major pull factors are its ability to offer visitors the opportunity to relax, safety, friendliness of residents, activities and favourable climate (Prideaux, McNamara, & Blakeney, 2009).

2. *A realistic assessment of the 'push' factors that motivate an individual to undertake travel to a destination.* Push factors may be described as the socio-psychological motives that influence individuals to travel. Push factors are internal (Uysal & Jurowski, 1994) and include the desire for rest and relaxation, escape, learning, status and prestige and social interaction (Crompton, 1979a; Dann, 1977; Ryan, 2003). A number of researchers have argued that push and pull factors work in parallel to create tourism markets (Jang & Cai, 2002; Uysal & Jurowski, 1994; Yuan & McDonald, 1990). Push factors provide a destination with a useful measure of the type of attractions, activities and, importantly, infrastructure that must be developed to attract specific tourism segments.

3. *The ability to respond to consumers' push factors will be determined by the destination's ability to harness its pull factors to create tourism experiences.* Products are developed by bundling pull factors into experiences and products, developing a destination that is tourist-friendly, the marketing process that communicates the destination's attractions to consumers and finally the distribution process that facilitates conversion of interest to a purchase. Important components of the marketing process include branding, promotion, advertising and distribution channels.

4. *Recognition of the changing nature of push factors.* To ensure long-term success destinations must be alert to changes in consumer demand and undertake periodic reassessment of

their product offerings. As part of this process, destinations should fund ongoing research into market segments and changes in seasonality, be aware of new products and services standards and be cognizant of the activities of competitors. If there are significant changes in consumer push factors, destinations may need to consider periodic brand refreshment or, in extreme cases, rebranding.

The push–pull theory of tourism is a useful model for understanding how destinations are able to achieve long-term sustainability. Because push factors are the primary drivers of an individual's decision to travel, destinations must be alert to changes that may occur over time in the weighting of various push factors. In the case of Norfolk Island, Prideaux and Glover (2009) suggest that recent changes in the composition of the island's senior market have resulted in the emergence of a consumer gap where much of the island's infrastructure that was developed for seniors who are members of the 'Builder' generation is now not able to meet the minimum standards demanded by baby-boomer generation seniors.

Pearce's (2005:1) conceptual framework (Figure 3.1) for understanding tourism builds on the basic push–pull concept to illustrate how the intersection of tourist's push factors and the destination's pull factors creates a destination (on-site) experience that in turn creates outcomes for the tourist, the host and the setting. The nature of these outcomes identifies areas where improvements can be made to better align the destination's pull factors with consumer push factors. For example, if one of the collective outcomes is dissatisfaction, the destination will need to improve product

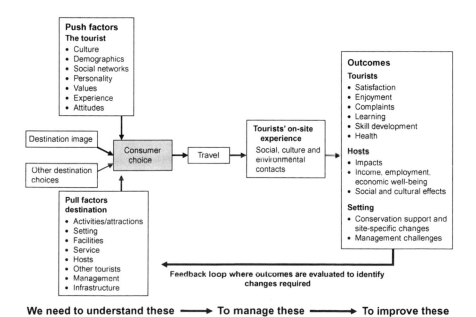

Figure 3.1 Conceptual framework for understanding tourist behaviour.
Source: Modified version of Pearce (1995).

delivery. If this is not possible, it may be necessary to look for new segments where the destination's pull factors have a better alignment with the target segment's push factors. The ultimate aim is to ensure that outcomes for tourists as well as the hosts are positive.

Generations

Generations, described as cohorts of persons born in a defined date range and sharing similar economic or cultural norms, are often used as a market segmentation tool. Generations are not universal between cultures. In China, for example, people born after the introduction of the one-child policy (1978) are members of the 'Little Emperor' generation, while in the West persons born between 1980 and 1994 are referred to as Generation Y. In the Australian context, the generation born prior to 1946 are termed the Builders (or alternatively the Silent generation by some sources), while persons born between 1946 and 1965 are members of the baby-boomer generation. Baby-boomers are generally more affluent than Builders and also more numerous. The number of Builders in the Australian population in 2007 was 3.5 million (17% of the population), while the number of baby-boomers was 5.3 million (26%) (http://www.mccrindle.com.au/fastfacts.htm). The members of the Builder generation are ageing rapidly and are therefore less inclined and increasingly less able to travel. Baby-boomers, however, are just beginning to retire in significant numbers, have access to far great superannuation resources than is the case with the Builders and on average have more disposable income available after retirement.

The Norfolk Island Tourism Industry

Norfolk Island, in common with many small islands, is heavily reliant on tourism as its main export sector, and tourism is a major employer and the main source of government revenue. Unlike many small island competitors in the Pacific, Norfolk Island enjoys a relatively high standard of living and stable administration. The island's main attractions are its convict heritage (see Figure 3.2), 'Bounty heritage', natural environment and way of life. After a long period of growth, tourism arrivals began to decline in 2004, recovering in 2007 before again declining (see Figure 3.3), leading to the island's administration commissioning a report into the future needs of the tourism industry. The result of this process was a *Five Year Tourism Strategy 2007/08–2011/12* (Global Leisure, 2007), which among other things noted that a major factor in declining arrivals was the failure of the destination to recognize that its major market segment, the seniors, was undergoing significant change in the destination's principal generating regions of Australia and New Zealand. In the generating regions, seniors who belonged to the Builders generation are being rapidly replaced by baby-boomer seniors. However, a corresponding change has yet to occur on Norfolk Island where the visitor base changed from 50% of visitors being aged 56 years or over in

Figure 3.2 The Kinston Heritage precinct. This precinct has been nominated for World Heritage listing and is Norfolk Island's principal heritage asset.
Photograph courtesy of Bruce Prideaux.

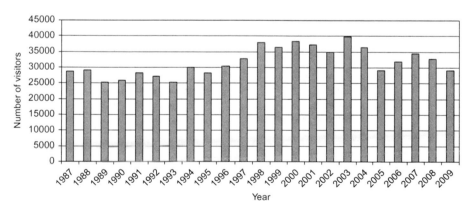

Figure 3.3 Annual arrivals in Norfolk Island, 1987–2009.
Source: Norfolk Island Government (2010).

1989 to 75.7% in 2007. The island's tourism industry has been slow to respond to this change, leading to a mismatch between the island's pull factors and the target sector's push factors, as illustrated in Figure 3.3. The failure to recognize that change was occurring in the consumers' push factors was compounded by the failure of the destination's tourism industry to investment in accommodation built to contemporary standards. This has resulted in the island's tourism offerings being locked into the current Builders generation market and to the exclusion of other target markets.

Figure 3.3 records visitor trends over the period 1989–2009. The period of decline that commenced in 2004 can be attributed to several factors, including the collapse of Norfolk Jet in 2005, the ageing of the Builder generation seniors and, arguably, an inability to effectively tap into the Australian baby-boomer market. At the same time, visitation from New Zealand fell from almost 10 000 in 2003 to under 7,000 in 2008.

The concept of a product gap developing as a result of a misalignment between the destination's product offering and its principal visitor segments was postulated by Glover and Prideaux (2009), and appears to offer one explanation for the problems faced by the Norfolk Island tourism industry. In Figure 3.4, curve 1 represents the Builder generation who constituted the bulk of the island's inbound market during the late 1980s through to the 2000s. The curve charts the rise in demand over time followed by a fall in demand as this segment ages and its members are less inclined to or less able to travel. Curve 2 illustrates a similar pattern of rising demand, in this case by baby-boomer visitors. By the time that the curves intersect, the destination should have entered a readjustment phase that will allow it to capitalize on the new market sector while still benefiting from the declining sector.

Norfolk Island has developed a tight market segmentation based on group travel by relatively low-yield seniors of the Builders' generation. This approach has been successful in the past but changes in the composition of the Australian seniors market, and changes in accommodation preferences have begun to impact on Norfolk Island. The declining demand for group travel has had a negative impact on arrivals, and the growing demand for quality accommodation has been largely ignored by the island's

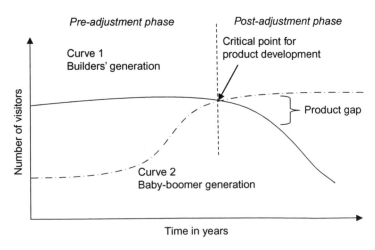

Figure 3.4 Emergence of a product gap. Note that demand curves 1 and 2 are illustrative only and are not drawn to scale.
Source: Glover and Prideaux (2009).

accommodation sector. If the destination's supply side fails to recognize changes in the pattern of consumer push factors and continues to target the consumer group that is in decline (Builders' generation), a product gap of the nature postulated in Figure 3.4 will occur.

From the perspective of the Tourist Area Life Cycle model postulated by Butler (1980), Norfolk Island appears to be entering a period of decline that will only be arrested by a rejuvenation phase. A decline in visitor numbers may occur for a number of reasons including a fall in the level of overall visitor satisfaction, loss of significant pull factor assets, fall in price competitiveness and ineffective marketing. Rejuvenation occurs when the destination is able to realign its pull factors to meet the demands of the market sectors it is targeting. A realignment of this nature requires three complementary steps:

1. *Step One*: the destination needs to make changes in its suite of products and services to reflect the standards and interests of its target market.
2. *Step Two*: destinations need to upgrade infrastructure to conform to contemporary consumer expectations.
3. *Step Three*: the destination may need to refresh its image in the marketplace to more closely align it with the push factors of its largest markets.

While there is growing recognition of the need for rejuvenation, Norfolk Island has yet to develop a comprehensive suite of strategies that will achieve this outcome. Strategies to implement Steps One and Two have yet to be put into place, while strategies to implement Step Three have centred on the rebranding process described later in this chapter.

Image and Branding

All destinations have an image that consumers regard as good, bad or are indifferent to (Hunt, 1975). Crompton (1979a:18) defined image as 'the sum of beliefs, ideas, and impressions that a person has of a destination'. For this reason it is important to identify the image or images of the destination that are held by consumers. Where images are negative remedial action may be required. In the destination context, branding is a process that strives to draw attention to positive images with the ultimate aim of converting interest into a purchase.

In large destinations that seek to attract a number of visitor segments the construction of a destination image is a complex task. If the image is to be multidimensional, it has to recognize the influences of the affective and cognitive spheres, which, according to Crompton (1979b), are created by an amalgam of personal feelings, beliefs, knowledge, opinions, expectations and impressions about a specific destination. As Henderson (2010) notes, there is a consensus in the literature that clearly defined and appealing images allow a destination to achieve a more desirable market position than those that are unknown or unattractive. This appeal also extends to the travel distribution system and potential investors. Achieving a successful place image in the marketplace relies on a range of interrelated factors. The initial factor is creating consumer interest through various elements of marketing, followed by converting interest to a purchase and then actual delivery. Branding assists this process by calling consumers' attention to the destination. As Pearce's model (Figure 3.1) suggests, the push factors of individual tourists and their actual experiences of the destination's pull factors produce outcomes that may range from satisfaction to disappointment. These are then fed back through the distribution system as positive or negative perceptions affecting future sales. In small destinations there is often limited scope to develop a broad image, hence the image may need to be developed to resonate with specific and well-defined target segments.

According to the American Marketing Association (cited in Tasci & Kozac, 2006:300), a brand is 'a name, term, symbol or design, or a combination of them, intended to identify the goods or services of one seller group or group of sellers and to differentiate them from those of competitors. Brands therefore, represent a mechanism for differentiation through logos, brand names and trademarks'. Branding, therefore should be a process of creating communications with consumers with the aim of developing recognition, trust and ultimately sales. According to Morgan, Pritchard, and Piggott (2002), strong destination brands create strong emotional meanings and are thus able to provide a high level of anticipation for potential visitors.

Image and branding are related although there is some dispute between researchers (Tasci & Kozac, 2006:304) on the extent that the concepts 'brand' and 'image' differ from or are associated with each other. Tasci and Kozac (2006) believe that brand development equates to destination image identity and argue that destination brand loyalty can only be built if visitors are given an experience that corresponds to their needs and also matches the images they have of the destination. Branwell and Rawding (1996) tend to support this contention by stating that projected images are the ideas and impressions of a place that are available for consumption by consumers.

While image and brand should support each other as suggested by Tasci and Kozac (2006), there is some danger in allowing image and brand to merge. Where there is a convergence of this nature, future rebranding may be difficult and will first require the separation of image from the brand. Brands should therefore remain subordinate to the image and be designed to support the desired image. In the case of Norfolk Island, image and brand have become intertwined.

Destinations face a number of difficulties in brand creation owing to the unique characteristics of the industry. Specifically tourism products are often intangible, perishable, heterogeneous and variable, and production and consumption are often inseparable (De Chernatony & Riley, 1999). Buhalis (2000) identified four principles for successful destination branding:

1. Collaboration rather than competition among stakeholders in brand development.
2. The brand must support the destination's values, including physical and cultural carrying capacity.
3. The brand must be orientated to a clearly defined target market.
4. The brand must support the destination's vision of development.

Positioning the brand is an important element in any branding exercise. The positioning task has three steps, according to Kotler *et al.* (1996). The first step is to identify competitive advantages that can be used to build the destination's position, effectively the destination's push factors. The second step is based on selecting the right competitive advantages for the desired target market or, in other words, matching destination push factors to consumer push factors. The third step is effectively communicating and delivering the position chosen to the selected target market or markets. According to Crockett and Wood (1999), successful brands have a clearly defined core personality or purpose that remains constant as the brand is used in new markets. Coca-Cola is an example of a brand that has a successful core personality that is able to appeal to consumers over a range of age, income and cultural differences.

Rebranding Norfolk Island

The Norfolk Island Five year Tourism Strategy 2007/2008–2011/2012 (2007:4) stated that 'If Norfolk Island is to further develop the benefits it seeks from tourism in an increasingly competitive, changing and demanding marketplace, it has no alternative but to change. The alternative will be a slow, lingering and painful decline of its tourism industry and of Norfolk Island's future.' The plan identified the need to transition the destination to the baby-boomer segment because it exhibits significant differences from the previous generation. The plan also noted that tapping into this target segment required a new approach including branding and image. The following discussion examines the rebranding approach taken by Norfolk Island.

One of the first difficulties that had to be confronted was the lingering effects of frequent changes in the island's marketing campaigns, taglines and messages, which had left the destination without an effective brand that could be reinforced with a marketing campaign. This situation dictated the need for a new brand that was supported by the Norfolk Island industry, government and community as well as the target market. To achieve this, a staged rebranding strategy was developed commencing with the establishment of a branding committee that represented a wide range of stakeholders. Regular updates of committee deliberations were issued to stakeholders to ensure that an effective two-way communications process was established. This approach ensured maximum ownership by stakeholders.

As part of this process, the committee commissioned SAI Marketing Counsel Pty Ltd. (2009) to identify which aspects of the tourism experience the island was good at and which groups of consumers would be interested in these experiences. The brief given to the consultant was to:

- develop a profile of visitors based on the type of accommodation they used;
- develop a profile of visitors based on the type of activities they participated in;
- identify the travel behaviour patterns of tourists in the generating regions and determine which of these segments fitted with the experiences offered by Norfolk Island.

As part of this process, existing plans were analysed and demographic and psychographic variables, including values, attitudes and lifestyles of potential visitors from both Australia and New Zealand, were assessed. A number of issues that were critical to brand development were identified, including:

- the need for any new target markets to be compatible with existing markets;
- Norfolk Island has a relatively low-carrying capacity;
- limitations imposed by the available accommodation mix;

- the mix of activities that are currently available;
- the need for new markets to be consistent with the host population's visions and values.

The consultant found that Norfolk Island's appeal stems from *three* core attributes (pull factors) described as place, past and people. Based on these attributes, the island's core pull factors are described as:

- no ordinary island (because of its uniqueness, diversity and distinct status as a self-governing territory);
- no ordinary history (based on a layered history of convicts, early settlers who were descendants of mutineers who had earlier settled on Pitcairn Island, and later arrivals);
- no ordinary folk (Norfolk Islanders who have their own distinctive language and culture).

Building on the three core pull factors previously discussed, the next step was to match the island's pull factors with consumer push factors. The findings of this exercise indicated that opportunities for participation in experiences offered by Norfolk Island were strongest among those aged between 35 and 54 years, those earning between \$52 000 and \$104 000 per annum and among young/midlife couples without children and couples with children aged 6–14 years. However, because of the restrictions imposed by accommodation discussed previously, it became apparent that the needs of many members of the target groups could not be supported and a narrower target market was required. After further analysis, the modified target market was identified as discerning travellers aged 50–64 or older, living in Eastern Australia and New Zealand, travelling as couples or in groups, looking for a week-long, short-haul holiday experience that is refreshingly different – physically engaging, mentally stimulating and emotionally bonding. This deviation from the broader segment placed a further limitation on the potential for the rebranding exercise to generate additional visitors.

The major positioning issues needed to attract the modified target segment were identified as:

- Norfolk Island is a subtropical (not tropical) Pacific island.
- The island is an Australian territory but in many ways different from Australia.
- The island lacks sandy beaches.
- The island has pine trees, not palm trees.
- The population lives on a Pacific island but ethnically are not Pacific Islanders (Polynesian or Melanesian).
- The island's small size belies its topography and intensity.

To attract the target segment, it became obvious to the branding committee that the benefits that needed to be conveyed by the new brand were that Norfolk Island is a South Pacific destination that offers a surprisingly unique and diverse experience; that it totally belies its size and combines nature, history, people and culture in a compact and easily accessible environment. To communicate the benefits highlighted by this core brand idea, Norfolk Island needed to be presented to potential visitor as a destination that is a totally different world. To achieve this change the destination image was repositioned as the World of Norfolk.

Figure 3.5 summarizes how the island was repositioned from the geographic place of Norfolk Island to a new experience called the World of Norfolk. Aspects that were previously seen as limitations were transformed into strengths to achieve very strong points of differentiation from competitors in the South Pacific. Size, for example, was repositioned from a weakness under the previous Norfolk Island brand to a strength under the new World of Norfolk brand.

It was also apparent that the brand promise needed a major overhaul, as illustrated in Figure 3.6. Again size was transformed from a disadvantage to an advantage designed to attract new visitors as well as reassure past visitors.

An important aspect of any branding campaign is developing a brand personality, which is described as the traits that would be associated with a brand if it were a living, breathing person. The brand committee determined that the brand personality for Norfolk Island should be young, energetic, proud, possessive, rustic, quirky, motherly, loving, generous, nurturing, resourceful, tenacious, spirited and humorous. The committee also recognized that the island's brand message must be developed to create an emotional connection based on available experiences, imagery and words. It also needed to contain an intellectual connection based on inclusions, itineraries and costs.

The final step in the process was the development of a 'unique selling proposition' for the brand. After some debate it was decided that the unique selling position of The World of Norfolk was an experience of pared-back natural simplicity,

Norfolk Island South Pacific	*Repositioned as*	The World of Norfolk South Pacific
From		**To**
Two dimensional; finite space		Three dimensional; infinite scope
Competes head on against other islands		Redefines category whilst retaining identity and location
Reinforces stereotype images		Breaks the mould, sets it apart
Small size a weakness		Size becomes a potential strength
Limited opportunity for claims		Implies uniqueness *and* diversity
Makes Destination Norfolk *different from* and *superior* to competition. Provides a unique, credible and sustainable positioning platform		

Figure 3.5 Repositioning the brand from one based on the geographic identity of Norfolk Island to a brand based on experience.

The World of Norfolk
Small world. No small wonder

Small world	**No small wonder**
Gives credence to *World of Norfolk* positioning	Reinforces wondrous nature of destination
Kindles visitor interest	Captures visitor emotions
Suggests surprise encounters	Elevates 'Be surprised' tagline to a new level
Signifies connectedness with people, environment and history	Contrasts with *Small world*
Makes a compelling brand promise	

Figure 3.6 The new brand identity.

Figure 3.7 The World of Norfolk campaign line.

untarnished by the worst trappings of modern world, a place with raw elemental beauty, no street lights so the sky's galaxies open up, a subtropical temperature never below 10°C or above 28°C, a biological showpiece, a relaxed, peaceful pace to savour every experience, where children can be free to roam, a remarkable sense of community, a local language blending of Old English seafaring and Tahitian and a telephone directory listed by nicknames. The campaign line used to convey this message was 'Welcome Back to Earth' (Figure 3.7).

The new 'World of Norfolk' campaign aimed to bring the people of Norfolk Island to life against a backdrop of the unique beauty of the island. It uses a sense of humour, taking the experiences of city life that frustrate people and contrasting these with Norfolk's unique meaning of the same terms and experiences. The aim was to show that Norfolk is able to provide an escape from such frustrations while highlighting its differences from other destinations in the South Pacific.

Conclusion

The ability to achieve long-term sustainability in the international tourism marketplace rests on a destination's ability to offer an experience or experiences that match the push expectations of the consumer. In the sense used in this chapter the product has two complementary elements, the experiences and activities component and the infrastructure component. Infrastructure includes hotels, shopping, transport, etc. Problems in either one of these two elements will create barriers to an effective matching of push and pull factors. On Norfolk Island it is apparent that the accommodation element of the island's pull factors is deficient and for this reason negates some of the pull opportunities that are present in the remainder of the island's suite of experiences. The development of the 'World of Norfolk' brand appears to have created an image that resonates with target segments in the Australian and New Zealand short-haul market. In the normal course of events, a brand that is based on an image that offers value to its intended target audience should succeed provided that the product is able to match the expectations that have been created by the brand.

According to Morgan et al. (2002), strong destination brands create strong emotional meanings and are thus able to provide a high level of anticipation for potential visitors. Where a new brand can remove the negative images associated with the previous brand, there is a realistic expectation that the new brand should work and be instrumental in increasing arrivals from the targeted segments. In the case of Norfolk Island, the new brand has significant potential to replace the previous image of the

Norfolk brand that had come to be seen as a quaint, slightly run-down place that only attracts 'oldies' (seniors and retirees). However to be effective the new brand needs to be supported by the destination's total sum of experiences and infrastructure. Given the problems noted earlier, this will be a difficult task.

The finding of the chapter is that while the new brand is likely to have strong consumer appeal of the nature suggested by Morgan *et al.* (2002), the failure to upgrade the island's tourism infrastructure will dilute the ability of the new branding and associated marketing campaigns to significantly increase visitor numbers. At best the new brand can be anticipated to halt the recent decline in visitor numbers by appealing to a new target segment that is not particularly sensitive to the inadequacies of the island's accommodation. On a positive note, the initial focus on a narrow target segment offers an opportunity to broaden the brands appeal at a later date when the other steps needed to achieve rejuvenation are implemented.

From a theoretical perspective, this finding highlights the need for destinations to pay close attention to changes in consumer push factors and, when changes in the type of experience desired are detected, to implement appropriate strategies to realign the destination's total stock of pull factors to match the new demands of the target segments. The rebranding exercise appears to have achieved this need by following the three steps advocated by Kotler *et al.* (1996); however, the problems caused by infrastructure remain. It is also worth noting the potential for rejuvenation that is demonstrated in the Tourist Area Life Cycle. If the destination can collectively admit that it has entered a period of decline, the potential for rejuvenation becomes greater. For Norfolk Island this may mean radical strategies to generate capital, possibly in the form of loans backed by a new taxation regime, to refurbish its infrastructure and to encourage investors to construct new high-quality accommodation.

Discussion Questions

1. It is apparent that the needs of target markets change over time. Many destinations cope with changes of this nature by readjusting their tourism product to match changes in consumer demand. What strategies might destination managers implement to ensure that product gaps of the nature highlighted in Figure 3.4 do not occur?
2. This chapter argues that there is a need to ensure that destination image and branding do not converge. Consider the difficulties that DMOs may encounter when convergence of image and brand does occur.
3. In this chapter generation membership was identified as a key factor in determining the characteristics of the destination's existing target markets. Consider the difficulties that may be encountered when a destination's image is closely aligned with a specific market segment based on a single characteristic such as generation membership.

References

Branwell, B., & Rawding, I. (1996). Tourism marketing images of industrial cities. *Annals of Tourism Research, 23*, 201–221.

Buhalis, D. (2000). Marketing the competitive destination of the future. *Tourism Management, 21*, 97–116.

Butler, R. (1980). The concept of a tourist area resort cycle of evolution: Implications for management of resources. *Canadian Geographer*, *14*(1), 5–12.

Crockett, S., & Wood, L. (1999). Brand Western Australia: A totally integrated approach to destination branding. *Journal of Vacation Marketing*, *5*, 276–289.

Crompton, J. (1979a). Motivations for pleasure vacation. *Annals of Tourism Research*, *6*(4), 408–424.

Crompton, J. (1979b). An assessment of the image of Mexico as a vacation destination and the influences of geographic location upon the image. *Journal of Travel Research*, *17*, 18–23.

Dann, G. (1977). Anomie, ego-enhancement and tourism. *Annals of Tourism Research*, *4*(4), 184–194.

De Chenatony, L., & Riley, F. (1999). Experts views about defining services brands and the principles of services branding. *Journal of Business Research*, *46*, 181–192.

Global Leisure. (2007). *Five year tourism strategy 2007/2008–2011/2012*. Sydney: Global Tourism and Leisure.

Glover, P., & Prideaux, B. (2009). Implications of population ageing for the development of tourism products and destinations. *Journal of Vacation Marketing*, *15*, 25–37.

Henderson, J. (2010). Uniquely Singapore? A case study in destination branding. *Journal of Vacation Marketing*, *13*, 261–274.

Hunt, J. (1975). Image as a factor in tourism development. *Journal of Travel Research*, *13*, 1–7.

Jang, S., & Cai, L. (2002). Travel motivations and destination choice: A study of British outbound markets. *Journal of Travel and Tourism Marketing*, *13*(3), 111–131.

Kotler, P., Bowen, J., & Makens, J. (1996). *Marketing for hospitality and management*. Upper Saddle River, NJ: Prentice Hall.

McCrindle Research. http://www.mccrindle.com.au/fastfacts.htm. Last accessed 10 March 2010.

Morgan, N., Pritchard, A., & Piggott, R. (2002). New Zealand, 100% pure: The creation of a powerful niche destination brand. *Journal of Brand Management*, *9*, 335–354.

Norfolk Island Government. (2010). *Visitor statistics, 1979-2009*. <http://www.info.gov.nf/reports/visitor%20statistics/ >. Visited 10 April 2010.

Pearce, P. L. (1995). Pleasure travel motivation. In R. W. McIntosh, C. R. Goeldner, & J. R. Brent Ritchie (Eds.), *Tourism: Principles, practices, philosophies* (7th ed.) (pp. 167–190). New York: John Wiley.

Pearce, P. (2005). *Tourist behaviour: Themes and conceptual schemes*. Clevedon: Channel View Publications.

Prideaux, B. (2007). Potential impacts of generational change on destinations: A case of Norfolk Island. *Advances in Hospitality and Leisure*, *3*, 49–70.

Prideaux, B., McNamara, K., & Blakeney, K. (2009). *Shopping on Norfolk Island: 2008 survey [prepared for Norfolk Island tourism]*. Cairns: James Cook University.

Ryan, C. (2003). *Recreational tourism: Demand and impacts*. Clevedon: Channel View Publications.

SAI Marketing Counsel Pty Ltd. (2009) *Making a world of difference to the Norfolk Island brand: Repositioning destination Norfolk – A strategy framework*. New South Wales: SAI Marketing Counsel Pty Ltd.

Tasci, D., & Kozac, M. (2006). Destination brands vs destination images: Do we know what we mean? *Journal of Vacation Marketing*, *12*, 299–317.

Uysal, M., & Jurowski, C. (1994). Test the push and pull factors. *Annals of Tourism Research*, *21*(4), 844–846.

Yuan, S., & McDonald, C. (1990). Motivational determinates of international pleasure time. *Journal of Travel Research*, *24*(1), 42–44.

4 British and French Visitors' Motivations and Images of Mauritius: A Qualitative Approach

Girish Prayag

SKEMA Business School, France

Introduction

The purpose of this chapter is to provide a qualitative interpretation of visitors' motives for destination choice and images of Mauritius. Existing research on destination image reveals that unstructured methodologies involving conversations with visitors have been the least utilized method of research. Until now, there has been limited application of neural network software in understanding visitors' perceptions of place. Linking visitors' motivations and perceptions arguably provides a richer understanding of tourist behaviour *in situ*. Hence, this chapter attempts to address these issues with specific reference to perceptions of British and French international visitors to Mauritius. A dual perspective was used in analysing the data. Initially, thematic analysis was employed to identify broad themes, and these were triangulated with content analysis from CATPAC that enabled the identification of similarities and differences in perceptions between the two key generating markets for the island. Consequently, this chapter is structured as follows. First, the research context of Mauritius is described. Second, the theoretical framework of the study is outlined. The methodological issues are then discussed, followed by the findings. Finally, the strategic implications for marketing are discussed.

Mauritius: Key and Star of the Indian Ocean

Long described as the key and star of the Indian Ocean, Mauritius is a well-established tourist destination for visitors from Europe and a highly competitive player in the Southern African region (Archer, 1985; Khadaroo & Seetanah, 2007; Wing, 1995). Mauritius has, to date, been positioned as a resort 'enclave' with its sun, sand and sea products. This positioning has emanated from a clear emphasis in government's tourism policy of attracting high-spending visitors in the 1980s, developing luxury resorts in the 1990s and attracting internationally recognized brand names of hotels such as Hilton and Sheraton in the new millennium. However, like all 'stars', fading of its appeal was inevitable. The period 2000–2005 saw the yearly tourism growth plummeting to levels below 5% on average in comparison to previous years where double-digit

Marketing Island Destinations. DOI: 10.1016/B978-0-12-384909-0.00004-0

figures were common. This prompted the government and tourism authorities to review destination development and tourism policies. In an effort to revamp tourist arrival numbers, the island embarked on a branding initiative in 2006, which, among others, had the goal of diversifying the image and repositioning the destination in its various target markets. New products for niche markets such as adventure tourism, golf tourism, cultural tourism and wellness/spa tourism were developed to capture the interest of existing and new markets such as China, Eastern Europe and Russia.

The year 2007 turned out to be exceptional, with an estimated 906 971 international tourist arrivals, representing an increase of 15.1% from 2006 figures. However, with the global financial crisis and economic downturn, international tourist arrivals grew by only 2.6% in 2008 (Handbook of Tourism Statistics, 2008). The branding process was completed, and the brand 'Mauritius' with the tag line *C'est un plaisir* was launched in October 2009. While it is too early to assess the effectiveness of the branding strategy for Mauritius, in a period of economic downturn branding theory suggests that a more focused communication strategy, a clear brand value proposition and positioning, and consistency in image marketing are critical for survival (Kapferer, 2008). Hopefully, the new brand image for Mauritius will enable the destination to maintain its popularity in its various target markets. To date, the French market remains the leader in generating countries for Mauritius, with an estimated international tourist arrivals of 240 028 in 2007, followed by the United Kingdom (107 297), Germany (65 165) and Italy (69 510). In the Southern African region, South Africa and Reunion Island remain the two main generating markets, with an estimated 81,733 and 95,823 international tourist arrivals, respectively. India (42,974), China (7739) and Australia (19,635) remain the main generating markets for the region of Asia and Australasia (Handbook of Statistics, 2007). Therefore, some evidence exists to suggest that market diversification and new product development strategies have contributed to reverse the decline in tourist numbers for the island. This context sets the scene for understanding whether British and French visitors' perceptions of the island have changed as a result of new products being marketed by the destination.

Theoretical Framework

Travel Motivations

When destinations alter their product mix and target markets, it is necessary to understand whether tourist perceptions and behaviour change accordingly. As a result, a significant amount of research has been devoted to understanding visitors' destination choice factors. These factors can be categorized into pull and push components (Andreu, Kozak, Avsi, & Cifter, 2005; Crompton, 1979; Hong, Kim, Jang, & Lee, 2006; Jang & Cai, 2002; Klenosky, 2002; Meng, Tepanon, & Uysal, 2008). Push factors are internal to the individual and instill a desire to travel (Mill & Morrison, 1998). They are related to motivational factors such as the needs for relaxation, personal development, social interaction and new cultural experiences, among others, and are often associated with Maslow's hierarchy of needs (Andreu *et al.*, 2005; Chon, 1990;

Crompton, 1979; Klenosky, 2002; Swarbrooke & Horner, 2004). Pull factors are external to individuals, and affect when, where, and how people travel, given the initial desire to travel, and often determine the attractiveness of a destination to visitors. Strong linkages between travel motivations and destination attributes have been documented in the literature (Jang & Cai, 2002) but few have investigated these from an interpretive approach. Nonetheless, it is usually accepted that push factors are present before pull factors can be effective (Mill & Morrison, 1998; Meng *et al.*, 2008), and destination image has been described as a significant pull factor (Hong *et al.*, 2006; Klenosky, 2002).

Destination Image Formation

Published research into destination image shows that it is a critical element in destination choice (Baloglu & McCleary, 1999; Beerli & Martin, 2004; Gartner, 1993; Lin, Morais, Kerstetter, & Hou, 2007; Um & Crompton, 1992). For example, Um and Crompton (1992) suggest that potential tourists frequently have limited information and knowledge about a destination that they have not previously visited, and therefore the image of a destination takes a holistic position in the visitor's decision process. The literature distinguishes between two types of images, organic and induced. Organic image refers to images derived from non-commercial information sources such as word-of-mouth and actual visitation. Induced image refers to the marketing efforts of destination promoters (Gartner, 1993; Tasci & Gartner, 2007). Actual visitation creates an image more realistic than initial expectations and is referred to as the 'complex' image of a place (Chen & Hsu, 2000).

An alternative view of destination image was proposed by Echtner and Ritchie (1991, 1993) who suggested that the construct comprises of attribute-based and holistic components. The attribute-based component refers to perceptions of individual features of a destination such as scenery, hospitality and tourist attractions. The holistic component has been described as the overall image of a destination (Lin *et al.*, 2007). The framework put forward by these authors also suggests that these two components possess functional and psychological characteristics as well as attributes that are either common to all destinations or unique to a place. This alternative conceptualization of destination image has been the most utilized and operationalized through the measurement of three components: cognitive, affective and conative. The first component refers to beliefs and knowledge about a destination and is measured through a list of functional attributes of a place (Echtner & Ritchie, 1993; Gartner, 1993). The affective component refers to feelings toward a place (Gartner, 1993) and is measured using Russel, Ward, and Pratt's (1981) affective grid scale (arousing–sleepy, pleasant–unpleasant, exciting–gloomy and relaxing–distressing). A conative component develops as a result of the interaction between cognitive and affective components and refers to intended behaviour towards the destination (Pike & Ryan, 2004).

While there seems to be agreement on the types and components of the construct, its measurement remains an area of contention. Three distinct measurement approaches have emerged over the years. The positivistic approach employing structured methodologies remains the most utilized (Gallarza, Saura, & Garcia, 2002;

Pike, 2002), while the use of mixed methods (Echtner & Ritchie, 1993; Pike & Ryan, 2004) has gathered some momentum in the last decade. However, the use of unstructured methods relying on conversational data, projective techniques and photography (Espelt & Benito, 2005; Prayag, 2007; Prebensen, 2007; Ryan & Cave, 2005; Tapachi & Waryszak, 2000) has been the favoured approach more recently. This is because destinations are increasingly viewed as social (Espelt & Benito, 2005) and individual constructions (Gallarza *et al.*, 2002; Ryan & Cave, 2005). Hence, qualitative methods offer arguably a richer and deeper understanding of visitors' perceptions and emotional attachment to a place (Prebensen, 2007; Ryan & Cave, 2005; Trauer & Ryan, 2005). They also allow both attribute-specific and holistic images to be captured (Echtner & Ritchie, 1991), while the use of conversational data allows the motives underlying visitors' choice of a destination to be identified (Tapachi & Waryszak, 2000).

The Relationship Between Motivation and Destination Image

The relationship between motivations and images has been of lesser interest to researchers (Beerli & Martin, 2004; Martin & Del Bosque, 2008). According to Moutinho (1987), motivations play an important role in destination image formation in a conscious or unconscious way. It has been argued that the cognitive component of destination image is related to the individual's beliefs about the place while the affective component is more strongly related to psychological motivations (Gartner, 1993; Martin & Del Bosque, 2008). Gartner (1993) points out that the affective component is the value that individuals attach to the place based on motivations. The affective dimension may also influence, either directly or indirectly, the overall image of the destination (Beerli & Martin, 2004). However, others (Baloglu & McCleary, 1999; Beerli & Martin, 2004) have only shown a weak relationship between these two concepts. Hence, the methodology employed for this research seeks to uncover the relationships between different motivations and images, and is described next.

Methodology

The research approach adopted was based on phenomenology. 'Phenomenology uses the familiar methodological principle that scientific knowledge begins with a fresh and unbiased description of its subject matter' (Wertz, 2005:167). Therefore, the researcher is required to 'bracket-out' during the interview in order to allow the participant to narrate their 'lived' experiences. The phenomenological approach typically involves a highly intensive and detailed analysis of the accounts produced by a comparatively small number of participants. The verbatim comments are generally captured using semi-structured interviews, focus groups or diaries, and the analysis proceeds such that patterns of meaning are developed, and reported in a thematic form (Larkin, Watts, & Clifton, 2006). As a result, a convenience sample of 40 visitors (20 British and 20 French) was interviewed using the semi-structured format. This sample size was determined using personal construct theory, which suggests that, in any series of interviews, a researcher will find repetition of common ideas, and therefore consensual realities about visitors' experiences can be identified through sample sizes of 20–25 for exploratory studies (Ryan & Cave, 2005). On average, these interviews lasted for 30 minutes and took place at the international airport of Mauritius. This location provided a sample of visitors whose experiences were 'complete' and 'fresh' in their mind. They were asked two broad questions (what made you choose Mauritius for holidays? and how do you feel about the place?). These questions were similar to those of Echtner and Ritchie (1991) and Ryan and Cave (2005).

The verbatim comments of participants from these interviews were analysed from a dual perspective. First, thematic analysis using the stepwise procedure (see Table 4.1) recommended by Braun and Clarke (2006) enabled the identification of common themes in the data. Thereafter, content analysis using CATPAC, a neural network software, was performed to identify relationships between words in the data. CATPAC generates a frequency counts of the most frequent words used in the textual data and uses a clustering algorithm to produce a dendogram that shows relationships between the most frequent words (Govers, Go, & Kumar, 2007). Given that thematic analysis is an interpretation of the researcher's level of understanding of the textual data, while CATPAC offers an independent interpretation, similarities between the two would establish the credibility of the findings.

Findings

The demographic profile of the sample (Table 4.2) indicates slightly older participants, more females interviewed and a reasonable level of repeat visitation.

Motives for Choice

The application of Braun and Clarke's (2006) approach for thematic analysis revealed the existence of three major motives for choosing the island.

Table 4.1 Stepwise Procedure for Thematic Analysis

Steps	Description of the process
1. Familiarization with the data	Transcribing data, reading and re-reading the data, noting down initial ideas.
2. Generating initial codes	Coding interesting features in the data in a systematic way across the entire data set.
3. Searching for themes	Collating codes into potential themes.
4. Reviewing themes	Checking if the themes work in relation to the coded extracts and the entire data set.
5. Defining and naming themes	Ongoing analysis to refine the specifics of each theme, and the overall story the analysis tells.

Source: Adapted from Braun and Clarke (2006).

Table 4.2 Demographic Profile of Sample

Demographics	British	French
Average age	44.7	41.9
Male	30%	40%
Female	70%	60%
Average length of stay	12.7 days	10.6 days
Main purpose of visit	Holidays (95%) MICE (5%)	Holidays (85%) MICE (15%)
Repeat visitors	25%	25%

Note: MICE refers to Meetings, Incentives, Conferences and Exhibitions.

Escape from a Mundane Environment

The need to be away from routine was a frequently expressed motive for respondents. For example, one participant commented:

> Recommendations from friends. It's our first time here, we have never been to this destination before. We have been to Caribbean islands before but never to Indian Ocean islands. I was looking for hot weather for Easter and we need to travel away from Europe over that period [need for escape].
>
> British visitor

In many cases, the transcripts showed that destination choice based on this motive was also dependent on either recommendation from others for first-time visitors or personal experiences for repeaters. For example, another participant commented:

> I was here before for holidays so I know the destination, it's different. The knowledge I have about the destination makes it an easy choice. I have learnt a lot about the place from previous trips here [need for learning]. It's a very beautiful country.
>
> French visitor

As for repeat visitors, it seems that the need for learning is an important motive guiding choice of previous visits, which then confirmed the destination as being appropriate for fulfilment of need for escape in subsequent trips. This motive is similar to findings in other studies (Beerli & Martin, 2004; Crompton, 1979; Martin & Del Bosque, 2008; Mill & Morrison, 1998; Swarbrooke & Horner, 2004).

Enhancement of Kinship and Social Interaction

It was evident that another important motive for choosing Mauritius was to reconnect with friends and relatives or to develop closer relationships among family members, as indicated in these quotes:

> My husband was from Mauritius so I came to visit with my sons as we have relatives here. We have been three times here before, but we have not been here in the last

10 years. It has changed a lot, there are much more buildings, more shops but it is still a beautiful place and we had a good time here.

British visitor

We have direct flights to here [from France], so it's an easy place to get to. But also my brother is married to a Mauritian, so we came to see how the place was and meet the new relatives.

French visitor

These quotes also suggest that the vacation served as a medium to meet new people in a different location and could potentially be the opportunity for these visitors to develop more permanent relationships with locals, as suggested by others (Beerli & Martin, 2004; Crompton, 1979; Meng *et al.*, 2008).

Specific Events

Another motive for choosing the island seems to be related to specific events in the life of the visitor. For example, some participants mentioned weddings, anniversaries and Easter holidays as the significant motivators of their choice, while others reported that the choice was made either by family members or their workplace. A participant mentioned that:

I did not choose, I am here on an incentive travel package for the organization I work for. I came here 15 years ago, it was nice to see how the place has evolved.

French visitor

This motive is also indicative of the influence of travel intermediaries on the choice process given that the island is positioned as a wedding or honeymoon destination in its European markets.

Images within Motives

In most cases, motives were closely associated with cognitive images of the place. For example, one participant commented:

I came because of the wedding of a friend, I was the bridesmaid. It's such a lovely location for a wedding, everything is just amazing, the sand, the beach, the sea, the sky ... it is an idyllic place for a wedding I guess. The couple was so happy. The food was good and tasty, a lot of variety to choose from, from Mediterranean, to Chinese, Indian, Italian, seafood, great stuff. The wedding dinner was great, excellent menu.

British visitor

This quote illustrates how the physical attributes of the place (sand, beach, sea and food) associated with a specific event (wedding) can be a significant motivator for choice. The quote below indicates that need for kinship and social interaction is also dependent on the physical attributes of the place, natural beauty and hospitality of locals in this case:

> We have family here, so we came to visit them. We know the place has nature, it's a very green place and the Mauritians, we like their kindness.
>
> French visitor

Content Analysis

Following thematic analysis, the original transcripts were entered into CATPAC to identify relationships between words for each group of visitors. The dendogram for British visitors showed the existence of five different clusters of words. The first cluster showed a strong relationship between words such as 'Mauritius', 'good', 'scenery', 'weather', 'family' and 'friends', indicating that cognitive images and visiting family and friends were important factors influencing destination choice. The second cluster showed a relationship between three words, namely 'Indian', 'Ocean' and 'islands', indicating that the geographical location of the place was a significant pull factor. The third cluster showed a relationship between 'nice' and 'place' and the fourth cluster showed a relationship between words such as 'always', 'come' and 'people'. Both clusters (3 and 4) are indicative of holistic impressions of the destination. The fifth cluster indicated the motive of escape and specific events, given that a relationship was found between words such as 'wanted', 'liked', 'different', 'Easter' and 'holidays', suggesting that visitor choice was guided by these factors.

As for the French sample, the dendogram suggested the existence of six clusters of words. The first cluster reflected the need for learning as suggested by the relationship between words such as 'chose', 'come', 'learn', 'people' and 'place'. Visiting friends and relatives was another motive, given the existence of a relationship between the words 'direct' and 'family'. The third cluster seems to be related to the need for familiarity, given that words such as 'Mauritian', 'like', 'know', 'holiday' and 'destination' clustered together, suggesting that visitors knew of the place. The fourth cluster showed a relationship between three words, 'incentive', 'travel' and 'package', indicative of specific events as an important motivator. Cognitive images such as 'sun' and 'beach' clustered together in the fifth cluster, while holistic impressions were evident from the sixth cluster, given that two words, namely 'everything' and 'really' clustered together.

These results indicate both similarities and differences between the two samples. It seems that French visitors have more motives for choosing the island, but the results overall confirm the earlier derived themes.

Cognitive Images

The frequency counts of words most used in the transcripts enabled the identification of cognitive images for Mauritius, and these can be expressed diagrammatically as shown in Figure 4.1, where n represents the number of times the word was used. Interestingly, there are some similarities between French and British visitor images

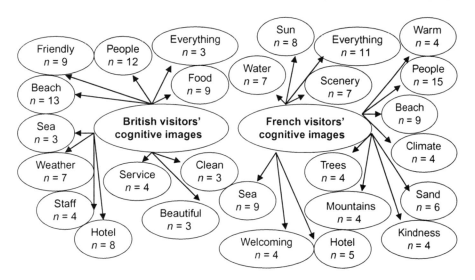

Figure 4.1 Cognitive images for Mauritius.

associated with 'beach', 'people', 'sea', 'weather/climate' and 'hotel', albeit minor discrepancies in the number of times these words were used. These images reflect the nature of the product sold but also suggest that images associated with new products such as golf and cultural tourism do not feature prominently in visitors' perceptions of the place. These findings confirm the existence of common attributes for a destination as suggested by Echtner and Ritchie (1991, 1993). In addition, Figure 4.1 shows the existence of holistic images as suggested by the use of the word 'everything' to describe images of Mauritius. However, holistic impressions seem to be more prevalent among French visitors. These visitors used more words to describe cognitive images relating to psychological attributes such as 'kindness' and 'welcoming'.

Affective Images

Thematic analysis of the question 'how do you feel about the place' revealed the existence of two major affective image components, namely relaxation and well-being.

Relaxation

Feelings of relaxation were a constant theme in the transcript. For example, a participant mentioned:

> It [Mauritius] is a lovely place. I just hope that it does not get spoilt due to overdevelopment. They need to keep it natural. There is not much motorized sports here compared to other places. It is an exclusive destination [need for prestige] and it needs to keep that. It made us feel serene, relaxed, comfortable, not feel threatened at all [need for safety]. It is very nice to have spent holidays here.
>
> British visitor

Within this quote, it can be seen that motives such as the need for prestige and safety were involved in their destination choice. Another respondent mentioned:

> It's nice to feel that the place is different from back home [need for escape], it's nice to see that it is different [need for novelty] from bigger countries that I have visited. I think I am feeling sad to leave. It [Mauritius] has very varied scenery, sea, beaches, the inside of the country, all beautiful, also for those interested in sea diving. I felt relaxation, calm, and no stress.
>
> French visitor

This quote illustrates an interplay between motives (need for escape and novelty) and cognitive images (scenery, sea, beaches and diving) in determining affective images (relaxation, calm and no stress) of a place. Hence, this finding seems to confirm the hierarchical relationship between cognitive and affective images and their relationship with motivation factors.

Well-being

A feeling of well-being at the end of their vacation was common among participants. For example, one participant mentioned:

> It's a very nice, very pleasant feeling. I am impressed always by the place and the development happening here. It is with anticipation mixed with joy that I look forward to visiting. There is a certain degree of carelessness and laid-back about the place that make me feel less stressed.
>
> British visitor

Another participant commented:

> I am very satisfied with my trip. I felt relaxed and the country is continuing to progress economically each time I come here. I also discover new places [need for novelty] for each visit, so it keeps me wanting to come back.
>
> French visitor

This quote specifically illustrates a relationship between affective images and motives as well as the influence these two factors have on trip evaluation (satisfaction) and future behaviour, which is indicative of the conative component of image. Therefore, these results seem to suggest a complex relationship between motivations, image components, satisfaction and future behaviour.

The dendogram (Figure 4.2) generated for this question from CATPAC revealed the existence of five clusters of words for British visitors. From the right, the first cluster showed a relationship between five words, namely 'relaxed', 'pleasant', 'place', 'nice' and 'lovely'. Going back to the original transcripts, the interpretation that can be offered is that visitors associated these emotions with the place during their stay. The second cluster shows a relationship between two words 'good' and 'time', which indicates the good time they spent at the destination. The third cluster

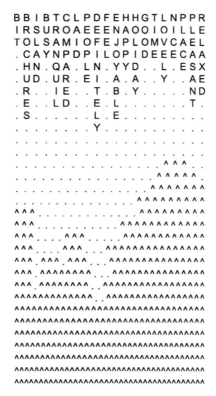

Figure 4.2 British visitors' dendogram for affective images.

shows a relationship between five words, which indicates that visitors 'definitely' 'feel' 'happy' and had an 'enjoyable' 'holiday'. The fourth cluster showed a relationship between words such as 'people', 'laid', 'compared', 'tranquil' and 'busy'. From the transcripts, it was clear that visitors perceived local people as 'laid-back', and this contributed to the perception that they felt the place was tranquil in comparison to their busy life elsewhere. The final cluster showed a relationship between three words, namely 'island', 'brochures' and 'bit' indicative of the 'island' experience being a 'bit' similar to the 'brochures' that visitors consulted as suggested in the transcripts.

As for French visitors, the dendogram (Figure 4.3) indicated the existence of four clusters of words. From the right, the first cluster consists of six words, indicative of the 'good' 'time' visitors had and positive feelings associated with 'beautiful' 'scenery', 'country' and 'people'. The second cluster shows a relationship between the word 'nothing' and 'experience'. The transcript revealed that some visitors mentioned that they felt nothing in particular about their island experience. This is perhaps indicative of the destination experience either being not differentiated enough from other holiday experiences or that visitors did not have any out-of-the ordinary experiences that stand out on this trip. The third cluster shows the reverse of the previous relationship, given that the three words, namely 'nice', 'feel' and 'different',

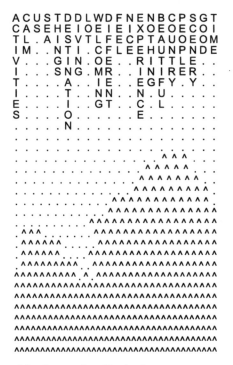

Figure 4.3 French visitors' dendogram for affective images.

are suggestive of visitors feeling that the destination experience is nice and different. The fourth cluster of words shows a weaker relationship between words such as 'lot', 'diving', 'destination', 'things', 'sea', 'us', 'calm' and 'activities'. An examination of the transcripts revealed that this relationship is indicative of the activities such as sea diving undertaken by visitors and that the destination offers many things to do but still left them feeling calm and relaxed.

An examination of these two dendograms suggests that French visitors describe their feelings for the destination based more on cognitive images while British visitors tend to describe mostly emotions associated with their experiences. These findings suggest that the two themes of relaxation and well-being derived from thematic analysis can be confirmed, given that words such as 'relax', 'happy', 'nice' and 'calm' appear in the dendograms, lending support to the use of neural network software to enhance the credibility of findings derived from thematic analysis.

Strategic Marketing Implications

These findings have a number of implications for strategic image management and destination marketing. While the identification, development and dissemination of a strong positive image of a place is necessary for visitors to consider a destination as a potential holiday place, the findings of this study tend to suggest that underlying motives play a greater role in influencing the decision process in comparison to cognitive images. Hence, destination marketers should have a thorough understanding of visitors' motives, and these should feature prominently in marketing and advertising campaigns. For example, the motive of escape from normal routine can be portrayed in advertising campaigns and brochures using images of empty beaches, underdeveloped coastlines, warm weather and blue sea. It is also apparent from the results that motivations seem to influence both cognitive and affective images. Hence, destination marketing organizations would benefit from understanding the structure of destination image as this enables the relevant attributes of a destination to be marketed to different target markets. For example, those seeking utilitarian benefits, such as relaxation, stress relief and escape, would not necessarily respond positively to advertising campaigns depicting shopping in busy streets or crowded places or cultural/historical attractions fulfilling the need for learning.

The results of the study also reveal that the traditional positioning of Mauritius as offering 'sun, sand and sea' products and stereotypical images of island destinations in general seem to persist. This is not surprising given that visitors' perceptions are difficult to change in the short term, as suggested by others (Tasci & Gartner, 2007). However, there seems to be the need for realigning communication mix elements of the destination. First-time visitors seem to be influenced more by word-of-mouth and travel intermediaries, while repeaters are influenced more by personal experiences. Therefore, communication in mass media may not be the most effective communication channel for British and French visitors. Incentives for travel intermediaries would be necessary to push the product in the distribution channel in France and the United Kingdom. The findings also suggest multiple motives and images influencing visitors' choices, which may suggest the need for segmentation if marketing resources are to be used efficiently.

Conclusion

The nature of this study neither allows for generalization of findings nor provides empirical evidence of the relationships between motivations, cognitive and affective images, and future behaviour. These relationships need to be explored in a quantitative study. However, this study shows the usefulness of conversational data in elaborating on the complexities involved in understanding motives and images of place. It also emphasizes the need for establishing credibility of findings derived from thematic analysis, which can be achieved through the use of neural network software such as CATPAC. The richness of a qualitative approach in understanding visitors' perceptions as illustrated in this chapter seems to explain the increasing popularity of qualitative techniques in destination image research.

Acknowledgement

The author would like to thank Prof. Chris Ryan from the Waikato Management School, New Zealand, for his contribution to this study.

Discussion Questions

1. What are the reasons that would explain why the traditional images of sun, sand and sea for island destinations such as Mauritius persevere despite attempts for market and product diversification?
2. Do you think that qualitative methodologies for destination image research are better at capturing relationships between image components and motivation factors?
3. In a period of global economic downturn, how could Mauritius ensure that its new destination 'brand' remains relevant for its European, Southern African and Asian markets?

References

Andreu, L., Kozak, M., Avci, N., & Cifter, N. (2005). Market segmentation by motivations to travel: British tourists visiting turkey. *Journal of Travel & Tourism Marketing, 19*(1), 1–14.

Archer, B. (1985). Tourism in Mauritius: An economic impact study with marketing implications. *Tourism Management, 16*(1), 50–54.

Baloglu, S., & McCleary, K. W. (1999). U.S. international pleasure travelers' images of four Mediterranean destinations: A comparison of visitors and non-visitors. *Journal of Travel Research, 38*(2), 144–153.

Beerli, A., & Martin, J. D. (2004). Factors influencing destination image. *Annals of Tourism Research, 31*(3), 657–681.

Braun, V., & Clarke, V. (2006). Using thematic analysis in psychology. *Qualitative Research in Psychology, 3*(1), 77–101.

Chen, J. S., & Hsu, C. H. C. (2000). Measurement of Korean tourists' perceived images of overseas destinations. *Journal of Travel Research, 38*(4), 411–416.

Chon, K. (1990). The role of destination image in tourism: A review and discussion. *Tourist Review, 45*(2), 2–9.

Crompton, J. L. (1979). Motivations for pleasure vacation. *Annals of Tourism Research, 6*(4), 408–424.

Echtner, C. M., & Ritchie, J. B. R. (1991). The meaning and measurement of destination image. *Journal of Tourism Studies, 2*(2), 2–12.

Echtner, C. M., & Ritchie, J. B. R. (1993). The measurement of destination image: An empirical assessment. *Journal of Travel Research, 31*(4), 3–13.

Espelt, N. G., & Benito, J. A. D. (2005). The social construction of the image of Girona: A methodological approach. *Tourism Management, 26*(5), 777–785.

Gallarza, M. G., Saura, I. G., & Garcia, H. C. (2002). Destination image: Towards a conceptual framework. *Annals of Tourism Research, 29*(1), 56–78.

Gartner, W. C. (1993). Image formation process. *Journal of Travel & Tourism Marketing, 2*(2/3), 191–215.

Govers, R., Go, F. M., & Kumar, K. (2007). Virtual destination image: A new measurement approach. *Annals of Tourism Research, 34*(4), 977–997.

Handbook of Tourism Statistics (2007). Ministry of Tourism, Leisure & External Communications, Mauritius.

Handbook of Tourism Statistics (2008). Ministry of Tourism, Leisure & External Communications, Mauritius.

Hong, S., Kim, J., Jang, H., & Lee, S. (2006). The roles of categorization, affective image and constraints on destination choice: An application of the NMNL model. *Tourism Management, 27*(5), 750–761.

Jang, S., & Cai, L. A. (2002). Travel motivations and destination choice: A study of British outbound market. *Journal of Travel & Tourism Marketing, 13*(3), 111–133.

Kapferer, J. N. (2008). *New strategic brand management: Creating and sustaining brand equity long-term.* Padstow: MPG Books Ltd.

Khadaroo, J., & Seetanah, B. (2007). Transport infrastructure and tourism development. *Annals of Tourism Research, 34*(4), 1021–1032.

Klenosky, D. B. (2002). The 'pull' of tourism destinations: A means–end investigation. *Journal of Travel Research, 40*(May), 385–395.

Larkin, M., Watts, S., & Clifton, E. (2006). Giving voice and making sense in interpretative phenomenological analysis. *Qualitative Research in Psychology, 3*(1), 102–120.

Lin, C. H., Morais, B., Kerstetter, D. L., & Hou, J. S. (2007). Examining the role of cognitive and affective image in predicting choice across natural, developed, and theme-park destinations. *Journal of Travel Research, 46*(November), 183–194.

Martin, H. S., & del Bosque, I. A. R. (2008). Exploring the cognitive–affective nature of destination image and the role of psychological factors in its formation. *Tourism Management, 29*(2), 263–277.

Meng, F., Tepanon, Y., & Uysal, M. (2008). Measuring tourist satisfaction by attribute and motivation: The case of a nature-based resort. *Journal of Vacation Marketing, 14*(1), 41–56.

Mill, R., & Morrison, A. (1998). *The tourist system: An introductory text* (3rd ed.). Dubuque, IA: Dendall/Hunt Publishing Company.

Moutinho, L. (1987). Consumer behavior in tourism. *European Journal of Marketing, 21*(10), 3–44.

Pike, S. (2002). Destination image analysis – A review of 142 papers from 1973 to 2000. *Tourism Management, 23*(5), 541–549.

Pike, S., & Ryan, C. (2004). Destination positioning analysis through a comparison of cognitive, affective, and conative perceptions. *Journal of Travel Research, 42*(May), 333–342.

Prayag, G. (2007). Exploring the relationship between destination image and brand personality of a tourist destination: An application of projective techniques. *Journal of Travel & Tourism Research, 2*(Fall), 111–130.

Prebensen, N. K. (2007). Exploring tourists' images of a distant destination. *Tourism Management, 28*(3), 747–756.

Russel, J. A., Ward, L. M., & Pratt, G. (1981). Affective quality attributed to environments: A factor analytic study. *Environment and Behaviour, 13*(3), 259–288.

Ryan, C., & Cave, J. (2005). Structuring destination image: A qualitative approach. *Journal of Travel Research, 44*(November), 143–150.

Swarbrooke, J., & Horner, S. (2004). *Consumer behaviour in tourism.* Oxford: Butterworth-Heinemann.

Tapachi, N., & Waryszak, R. (2000). An examination of the role of beneficial image in tourist destination selection. *Journal of Travel Research, 39*(1), 37–44.

Tasci, A. D. A., & Gartner, W. C. (2007). Destination image and its functional relationships. *Journal of Travel Research, 45*(May), 413–425.

Trauer, B., & Ryan, C. (2005). Destination image, romance and place experience – An application of intimacy theory in tourism. *Tourism Management, 26*(4), 481–492.

Um, S., & Crompton, J. L. (1992). The roles of perceived inhibitors and facilitators in pleasure travel destination decisions. *Journal of Travel Research, 30*(3), 18–25.

Wertz, F. J. (2005). Phenomenological research methods for counseling psychology. *Journal of Counseling Psychology, 52*(2), 167–177.

Wing, P. (1995). Tourism development in the South Indian Ocean: The case of Mauritius. In M. V. Conlin & T. Baum (Eds.), *Island tourism: Management principles and practice* (pp. 229–235). New York: John Wiley & Sons.

5 Market Positioning: The Case of Barbados

Jennifer V. Barrow and Sherma Roberts

The University of the West Indies, Cave Hill, Barbados, West Indies

Introduction

Market positioning can be viewed as the interface between brand identity and brand image. Positioning has two major advantages, both of which are beneficial to the destination management organization. First is that it allows the consumer to easily differentiate the brand from other similar destinations, and second, the destination through its positioning can gain competitive advantage by virtue of its distinctiveness. Barbados has arguably been able to benefit from a distinctive market position as a luxury high-end destination, perhaps having more to do with fortuitous factors of its historical relations rather than the pursuit of well-defined marketing strategy. This chapter examines the island of Barbados and the way in which its market positioning has been influenced by the overall visitor perception. Market positioning with image and attributes as the key constructs is reviewed within the context of the National Marketing Policy Framework. Using secondary data collected longitudinally, the chapter seeks to identify the extent to which product attributes and customer perceptions mirror official destination positioning.

Market Positioning

Given its foreign exchange earning and employment potential, tourism is touted as a vehicle for development in many developing countries (Holloway, 1998). As such, many destinations offering sun, sea, sand and, most recently, culture and lifestyle elements are emerging and competing for the same global travel market. Making a similar point, Gunn (1972) notes that there is an ever-increasing option of available tourism destinations for travellers to choose from and which has resulted in a case for substitutable options, as well as increased confusion. To differentiate themselves, destinations must be able to transform their comparative advantage into competitive advantage, so that their destination is not easily substitutable. The destination attributes and image therefore are important in applying this concept of product differentiation. This takes research and focused strategy in order to ensure the end result meets the needs of the customer (Kotler, Bowen, & Makens, 2006).

Marketing Island Destinations. DOI: 10.1016/B978-0-12-384909-0.00005-2

As Ries and Trout (1981) posit, market positioning is how the consumer views or perceives the product in relation to other similar products. Kotler *et al.* (2006:281) put forward three steps for the positioning strategy of a tourism entity. They include: (1) identifying a set of possible competitive advantages upon which to build a position, (2) selecting the right competitive advantages and (3) effectively communicating and delivering the chosen position to a carefully selected target market. The large number of players all with their own select messages aimed at the consumer can generate confusion in the mind of the target market. The consumer then has to filter this information in order to best retrieve and keep what is important to them, often using prior knowledge and experience. This process can lead to oversimplification of the product to a specific image, and therefore this is where perception plays a large part in decision-making. It is the responsibility of the tourism destination marketing organization (DMO) to guide the consumer in its perceptions by sending clear, simplified messages on the product being marketed. Generally this comes down to images and attributes as part of the market positioning framework, as these can determine the overall success of the marketing strategy and the resulting outcome of the destination's tourism sector in general.

The tourism destination must therefore look both internally at the product attributes and externally at the competitive set in order to effect strategic market positioning. However, the fact cannot be ignored that all destinations are not created equal and therefore do not all have a multitude of competitive advantages that cannot be easily replicated by the competition. This situation of minimum advantages creates the need for ongoing review of the product and strategic implementation of new advantages if a destination is to remain competitive (Kotler *et al.*, 2006; Hooley *et al.*, 2008; Melian-Gonzalez & Garcia-Falcon, 2003). The positioning can be based on specific product attributes or against another product class, such as the cruise ships, against destinations, against a competitor or against a specific class of user.

Successful strategic marketing and effective product positioning require that the tourism organization be constantly in touch with the changing needs, tastes and preferences of its target market Poon (1994). In other words, a clear understanding of the present and potential customer perception of the product on its own and relative to its competitors is critical to effective positioning (Echtner & Richie, 1991; Witt *et al.*, 1995; Hsu *et al.*, 2009; Prentice & Andersen, 2000). The perceptions need to be identified, segmented and acted upon with the appropriate marketing mix. This can only be accomplished through ongoing market research and concomitant tactical planning.

Product Differentiation

Inherent in the theory of competitive advantages is the concept of product differentiation across or within market segments. These advantages can be segmented as physical attribute, service, personnel, location or image, according to Kotler *et al.* (2006). Buhalis (2000) proposes that there is a need for the coordination of the delivery of the tourism product through the development of partnerships between public and private sectors in addition to differentiation of the product as several entities deliver the various segments of the product. An objective for consideration at all times is that for the position strategy to work there is the need to reinforce the company or brand image in a positive light, thereby supplanting any negative or bleary images already held by the target audience (Baloglu & McCleary, 1999). This further reiterates Ries and Trout's (1981) theory of market positioning battles being fought in the consumer's mind.

One issue that arises is whether image is the key construct in destination positioning. The image construct has been identified as influencing destination image and ultimately consumers' buyer behaviour and satisfaction with the end product (Chacko, 1997). There are, however, issues of what constitutes a destination image and how consistent this image construct is across markets and products in terms of a relevant theory (Echtner & Ritchie, 1991). In this chapter the image construct is defined as the perception of a place.

While maintaining its upmarket image, Barbados shifted its promotional tagline from a global view of 'Just Beyond Your Imagination' to 'Experience the Authentic Caribbean'. In so doing, the destination made a contracting move to position itself as a regional competitor in the customer's mind. Previous positioning taglines included 'The Best It Can Be' and 'Just Beyond Your Imagination', both of which showcased the destination's ability to capture the customer's imagination and allow customers to conjure up their own images based on the pull attributes without the direct reference to a single competitive set.

Tourism Development in Barbados

Barbados is one of the more mature Caribbean destinations, arguably located on the development stage of the Butler's life cycle (Butler, 1980). It has been identified by the United Nations as a successful small island developing state in terms of quality of life index, and this position has been attained while the economy is being driven by the tourism sector. While Barbados has had a long history of tourism dating back to the eighteenth century, it was not until the introduction of the Hotel Aids Act in 1956 and the establishment of the Barbados Tourism Authority (BTA) in 1958 that tourism in Barbados was formalized.

Barbados' reliance on tourism as the main driver of its economy is strong. At present tourism accounts for approximately 12.4% of the GDP (Central Bank of Barbados, 2004). In 2008, tourist expenditures amounted to $2.4 billion. As noted in the Inter-American Development Bank's (IADB) economic status special report on Barbados in 2006, given Barbados' size and development status, it displays strong social indicators in terms of income per capita, the poverty rate and literacy rate, placing the island 31st on the UN Human Development Index, which is among the more advanced economies in the high development group.

A mass tourism destination since the 1950s, Barbados offers the traditional three Ss (sun, sea and sand) as its primary attraction. Originally, a winter destination for the wealthy, the island in the summer would attract the less wealthy tourists who sought to emulate the lifestyle of the rich (Francis, 1992, cited by Tourism Concern,

1996). Contemporary Barbados now offers sports, heritage, cultural and eco-tourism attractions (BTA, 2001). This latter diversification has arisen in part from the democratization of travel and the increase in the more discerning, value-conscious and socially and environmentally responsible tourist, who is no longer content to just lie on the beach (Poon, 1993). An increased dependence on tourism by other warm-weather destinations has also put added pressure on Barbados to differentiate itself, and offer something more to the visitors that choose the region each year. Its global outreach as more than a beach is therefore at the forefront when positioning.

During the 1950s and 1970s, Canada was Barbados's major source market, while the United States took the lead in the 1960s and 1980s. The United Kingdom became the major source market in the 1990s and has continued to maintain this position until the present time. Currently, the island's major source markets are the United Kingdom, United States and Canada, respectively (see Table 5.1), all of which have suffered as a result of the slowdown in global economic conditions that started in 2008. These markets are supplemented by visitors from the rest of Europe and the Commonwealth Caribbean. Of note is that over the years the BTA appears to have managed to respond quite quickly to changes in its source markets and in so doing has maintained a certain level of competitiveness. It has also always positioned from a global offering rather than restricting itself to being seen as just competing with its Caribbean neighbours.

In 2008, despite challenges in main source markets, tourism contributed its highest foreign exchange earnings – a record BDS $2.4 billion. Barbados was host to 563 118 stay-over visitors and 597 523 cruise passengers (www.barstats.gov.bb). While the Caribbean as a region receives the majority of its visitors from the United States, due to the close proximity and ease of access, the arrivals to Barbados are dominated by the UK market, which contributed approximately 40% of total stay-over visitors to the country in 2008. Over recent years, the strength of the UK economy, coupled with ample scheduled and charter air access, including the luxury Concorde flights until its retirement, served to solidify the dominance of the UK market and distinguish Barbados as a quality destination.

In spite of being actively involved in tourism for a long time, Barbados does not have a strong international branded presence in the accommodation sector. Currently, the sector is dominated by independently owned and operated properties. This is seen by some in the industry as a weakness as an international brand is considered necessary for higher capture rates in the major source markets. It is thought that established brands offer some level of assurance to travellers familiar with the brands as consumers know what to expect in terms of quality service, standards and value-added. Additionally, an integral aspect of this is the increased marketing funds that could be brought to bear by the international brand company to help supplement the public funds of the BTA. However, small boutique properties have been able to successfully exist as part of the Barbados product offering giving credence to Buhalis' (2000) theory that *inter alia* a destination's characteristics are important factors in any marketing strategy.

Buhalis (2000) contends that there is a need to understand the various types of destinations and their characteristics in order to effectively market. He refers to the matching of demand based on the type of destination and the impact of travel

Table 5.1 Source Markets for Tourists to Barbados, 1960

Long-stay Visitor and Cruise Passenger Arrivals 1960–2008

Year	United States	Canada	United Kingdom	Europe	Carribean	Other	✈	% change	🚢	% change
1960	9716	3755	2102	na	14638	5324	35535	17.5	24172	41.8
1961	10522	5429	2901	na	14747	3461	37060	4.3	26943	11.5
1962	11688	7944	3363	na	17120	4143	44258	19.4	24658	-8.5
1963	13154	9991	4765	na	17773	4944	50627	14.4	27184	10.2
1964	15138	10923	6174	na	20104	5286	57625	13.8	41671	53.3
1965	19811	14212	6673	na	23264	4458	68418	18.7	52664	26.4
1966	23827	16372	8304	na	18654	11947	79104	15.6	51593	-2.0
1967	29813	18293	9622	na	16953	16884	91565	15.8	45451	-11.9
1968	41287	27879	11493	na	27707	7331	115697	26.4	75981	67.2
1969	52689	31617	10168	na	25517	14312	134303	16.1	80899	6.5
1970	57111	39609	12083	3719	33450	10445	156417	16.5	79635	-1.6
1971	68487	53690	13621	6379	33893	13005	189075	20.9	79159	-0.6
1972	75525	61918	14851	9187	36608	12260	210349	11.3	100086	26.4
1973	73280	68712	17680	11165	39443	11800	222080	5.6	116469	16.4
1974	66237	77246	23782	13039	37583	12831	230718	3.9	119524	2.6
1975	54894	75517	24802	14730	38882	12751	221576	-4.0	98546	-17.6
1976	56041	73005	25843	16784	38469	14172	224314	1.2	99406	0.9
1977	70389	83749	25841	22870	49346	17119	269314	20.1	103077	3.7
1978	85473	90992	36432	30915	55544	17527	316883	17.7	125988	22.2
1979	91354	92745	49430	41031	75966	20390	370916	17.1	110073	-12.6
1980	85526	84934	56226	38354	85408	46022	396470	6.9	156461	42.1
1981	74472	69897	72090	29621	87415	19096	352591	-11.1	135782	-13.2
1982	75511	59619	51145	21588	81864	14068	303795	-13.8	110753	-18.4
1983	113989	53198	47662	17334	83789	12366	328338	8.1	102519	-7.4
1984	140202	67307	46274	16820	83999	13050	367652	12.0	99166	-3.3
1985	148093	70573	38922	16666	71066	13915	359235	-2.3	112222	13.2

(Continued)

Table 5.1 Source Markets for Tourists to Barbados, 1960 (*Continued*)

				Long-stay Visitor and Cruise Passenger Arrivals 1960–2008						
Year	United States	Canada	United Kingdom	Europe	Carribean	Other	✈	% change	🚢	% change
1986	166 250	60 285	47 590	19 082	61 701	14 862	369 770	2.9	145 335	29.5
1987	175 093	64 349	79 152	23 598	64 356	15 311	421 859	14.1	228 778	57.4
1988	170 773	65 622	101 231	34 404	63 410	16 045	451 485	7.0	291 053	27.2
1989	154 269	65 564	118 122	43 949	62 840	16 515	461 259	2.2	337 100	15.8
1990	143 295	57 830	94 890	57 873	62 298	15 881	432 067	−6.3	362 611	7.6
1991	119 069	46 286	88 166	65 788	57 988	16 925	394 222	−8.8	372 140	2.6
1992	110 685	49 999	88 759	65 518	52 831	17 680	385 472	−2.2	399 702	7.4
1993	112 733	49 190	100 071	61 871	52 462	19 652	395 979	2.7	428 611	7.2
1994	109 092	52 286	123 455	68 077	51 487	21 235	425 632	7.5	459 502	7.2
1995	111 983	53 373	126 621	70 462	58 635	21 033	442 107	3.9	484 670	5.5
1996	111 731	54 928	139 588	62 418	56 752	21 666	447 083	1.1	509 975	5.2
1997	108 095	58 824	155 986	64 632	63 581	21 172	472 290	5.6	517 888	1.6
1998	106 300	59 946	186 690	65 045	70 358	24 058	512 397	8.5	506 610	−2.2
1999	104 953	57 333	202 772	41 221	86 127	22 208	514 614	0.4	432 854	−14.6
2000	112 153	59 957	226 787	33 988	87 424	24 387	544 696	5.8	533 278	23.2
2001	106 629	52 381	217 466	28 659	80 085	21 858	507 078	−6.9	527 597	−1.1
2002	123 429	46 754	192 606	25 328	89 505	20 277	497 899	−1.8	523 253	−0.8
2003	129 326	49 641	202 564	29 526	96 809	23 345	531 211	6.7	559 119	6.9
2004	129 675	50 025	213 945	30 030	104 754	23 073	551 502	3.8	721 270	29.0
2005 ®	131 005	47 690	202 765	26 852	114 775	24 447	547 534	−0.7	563 588	−21.9
2006	130 767	49 198	211 523	29 400	117 469	24 201	562 558	2.7	539 092	−4.3
2007 ®	133 519	52 981	223 575	27 058	99 383	36 421	572 937	1.8	616 354	14.3
2008 (P)	131 795	57 335	219 953	31 825	100 639	26 120	567 667	−0.9	597 523	−3.1

Source: Barbados Statistical Services (2009).

motivations to develop suitable product offerings. This also contributes to positioning brand to the appropriate target market both present and potential. Buhalis (2000) further contends that tourism product selection entails a wide array of criteria depending on the purpose and features of the planned travel process, citing detailed customer behaviour studies undertaken by such analysts as Gilbert and Gilbert: Swarbrooke and Homer (1999); Goodall and Goodall; Kent (1991); Mansfeld (1995); Mayo and Jarvis (1981); Sirakva, McLellan, and Uysal (1996); Mazanec (1989); Mazanec and Zins (1994); Moutinho (1987); Ryan (1997); Woodside and Lysonski (1989).

Barbados' Attributes and Image

Over the years, there have been some specific studies on Barbados' image and attributes as a tourism destination, which have contributed to the collation of secondary data on the constructs being reviewed. These studies look at data covering both the winter, high season and the summer low season based on the seasonality aspect of tourism in Barbados. They take into consideration the major source markets of the destination, including some specifics on the United Kingdom that have led the growth in Barbados in recent years (Ibrahim & Gill, 2005; Phillips Group, 2007; Poon & Thomas, 2006; Tourism Intelligence International, 2000; Vanterpool-Fox, 2008).

The brand elements highlighted for Barbados deal with such areas as its common reference as 'Little England' being a catalyst for the growth of tourist arrivals into the Caribbean from the United Kingdom. The destination was noted as having an aspirational appeal and the image as the 'wintering ground of the rich and the famous' (Poon & Thomas, 2006). A consistent pattern for attributes prioritized the climate and beaches. The IADB (Poon & Thomas, 2006) report looked at six attributes using a maximum grade of importance of 10. The attributes included climate/beaches, accessibility, heritage/culture, closeness to nature, sports/games and another option. Poon and Thomas (2006) also sought to examine the attributes by considering the appeal of the destination segmented by season.

It must be noted that arrivals into Barbados are seasonal, with the winter months receiving some 44% of its annual arrivals in the year (Poon & Thomas, 2006). However, the performance in the low season of July and August revealed high performance of these two months to the tune of 19% of total arrivals. The data showed the significance of the contribution made by returning nationals living abroad and confirmed that the destination remains a winter escape to the tropics. The use of events marketing to fill the decline in the low season also resulted in those months having the highest percentage of visitors. This reflects the role of special events marketing in boosting the industry.

The two-tiered structure with two distinct product lines covering different economic groups in terms of destination activity for the West Coast and South Coast products is also noteworthy and significant to Barbados. The West Coast properties and attractions cater to a luxury market while the South Coast attracts a more moderately priced market and myriad attractions Poon and Thomas (2006). The two-tiered structure reveals some aspect of diversification within the tourism industry that represents some resilience as the two markets are not equally affected by business cycles and economic shocks (Poon & Thomas, 2006).

Barbados experiences a high percentage of repeat visitors, showing strong levels of customer loyalty with more than 40% of the visitors being on repeat visits. The high repeat visitor factor is directly linked to high customer satisfaction with the Barbados experience. There is also a competitive element in terms of characteristics of the destination using seven other sun destinations for comparison, namely Antigua, Bahamas, Cuba, Dominican Republic, Jamaica, Mexico and St Lucia. Barbados performed in the top position overall and led the way in the areas of service quality, safety and security, accommodation, airline connections, immigration and customs, restaurants, water sports and environment. This study done by Poon and Thomas (2006) showed some similarities to that by Uysal *et al.* (2000) comparing Virginia with 10 other states.

Ibrahim and Gill (2005) used 19 attribute statements for feedback from actual visitors. Some key areas that contribute to market position strengthening include variables such as customers' perception and satisfaction linked to the sun, sea and sand image and friendliness of the people. There is also a close association of being in a relaxing and laid-back atmosphere while in Barbados. While shopping was not seen as a differentiating factor, according to Ibrahim and Gill (2005), it is interesting to note that the BTA's image perception for the Caribbean and Latin American market includes shopping and employs the marketing tagline of 'Never a Dull Moment'. Also, the UK Tourism Intelligence survey reinforced this attribute relative to the UK market in terms of the significant amount of shopping carried out in Barbados.

The strengthening of the destination's attributes and image was also seen in another study conducted by Vanterpool-Fox (2008), using an adaptation of Aakers' (1996) destination personality brand. The study highlighted the dominant characteristics of the destination brand as friendly, relaxing, outdoorsy, good-looking, secure and independent when reviewed in terms of the dimensions of 22 personality traits. In addition, the image of the destination was divided into the two clearly identified dimensions of effective/emotional and cognitive/functional. The results showed that the traits of relaxing, friendly and interesting were the top destination characteristics, gaining 5.95 out of a possible 7.00 score. Another opportunity for cross-referencing data was referred to in the Vanterpool-Fox (2008) study with the Barbados Brand Perception Study undertaken by the Phillips Group in 2007. This offered another opportunity for comparing additional data to see where the studies converge with national marketing policy.

All the studies showed that there was consistency in the key Barbados brand associations of relaxation, safety, conviviality and multi-dimensionality (Phillips Group, 2007, cited by Vanterpool-Fox, 2008). A brand descriptor of aspirational is also associated with the Barbados brand. This is linked to psychological/ emotional reasons tied to visitor self-concept and Barbados' history of premium price positioning. Also there is data to support a position on attributes such as safety, relaxed environment, friendliness and competence of the people in addition to good infrastructure and reliable utilities (Phillips Consulting Group, 2007, as cited in Vanterpool-Fox, 2008).

Destination Attributes/Marketing Policy Convergence

In positioning Barbados it cannot be taken out of its context as a part of the wider English-speaking Caribbean. The images of beautiful beaches, friendly people and warm climates are standard for the region and seen in the various collateral material used in the marketing activities. Barbados' official tourism website (www.visitbarbados. org) opens on its home page with the words:

> The Island of Barbados is recognized around the world for its sheer natural beauty, the richness of its culture and above all the friendliness of its people.

The mission of the tourism marketing organization is to position Barbados as the premier, globally competitive, year-round, warm-weather destination, contributing to a sustainable quality of life for its people. This image portrayed is the one the national tourism marketers have presented to the world. Any correlation to what is perceived by the Barbados visitor needs to be confirmed in order to assess whether the BTA's marketing positioning strategy is effective in driving the tourism sector.

Previous studies indicate there are specific common trends in the images and attributes across seasons and markets, as seen in Figure 5.1. These pull factors or external motivators that influence the decision-making process and ultimate destination choice are part of the image and attributes construct of destination marketing (Camprubi, Guia, & Comas, 2008).

According to the BTA, the island's market positioning is based on the destination being perceived as upmarket and therefore an aspirational buy. This is seen as leading to a trickle-down effect to induce the discerning traveller to want to visit the destination.

Conclusion

Effective positioning of Barbados is dependent upon a clear understanding of the needs and wants of the identified target markets. The customers' perception of the destination product influences their decision-making process in terms of choice of destination, especially where there are common aspects shared by the choices under consideration (Chacko, 1997).

The Caribbean as a tourism area has traditionally been known as a winter escape. The sun, sea and sand remain very important components of Caribbean islands including Barbados. This is particularly important for winter-weary travellers. However, for Barbados there is a distinct winter/summer customer and West Coast/South Coast element in terms of differentiation. What is constant across the year and markets and timeframes under review is the commonality of attribute construct elements of above-average safety, hospitality and diverse nature. However, it is important that the relevant authorities do not dismiss the original pull factors of sun, sea and sand in a rush to embrace niche-specific activity, and the 3S appear to remain the primary image before the others can come into consideration.

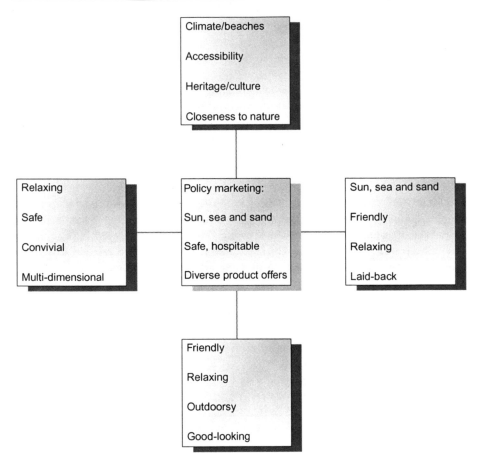

Figure 5.1 Independent attributes/images in relation to policy marketers' position.

It is therefore recommended that the market positioning should remain closely linked to the customer perception as there is convergence with national image. Regular reviews should be undertaken to ensure that this remains the case and, if not, adjustments would need to be made taking into consideration changing consumer wants and needs.

This chapter has reviewed market positioning using the key constructs of image and attributes. The review of secondary data on Barbados was collated by a review of studies undertaken over different periods of time. In looking at market positioning, the authors have sought common trends and any links to the national marketing policy position objectives while reviewing the taglines used to strengthen the image being portrayed to influence customer buying behaviour. There are commonalities, and there is the resulting inference that the national position takes into consideration the needs and wants of the target market based on their perception of the destination product. However, Barbados needs to maintain a global focus in market positioning rather than restrict itself to a regional competitive stance. In this way, it can also enhance its branding potential.

For Barbados to remain competitive it must undertake ongoing research. Further surveys are recommended across a one-year time period to encompass both summer and winter visitors at the destination in addition to including focus groups in the source markets for correlations of those who have visited and those who have not. However, although a weakness may be inferred, as based on Porter (1979), a brand positioning analysis is incomplete without a competitive point of reference, as image as a perception of place does not lend itself to clear definition of market positioning analysis. However, Kotler *et al.* (2006) contend that positioning can look at the product attributes and whether their needs or wants are being fulfilled in order to position to specific class of users or against an existing competitor as this chapter has sought to do. Barbados has been successful over the years in positioning specifically to class of user. Its attempt at positioning against existing competitor was short-lived. The destination therefore needs to continue in the more expansive approach of class of user positioning rather than with a more restrictive positioning against an existing competitor. Its historical strength has remained valid over time. As Chacko (1997) indicated, for a truly strong market position, it is necessary for a destination to differentiate itself from its competitors on meaningful attributes for the customer as this offers a competitive edge.

Discussion Questions

1. What variables might be used to segment Barbados' target market?
2. Explain how Barbados' positioning can impact overall destination performance.
3. What potential new markets could the BTA target based on their main attributes?

References

Aaker D. A. (1996). *Building strong brands*. New York: The Free Press

Baloglu, S., & McCleary, K. W. (1999). A model of destination image formation. *Annals of Tourism Research*, 26(4), 808–889.

Barbados Ministry of Tourism. (2001). Green paper on the sustainable development of tourism in barbados – A policy framework. Government of Barbados.

Barbados Statistical Services. http://www.barstats.gov.bb. Accessed 6 July 2009.

Barbados Tourism Authority. (2001). *Annual report 1999–2000*. Barbados: The Barbados Tourism Authority.

Buhalis, D. (2000). Marketing the competitive destination of the future. *Tourism Management*, 21(1), 97–116.

Butler, R. (1980). The concept of a tourist area cycle of evolution. *Canadian Geographer*, 24, 5–12.

Camprubi, R., Guia, J., & Comas, J. (2008). Destination networks and induced tourism image. *Tourism Review*, 63(2), 47–58.

Caribbean Tourism Organization. (CTO). http://www.onecaribbean.org. Accessed 6 July 2009.

Central Bank of Barbados (2005). *2004 Annual Report Barbados*. Central Bank of Barbados.

Central Bank of Barbados. (2008). *Annual report 2008*. Barbados.

Chacko, H. (1997). Positioning a tourism destination to gain a competitive edge. *Asia Pacific Journal of Tourism Research*, *1*(2), 69–75.

Echtner, C. M, & Ritchie, J. R (1991). The meaning and measurement of destination image. *The Journal of Tourism Studies*, *2*(2), 2–12.

Gunn, C. (1972). *Vacationscape: Designing tourist regions*. Austin: University of Texas, Bureau of Business Research.

Holloway, J. C. (1998). *The business of tourism* (5th edn.). Harlow: Pearson Education.

Hooley, G., Piercy, N. F., & Nicoulaud, B. (2008). *Marketing strategy and competitive positioning* (4th edn.). Harlow: Pearson Education.

Hsu, T.-K., Tsai, Y.-F., & Wu, H.-H. (2009). The preference analysis for tourist choice of destination: A case study of Taiwan. *Tourism Management*, *30*, 288–297.

Ibrahim, E., & Gill, J. (2005). A positioning strategy for a tourist destination based on analysis of customers' perceptions and satisfactions. *Marketing Intelligence and Planning*, *23*(2), 172–188.

Inter-American Development Bank (IADB). (2006). Barbados: Meeting the challenge of competitiveness in the 21st century. In L. Rojas-Suarez & D. Thomas (Eds.), *Special publication on development no. 2*. Washington, DC: IADB Office of External Relations.

Kotler, P., Bowen, J. T., & Makens, J. C. (2006). *Marketing for hospitality and tourism* (4th edn.). Harlow: Pearson.

Melian-Gonzalez, A., & Garcia-Falcon, J. M. (2003). Competitive potential of tourism in destinations. *Annals of Tourism Research*, *30*(3), 720–740.

Nation Newspaper Getting on with Tourism. 20 June. Internet edition (2002). http://www.nationnews.com.

Poon, A. (1993). *Tourism, technology and competitive strategies*. Wallingford: CABI.

Poon, A., & Thomas (2006) as cited in IADB report, *Barbados: Meeting the challenge of competitiveness in the 21st century*.

Porter, M. (1979). How competitive forces shape strategy. *Harvard Business Review March–April*, 137–145.

Prentice, R., & Andersen, V. (2000). Evoking Ireland: Modeling tourist propensity. *Annals of Tourism Research*, *27*(2), 490–516.

Ries, A., & Trout, J. (1981). Positioning: *The battle for your mind*. New York: Warner Books.

The Phillips Consulting Group (2007). *Barbados Brand Perception Study*, October 2007 as cited in Vanterpool-Fox (2008).

Tourism Concern. (1996). *Trading places: Tourism as trade*. London: Tourism Concern.

Tourism Intelligence International. (2000). *How the British will travel 2005*. Report.

Uysal, M., Chen, J., & Williams, D. (2000). Increasing state market share through regional positioning. *Tourism Management*, *21*, 89–96.

Vanterpool-Fox (2008) Consumers' perception of the Barbados destination brand. MSc dissertation for Masters in Management, University of Surrey.

Witt, S. F., Brooke, M. Z., & Buckley, P. J. (1995). *The management of international tourism* (2nd ed.). London: Routledge.

World Tourism Organization. http://unwto.org.

WTO (World Tourism Organization). *Millennium tourism boom in 2000*. Press release, January. Internet edition (2001). http://www.world-tourism.org.

6 Investigating Marketing Opportunities of a Politically Challenged Island Destination: The Case of North Cyprus

Erdogan H. Ekiz*, Kashif Hussain* and Stanislav Ivanov[§]

*Taylor's University College, Malaysia; [§]International University College, Bulgaria

Introduction

Tourism is often regarded as the world's largest and most diverse industry and a major global economic force. According to the World Travel and Tourism Council's (2010:6) figures, tourism generates US$7.892 billion economic contribution world-wide (9.9% of all earnings) while employing 238.3 million people (8.4% of total employment), representing one in every 11.9 jobs. Jafari (2001:29) posited that tourism made a great improvement from humble figures to leading ones, in particular noting that '… in 1950, 25.3 million international tourists arrivals resulted in 2.1 billion USD receipts … in 1998, 625 million international tourists generated $445 billion receipts'. This figure reached to 922 million international tourists in 2008 creating over US$1.1 trillion, corresponding to US$3 billion a day, with a 1.7% increase in real terms (United Nations World Tourism Organization, 2010).

Tourism is becoming an increasingly important component in the economies of many developing nations, but not without controversy (Honey, 1999; Mowforth & Munt, 1998). In particular, some developing nations have promoted themselves as international tourism destinations, as a means of attracting foreign investment and incoming cash flow. The shape and path of tourism development has differed considerably between countries, depending not only on their natural attractions, but also on accessibility, infrastructure, government policies and market moves by major international tourism operators (Holloway, Humphreys, & Davidson, 2009). Very broadly, for example, the Caribbean has become known for its coastal resorts, and East and Southern Africa for their wildlife. South-east Asia, Australia and Latin America are known for a combination of natural, cultural and adventure activities (Starr, 2003).

The above-mentioned economic benefits have meant that tourism has maintained its primacy in developing countries not to mention small island states, such as

Marketing Island Destinations. DOI: 10.1016/B978-0-12-384909-0.00006-4

North Cyprus. More specifically, earnings from the tourism industry are crucial for small island economies, yet they face many challenges as tourist destinations (Milne, 1992). Small islands are physically separated by water and long distance from the tourist-generating markets. As a result the accessibility of the destination suffers as tourists outside the island can reach there by only two means of transportation – air and water (excluding islands near coasts that can become accessible via bridges). Another challenge is the limited local market for capital, labour, food and water supplies and other products used in the tourism industries, which limits the competition among suppliers and increases prices. Furthermore, according to Hall (1994), political stability is also an essential prerequisite for attracting international tourists to a destination and a fundamental precondition to the successful establishment, growth and survival of a successful tourism industry. One example is the divided island of Cyprus where North Cyprus has been suffering from political instability (Ioannides & Apostolopoulos, 1999; Seddighi, Theocharous, & Nuttall, 2002) and facing several challenges to market itself as a tourist destination. Embargoes and sanctions placed on North Cyprus, an unrecognized island state in the world, are affecting its economy, transportation sector (no direct transportation means except the ports of Turkey), arrivals figures, producers and farmers, and the construction sector. All of these obstacles impact negatively upon tourism development and pose a challenge for the state to market itself as a tourist destination.

The Competitive Destination

Kotler, Haider, and Irving (1993) acknowledge that we are living in a time of 'place wars', where places and destinations are engaged in competitive behaviour within the tourism industry. The Mediterranean, the most visited tourism region of the world, is also affected by increasing competition from many new, more exotic and cheaper destinations that offer the same core sun-lust tourism product (Buhalis, 1999). The attractiveness or competitiveness of a destination is often dependent on a mix of push and pull factors, and varies from one destination to another. Weaver and Lawton (2002) suggest that some of these pull factors are geographical proximity to markets, accessibility to markets, availability of attractions, cultural links, availability of services, affordability, peace and stability, positive market image and pro-tourism policies. Similarly, Mathieson and Wall (1982) argue that the characteristics of potential destinations play an important role in the final choice of the destination. For example:

- *Environmental features and processes*: These include for instance what kind of nature the destination has (mountains, lakes, sea), amount of sunshine, the types of animals, temperature and other environmental processes.
- *Economic structure*: This includes among other things the level of economic development and the diversity of the economic base.
- *Political organization*: The political structure of the destination is essential. Factors such as existence of capitalism or socialist principles; incentives and constraints; the roles of national, regional and local tourist organizations have an influence on tourists.

- *Level of tourist development*: This category encompasses the level of local involvement in tourism, nature and diversity of attractions, types and quality of accommodation the destination has to offer, activities and eating facilities.
- *Social structure and organization*: This category includes factors such as the demographic profile of the host population, the strength of local culture and the levels of health and safety. In addition for some tourist things like religion, women in workforce and moral conduct have an enormous effect on the decision about the choice of the final destination. Perceptions, attitudes and values towards language, traditions and gastronomic practices affect on the decision as well.

It is to the political challenges that hamper North Cyprus's marketing efforts and by extension its ability to optimize its economic potential that the discussion now turns.

Background of Political Dispute in Cyprus

The island of Cyprus is situated in the eastern part of the Mediterranean Sea, and is its third largest island, at 224 km long and 96 km wide, with 768 km of coastline. It is very rich in terms of landscape, history and cultural heritage, being the mythical birthplace of Aphrodite. Its history is filled with waves of conquest and colonization, and during the past five thousand years it has been occupied by the Phoenicians, Assyrians, Arabs, Greeks, Normans, Franks, Genovese, Venetians, Ottomans and British. The Ottomans conquered Cyprus in 1571, and Ottoman rule was replaced by British annexation in 1878. In 1925 Cyprus was officially declared a British Crown Colony. The struggle for independence lasted until 1960, when Cyprus gained independence from Britain after the Greek and Turkish communities reached an agreement on a constitution, which was a '… complex power-sharing arrangement' (Fisher, 2001:310). The tensions between the Greek Cypriot majority and Turkish Cypriot minority came to a head in December 1963, when violence broke out in the capital of Nicosia following new proposals on the constitution in favour of Greek Cypriots (Hasguler, 2002). Despite the deployment of United Nations (UN) peacekeeping forces, random inter-communal violence emerged throughout the island in 1964. In 1974, a Greek-sponsored attempt to seize control of Cyprus (Symeonidou, 2005) was met by military intervention from Turkey. Then in 1983 the Turkish-held area declared itself the 'Turkish Republic of Northern Cyprus' (North Cyprus), but it is recognized only by Turkey (Fisher, 2001).

Although hosting two countries on one island is not an exception worldwide (e.g. Haiti and the Dominican Republic, and British St Martin and the Dutch St Maarten), the situation in the island of Cyprus is peculiar because currently North Cyprus is recognized only by Turkey (Gursoy, Ekiz, & Chi, 2007). Moreover, the two sides of the island share the same city as their capital – Nicosia for the Republic of Cyprus and Lefkosa for North Cyprus. North Cyprus covers an area of 3355 km^2, which is approximately one-third of the whole Island. The neighbours of North Cyprus are Turkey, Syria, Egypt, Israel, Lebanon, Greece and South Cyprus.

UN efforts to reach an agreement to reunite the divided island ended when the Greek Cypriots rejected the UN settlement plan in a referendum in April 2004. The aim of the referendum was to achieve a common will among the island's inhabitants for unification before the Republic of Cyprus entered the European Union. It was expected that with accession to the European Union, financial aid would be provided to the Constituent state in the north and that this would affect the economy positively, expand the number of tourists, increase the welfare of producers and farmers, develop the construction sector and remove the embargoes, besides giving Turkish Cypriots their own identity. Following the defeat of the UN plan in the referendum, there was no attempt to restart negotiations between the two sides until 18 April 2008. However, the island did enter the European Union on 1 May 2004.

Although the island has entered the European Union, only Greek Cypriots (South Cyprus) enjoy the full benefits of being an European Union Member State. Despite the fact that the results of the referendum were not in favour of North Cyprus, the state is developing several initiatives to give its tourism sector a brighter future. The present study therefore investigates the marketing opportunities of a politically challenged island destination – North Cyprus.

An Overview of Tourism in the Island of Cyprus

The Republic of Cyprus continues to be one of the most preferred locations for vacations in Europe. Despite the damage of the political and military problems in 1974, there was a fast recovery and tourist arrivals had exceeded the 1973 level by 1979, although it took several more years before the bed capacity recovered the levels of 1974 (Dana & Dana, 2000). The number of visitors was 24000 in 1960, growing to half a million in 1982, a million in 1988, 2 million in 1994 and 2.4 million in 2008 (Cyprus Tourism Organization, 2009). The expansion in tourist arrivals was facilitated by a parallel rise in the construction of new hotels, apartments and other tourist accommodation located almost exclusively in the coastal regions. There was an unprecedented rise in the number of beds from under 13000 in 1980 to over 78000 in 1995, and 96500 at the end of 2004, an average annual rate of increase of 12.8%. Tourism receipts in 2008 were CY£1.858 million (roughly US$2.506 million). Receipts from tourism represented 47.6% of the 2008 total receipts from exports of goods and services (Cyprus Tourism Organization, 2009).

In contrast to the South, which is a well-developed tourist destination, North Cyprus is still developing and its economy is handicapped by the international political and economic isolation of the country, as well as by the lack of private and governmental investment. The tourism industry's contribution has also not been optimal, given the political constraints of North Cyprus being an internationally unrecognized state and the imposition of political embargoes (Altinay, 1994). As Altinay, Altinay, and Bicak (2002:178) mention, 'in spite of its significant contribution to the North Cyprus economy, the tourism industry is lagging behind its competitive strength when compared with its main rivals'. While South Cyprus has turned into a well-established destination, North Cyprus has struggled to achieve economic growth and escape from its political and economic dependence on Turkey (Yasarata, Altinay, Burns, & Okumus, 2010).

Tourism Development in North Cyprus and Available Potential Segments

The tourism industry has been one of the main sectors for North Cyprus's economy. Despite its comparative advantage of rich geographical and natural resources, North Cyprus has not been able to fully harness that potential to enhance its competitiveness owing to the embargoes, restrictions in transportation (direct ferries/ships and direct flights) and competition with other countries. Since the second half of the 1980s, the tourism industry in North Cyprus has grown steadily, resulting in new travel agencies and the construction of new hotels, restaurants, bars, cafes and pubs and increasing competition between them. The North Cyprus tourism industry hosted 791 036 tourists, with a bed capacity of 13 000+, in 2008 (Statistical Yearbook of Tourism, 2009). Moreover, the ratio of net tourism income to the trade balance was 44.1% (US$303.2 million). The value added in the tourism sector in 2008 was almost US$376.2 million (Statistical Yearbook of Tourism, 2009). The main tourist-generating markets for North Cyprus were Turkey, Britain and Germany.

According to the Statistical Yearbook of Tourism (2009), there were 122 tourist accommodation venues in North Cyprus, with a total capacity of 13 000+ beds. This accommodation included 13 five-star hotels, 6 four-star hotels, 19 three-star hotels, 17 two-star hotels and 19 one-star hotels. There were also 48 special-class hotels, boutique hotels, bungalows, traditional houses or guesthouses. These establishments provided employment for 10 857 people, including 17 casinos, which constituted 7% of total employment (Statistical Yearbook of Tourism, 2009). There were 137 travel agencies. Adult entertainment, which although legal in North Cyprus, remains a sensitive issue and is difficult to investigate in terms of number of tourists, and the income generated. North Cyprus also boasted 46 nightclubs and nine pubs. The annual occupancy rate for hospitality organizations was estimated to be 30% in 2007.

Cansel, Bavik, and Ekiz (2008) argue that official tourism figures for North Cyprus might not reflect the real situation. In other words, they claim that official figures fail to include the earnings from the education, airline and accommodation sectors and the gambling industry. By considering these tourism-related activities, they calculated tourism revenue per capita for North Cyprus at US$1288. This figure is almost five times Turkey's per capita tourism income and half of that for South Cyprus.

According to Cansel et al. (2008), the main reasons for tourists visiting North Cyprus have been education, gambling, sex tourism and leisure. Existing infrastructure and growth in North Cyprus indicates that education, gambling, sex and sea, sun and sand (3S) tourism will continue to be the main potential segments of tourist expectation in the future (Cansel et al., 2008; Yasarata et al., 2010).

The education sector is one of the important income-generating sectors beside tourism, and generates over US$230 million per year for North Cyprus. There are some 37 000+ registered students, among which 25 000+ are from Turkey, 4000+ are from 65 different nationalities and the remainder are local students, studying at five public and private universities (two public and three private) in North Cyprus. In addition, the Middle East Technical University (METU) of Turkey, which is one of the oldest and most respected universities, has been accepting students for its campus in the Güzelyurt region of North Cyprus. Each of these foreign students spends approximately US$12000 on tuition fees, accommodation, food and other outlays.

As mentioned above, the UN has sanctioned boycotts prohibiting direct international flights to the North (Scott & Asikoglu, 2001). After 2002, following UN efforts and European Union interests, a bipartite agreement was signed between South and North Cyprus (with opening of the borders between the two states on the island, creating a new market), which led to the provision of better transportation links for foreign tourists, although there were still no direct flights. This policy change also meant that Greek Cypriots could now visit North Cyprus. The opening of the borders has also increased the potential of gambling and sex tourism as well as 3S tourism and the VFR (visiting friends and relatives) market. It has also created new hopes for the development of religious tourism as Cyprus possesses a rich cultural heritage.

According to *Forbes* magazine, money transactions generated by the gambling industry reached US$900 billion worldwide (http://www.ntv.com.tr/news). In 2006, there were 21 active casinos generating US$172153050 annually in North Cyprus (Ozgec, 2006). Some US$80 million of this amount was generated by Greek visitors to the island, and some US$90 million by gamblers from Turkey and other nationalities. The remaining US$2153050 is assumed to be generated by wealthy students to whom entrance to the casinos was officially forbidden. Likewise, it is also forbidden for local Turkish Cypriots to enter and play in casinos.

Beside 3S holidays, adult entertainment (sex tourism) was in high demand. In 2006, there were 336 prostitutes working with legal permits in licensed nightclubs and pubs. These clubs and pubs contributed approximately US$4714285 annually to the North Cyprus economy through permits, taxes, visa and passport fees, social security, reserve fund, weekly health checks in hospitals and so on (Cansu, 2006). If one prostitute earns approximately US$300 daily, an annual total of US$43800000 can be calculated. Assuming half of this money comes from tourists visiting North Cyprus, this accounts for a US$21900000 contribution to tourism revenue.

The national airline (Cyprus Turkish Airlines) and the monopolistic ferry company also contribute to tourism revenue. Other private airlines and shipping companies contribute by their taxes. Cyprus Turkish Airlines carried 946000 passengers paying approximately US$200 per person, generating a total of US$189.2 million in tourism revenue. The Sea Transportation Company carried over 300000 passengers paying US$50 per person, which makes US$15 million approximately. Conjecturally, half of these passengers are foreign tourists and contribute over US$102.1 million in total, with US$94.6 million from air and US$7.5 million from sea transportation.

The MICE (meeting, incentives, conferences and events) and niche markets, such as nature/adventure, religion and sport, are also growing in importance. However, these tourist segments are still fairly new so their contribution to the economy is not yet significant. There are also other investment opportunities available in North Cyprus tourism, such as marinas, golf and country clubs, theme parks and luxury retirement communities. Nonetheless, as an internationally isolated small island state, North Cyprus suffers from challenges such as scarcity of resources, a comparatively small domestic market, difficulties in forming and running businesses and accessibility to markets to promote the destination and its products (Altinay & Hussain, 2005; Gursoy *et al.*, 2007).

According to the Statistical Yearbook of Tourism (2009), currently, North Cyprus is unable to offer differentiated tourism products in comparison to neighbouring Mediterranean states. Consequently, demand for tourism is not effectively increasing. For the North, there is a need to revise its rules and regulations, and increase the variety of tourism products, which will generate competitive advantage and differentiated tourism products. SWOT analysis (Table 6.1) of North Cyprus's tourism sector

Table 6.1 SWOT Analysis of the Tourism Industry in North Cyprus

Strengths	Weaknesses
• Undiscovered and unspoiled • Hospitality of citizens • Mild climate of Cyprus, which provides an ideal situation for holiday in all seasons • Variety of flora and fauna • Beaches ideal for swimming and all kinds of water sports • Variety of Cyprus cuisines • High quality of natural resources • Richness of cultural and historical resources • Environmental-friendly accommodation establishments • Availability of new investment areas	• No direct flight from other countries (except Turkey) • Cheaper flights to other Mediterranean countries including South Cyprus • Lack of 'product image' • Lack of variety in provided services to meet changing market trends • Lack of public transportation • Political isolation • Lack of marketing segmentation and differentiation knowledge • Lack of infrastructure • Insufficient urban planning • Lack of financial resources
Opportunities	**Threats**
• Possibility of formation of an economically, environmentally and socially appropriate tourism product • Political determination and commitment to tourism • Possibility of using Gecitkale airport for tourist purposes • High tourism potential of the Eastern Mediterranean • Growing potential of special interest tourism worldwide • Growing collaboration between Turkey and Greece • Growing economic power of Turkey and possibility of European Union membership • Possibility of an agreement in Cyprus problem and European Union membership	• Competition with the other Mediterranean countries • Environment pollution in the Mediterranean region. • Political uncertainty in North Cyprus • Existing embargoes • Uncertainties in the Middle East • Possible conflicts in the Balkan region • Economic problems and crises in Turkey

outlines possible conditions for future tourism development. Creating differentiated tourism products based on comparative advantage over similar destinations may help to develop proper goals and strategies for North Cyprus's tourism industry. The North Cyprus tourism industry should focus on developing tourism based on regional differentiation in the Mediterranean. More specifically, it should adopt special inter- est tourism in addition to mass tourism and develop tourism to benefit from both natural and manmade environments. Also, a review of strengths and opportunities suggests that North Cyprus tourism industry should develop tourism in coordination with NGOs, local authorities, the private sector and universities. Tourism adminis- trators should focus on a tourism development model that is in harmony with other sectors, such as transportation and education. They should adopt appropriate models to meet the social, economic and physical transport facilities (especially to deal with direct flights). Finally, administrators should work towards structuring the tourism industry and policies free from political influence.

Current Trends in North Cyprus

When current trends are analysed, it can be clearly seen that preferences are shifting from the main 3S tourism stream to more specific niche segments. Destination coun- tries plan to use their strengths and comparative advantages to increase their share from these specific niches. Nature–adventure trips, ecotourism, purchasing and leas- ing land from exotic countries, culture, education and health tourism are increasing in popularity. Countries that use their unspoiled resources wisely are more likely to be the popular destinations of the future. North Cyprus, with its unspoiled natural and cultural resources, has this advantage.

Both Turkey and Republic of Cyprus are direct competitors of North Cyprus. However, this competition is concentrated on 3S tourism, where North Cyprus has no distinct strategic advantage. Since 2002, Turkey has pledged to establish a US$300 million investment project in North Cyprus with the help of Turkish businessmen. A part of these investments includes the Bafra region, which provides the region with six quality hotels, comprising 3 five-star, 1 three-star and 2 two-star hotels, creat- ing an increase of 3104 bed capacity. However, the target market is gamblers whose spend is often concentrated within the hotel and not spread among businesses located in the region.

Education industry in North Cyprus is also being challenged by a fall in univer- sity enrolment from Turkey. South Cyprus is also expanding into education tourism and is developing campuses for six new universities. This will create competition for foreign students planning to visit Cyprus island for education purposes. Education tourism has a 59.5% share of overall tourism revenue and has a vital importance for the North Cyprus economy (Cansel *et al.*, 2008). If, for any reason, a decline occurs in education tourism, this may create radical changes in per capita tourism revenues.

In view of the two-sided agreement between both administrative bodies of Cyprus (opening of the borders between the two states on the island in 2002), tourists recently have started to fly to South Cyprus and cross the border to the North Side by land transportation. This new development and the direct competition from the Turkish airline companies have led to a decline in the revenues of the national airline, Cyrus Turkish Airlines. As this situation continues, it will also cause a loss in North Cyprus tourism revenues. Other challenges that have affected tourism growth in North Cyprus include low levels of training, unacceptable service standards, poor public transportation, lack of personnel at ports of entry, English language deficiencies, duplicitous representations of North Cyprus by tour operators and unfair treatment of Turkish tourists (Altinay *et al.*, 2002; Altinay & Hussain, 2005; Cansel *et al.*, 2008; Scott & Asikoglu, 2001; Yasarata *et al.*, 2010).

Marketing North Cyprus

As mentioned, the main tourist-generating markets for North Cyprus have been Turkey, Britain and Germany, targeting tourists through traditional marketing channels. These are mainly magazines, brochures, websites, travel agencies, tour operators and international exhibitions. Magazines and brochures have been the mainstay for marketing North Cyprus for decades, but with the rise of technology and the Internet, many websites and fora have been developed for marketing. Given North Cyprus' political situation, the Government and Ministry of Tourism routinely monitor the content of these websites and highlight appropriateness to website developers. Several Internet-based fora have been launched in which the Turkish Cypriot expatriate community monitors the sites and spreads a positive word-of-mouth about North Cyprus. One of the most significant examples is the use of the social media, especially Facebook. The Ministry of Tourism in North Cyprus also offers incentives to local and international travel agencies and tour operators to attract tourists, e.g. for every tourist brought to stay more than three nights in North Cyprus the Government will pay $50 to participating travel agents or tour operators; also for mass tourism the Government is willing to share some of the promotional expenses. The best-known tour operators bringing tourists to North Cyprus routinely publish newspaper and TV advertisements in the main tourist-generating countries. The Ministry of Tourism facilitates and provides travel agents and tour operators a free airfare to international exhibitions. The state is also trying to enter the Russian market to attract tourists, although the lack of direct flights remains a problem.

Future Directions

Today, tourism is one of the largest industries in the world and is continuously expanding. One of the factors that have enabled the tourism industry to spread worldwide is the process of globalization. Over the last decade, globalization has led to increased competition and a need for cooperation. To be able to survive, companies and organizations within the tourism industry have to establish networks and cooperate (Fyall & Garrod, 2005).

Tourism destinations are probably one of the most difficult 'products' to market, involving large numbers of stakeholders and a brand image over which a destination marketing manager typically has little control. The diversity and complexity of tourism destinations is well documented, and this makes brand development difficult for national, regional and local tourism organizations. Destination branding necessarily involves the focused attention of all tourism-related organizations in a destination, and this can create major challenges in getting all stakeholders to develop a coherent theme for the destination brand.

North Cyprus currently generates a significant per capita income from tourism. However, this situation could deteriorate if changes and developments in the macro environment are not carefully monitored and analysed. If North Cyprus' forte of gambling, sex and education tourism niches is undermined, then other resources should be used to support infrastructural investments. These resources are rare, possessed by few other Mediterranean countries, and if well managed and utilized can provide significant tourism revenues for North Cyprus (see Table 6.1).

Only those destinations that have a clear market position and appealing attractions will remain at the top of consumers' minds when they book their holidays. In the highly competitive and dynamic global tourism environment, there is a need to develop a clear identity or 'brand' based on reality, while also reflecting the core strengths and 'personality' of the product. In this crowded marketplace, building and maintaining brand value is the key to business success and, as a result, brand management is quickly shifting from a peripheral marketing concern to the core business strategy. In this sense, it is important for policy makers in North Cyprus to target the right market using the correct mix of product, price and marketing communications. The following products and target markets are suggested:

- *Golf courses, country clubs and luxury summer residents*: Targeting the Middle East and selected European countries, this type of investment should attract international finance and know-how. It may present an opportunity to become a prestigious tourism haven and does not pose a threat to the environment.
- *Modern marinas, yachting clubs and facilities*: Developing attractive marinas and surrounding facilities can put North Cyprus on the map as a favoured destination for yachts, especially when convenient connections are made to country clubs and other tourist areas.
- *Luxury senior citizen care centres in combination with health facilities*: As health tourism gains momentum, it starts to generate large revenues for those countries with good health services and facilities. There is also a migration trend for retired people from expensive European countries to slow-paced, friendly-climate areas of the world. Creating excellent senior care facilities supported with excellent health facilities would attract many financially secure elderly to North Cyprus.
- *Facilities for international water sports and facilities for athletes and teams who need milder climates in winter time*: These types of facilities can play a major role in country promotion through recognizable event organizations, continuing the inflow of funds in the low season. Facilities for sports such as soccer, rugby, field hockey, water skiing and athletics can be developed, while wind surfing and jet skiing areas will undoubtedly appeal to the athletic youth of North Cyprus.

- *Facilities for ecological tourism*: Promoting ecotourism is crucial in the process of attracting environmentally conscious and high-income tourists. The facilities that support ecotourism must be designed with environmental conservation in mind.
- *Tours and accommodation for well-organized historical and religious sites*: North Cyprus possesses a wealth of cultural and historical sites that can be considered a world treasure. However, those riches are far from being well kept and displayed. Cleaning, restoring and landscaping the sites will provide a valuable tourism product for North Cyprus, helping trigger an inflow of funds and international interest for land and underwater archaeology.
- *Trekking, mountain bike and horse riding courses, adventure travel organizations and local handcrafting training*: Without harming the natural environment, various activities can be conducted to benefit both individual tourists and corporate training needs.
- *Aero-sports centres*: Skydivers, hang-gliers, and enthusiasts for ultralights and other small planes would enjoy the long season and surroundings. New airports would make transportation to and from the island more convenient.

The above examples could be increased. However, there is a pressing need for a national marketing plan for North Cyprus that includes target market analysis, setting of marketing objectives, the product mix, pricing decisions and an effective marketing communications mix in order to utilize the strengths of North Cyprus. If it is done properly, it would not be difficult for North Cyprus to equal or even surpass South Cyprus' per capita tourism income. A destination marketing organization (DMO) should be established in North Cyprus to serve and achieve these objectives. Other than the marketing plan, North Cyprus also needs a tourism master plan for urban areas and for the above-mentioned areas and sites. Master planning must be done by professionals who are independent of politics. Only then can the richness of the country's cultural and natural heritage survive and be transferred to the next generation. Setting environmental and urban standards and regulations will complete the planning. If this is done, North Cyprus will gain a positive image and take a big step towards becoming a prestigious tourism brand. It also requires qualified human resources, and embedding tourism principles and fundamentals in the North Cyprus education system would be a desirable strategic policy.

Conclusions

It is not easy for small island nations like North Cyprus to reach the elusive tourist. Limited marketing budgets, a wide array of competitors and an increasingly experienced and 'picky' tourist make it difficult to create and sustain a profitable industry. Even if the nation is successful in attracting the attention of the tourist, the challenge that remains for the provider is that of increasing the economic spend and yield associated with the industry. Tourist behaviour and attitudes are shaped by marketing campaigns, branding and the almost osmotic process of receiving information from the media and broader world around us. McKercher and Chan (2005) emphasized that it is critically important to understand why people visit a destination. At the end of the day, marketing is about achieving goals through understanding and responding to customers' needs (Clarke, 2005). The fact that the local tourist authorities in

North Cyprus have not carried out any qualitative marketing research raises questions about the appropriateness and effectiveness of their promotional campaigns and their new product development plans.

The current study has highlighted the impact of how politics can influence marketing and overall destination competitiveness for an island state. To overcome the challenge, it is necessary for North Cyprus to establish strong partnerships between the public and private sectors, taking greater advantage of new technologies and the Internet. Marketing must also lead to the optimization of tourism impacts and the achievement of the strategic objectives for all stakeholders. On an international level, it is vital for the tourism industry of North Cyprus to establish direct flight routes with the main tourist-generating countries as this will positively influence the accessibility of the destination and, by extension, the arrivals figures. However, it is likely that the political leaders of South Cyprus would consider direct flights as a signal for the international recognition of North Cyprus and would oppose such developments. In this light a more heretical idea can be raised – instead of both political entities on the island marketing their own individual destination, they could unite their efforts and market the island as a single destination. This would contribute not only to the steady growth of tourism on both sides of the border, but would be a further step to the political solution of the 'Cyprus question'. In this way, tourism would also practically prove that it is a viable tool to achieving peace.

Discussion Questions

1. What are the challenges of the island of Cyprus? How have these challenges impacted upon the marketing of North Cyprus?
2. How would the tourism industry of North Cyprus change if the island were politically united? What would be the potential impact on tourist arrivals and expenditure?
3. Considering the information given about the current situation of North Cyprus, what can the tourism official do to better market North Cyprus as a tourist destination?

References

Altinay, L., Altinay, M., & Bicak, H. A. (2002). Political scenarios: The future of the North Cyprus tourism industry. *International Journal of Contemporary Hospitality Management, 17*(3), 272–280.

Altinay, M. (1994). *Kucuk ada ulke ekonomilerinde turizm*. Famagusta, Northern Cyprus: Eastern Mediterranean University Press.

Altinay, M., & Hussain, K. (2005). Sustainable tourism development: A case study of North Cyprus. *International Journal of Contemporary Hospitality Management, 14*(4), 176–182.

Buhalis, D. (1999). Marketing the competitive destination of the future. *Tourism Management, 21*(1), 97–116.

Cansel, A., Bavik, A., & Ekiz, H. E. (2008). The unknown market in Mediterranean tourism: Turkish Republic of Northern Cyprus. *Journal of Tourism and Hospitality, 5*(2), 93–102.

Cansu, A. (2006). Eglence sektoro para basiyor. *Kibris Gazetesi/Cyprus Newspaper, April*(7), 1.

Clarke, J. (2005). Marketing management for tourism. In L. Pender & R. Sharpley (Eds.), *The management of tourism* (pp. 102–118). London: Sage Publications.

Cyprus Tourism Organization. (2009). *Tourism revenues and visitor arrivals for 2008/09*. Nicosia: Cyprus Tourism Organization Publications.

Dana, L. P., & Dana, T. E. (2000). Taking sides on the island of Cyprus. *Journal of Small Business Management, 38*(2), 80–88.

Fisher, R. J. (2001). Cyprus: Failure of mediation and the escalation of an identity-based conflict to an adversarial impasse. *Journal of Peace Research, 38*(3), 307–326.

Fyall, A., & Garrod, B. (2005). *Tourism marketing: A collaborative approach*. London: Cromwell Press.

Gursoy, D., Ekiz, H. E., & Chi, C. G. (2007). Impacts of organizational responses on complainant's justice perceptions and post-purchase behaviors. *Journal of Quality Assurance in Hospitality and Tourism, 8*(1), 1–25.

Hall, C. M. (1994). *Tourism and politics: Policy, power and place*. New York: Wiley.

Hasguler, M. (2002). *Kıbrıs'ta enosis ve taksim politikalarının sonu*. Istanbul: Iletisim Yayinlari.

Holloway, C., Humphreys, C., & Davidson, R. (2009). *The business of tourism* (9th ed.). New York: Prentice Hall.

Honey, M. (1999). *Ecotourism and sustainable development: Who owns paradise?* Washington: Island Press.

Ioannides, D., & Apostolopoulos, Y. (1999). Political instability, war, and tourism in Cyprus: Effects, management, and prospects for recovery. *Journal of Travel Research, 38*(1), 51–56.

Jafari, J. (2001). The scientification of tourism. In V. L. Smith & M. Brent (Eds.), *Host and guest revisited: Tourism issues of the 21st century* (pp. 28–50). New York: Cognizant Communication Corporation.

Kotler, P., Haider, D. H., & Irving, R. (1993). *Marketing places: Attracting investment, industry and tourism to cities, states and nations*. New York: The Free Press.

Mathieson, A., & Wall, G. (1982). *Tourism: Economic, physical and social impacts*. New York: Longman.

McKercher, B., & Chan, A. (2005). How special is special interest tourism. *Journal of Travel Research, 44*(1), 21–31.

Milne, S. (1992). Tourism and development in South Pacific island microstates. *Annals of Tourism Research, 19*(2), 191–212.

Mowforth, M., & Munt, I. (1998). *Tourism and sustainability: New tourism in the third world*. London: Routledge.

Uzgec, G. (2006). Gambling threats. *Kibris Gazetesi/Cyprus Newspaper, February*(27), 1.

Scott, J., & Asikoglu, S. (2001). Gambling with paradise? Casino tourism development in Northern Cyprus. *Tourism Recreation Research, 26*(3), 51–61.

Seddighi, H. R., Theocharous, A. L., & Nuttall, M. W. (2002). Political instability and tourism: An empirical study with special reference to the microstate of Cyprus. *International Journal of Hospitality & Tourism Administration, 3*(1), 61–84.

Starr, N. (2003). *An introduction to travel, tourism, and hospitality* (4th ed.). New Jersey: Prentice Hall.

Statistical Yearbook of Tourism. (2009). *Statistical yearbook of tourism – 2009*. Nicosia: State Printing House.

Symeonidou, S. (2005), Inclusive policy, segregating practice: A cultural analysis of the impairment discourse reflected in the official and hidden curricula in Cyprus, *Inclusive and Supportive Education Congress, International Special Education Conference, Inclusion: Celebrating Diversity?* 1–4 August, University of Cambridge, Glasgow.

United Nations World Tourism Organization (2010), Tourism highlights 2009 edition [Online], *World Tourism Organization.* Retrieved 11 January 2010, from http://unwto.org/facts/eng/pdf 20/highlights/UNWTO_Highlights09_en_HR.pdf.

Weaver, D., & Lawton, L. (2002). *Tourism management* (2nd ed.). Milton: John, Wiley & Sons.

World Travel and Tourism Council (2010), Progress and priorities 2008/2009 [Online], *World Travel and Tourism Council.* Retrieved 11 January 2010 from http://www.wttc.org/bin/pdf/original_pdf_file/ progress_and_priorities_2008.pdf.

Yasarata, M., Altinay, L., Burns, P., & Okumus, F. (2010). Politics and sustainable tourism development – Can they co-exist? Voices from North Cyprus. *Tourism Management, 31*(3), 345–356.

7 E-Marketing: An Evaluation of Tobago's Official Tourism Website

Sherma Roberts

The University of the West Indies, Cave Hill, Barbados, West Indies

Introduction

In comparison to many of its other Caribbean counterparts, the island of Tobago can be considered a relative newcomer to tourism. In fact, using Butler's Tourism Area Life Cycle (TALC) (Butler, 1980), Tobago can perhaps be positioned at the early to mid-stages of the development phase, given the growing levels of local and foreign investment in the tourism plant and services, an aggressive marketing campaign that seeks to distinguish Tobago as a premier leisure and ecotourism destination and a noticeable increase and acknowledgement by tourists and residents of negative social and environmental impacts, perceivably because of tourism development (Tobago News, 31 October 2008, 5 December 2008, 9 January 2009; Twining-Ward, 2008). Over the last few years, Tobago has also seen a modest increase in both its cruise and international arrivals. International arrivals grew from 23 111 in 1992 to 56 917 in 2008; and cruise passengers from 16 373 in 1996 to 22 253 in 2008 (Division of Tourism, 2009). Increased airlift from source markets, familiarization trips by travel agents, media and tour operators, representation at travel markets, personal selling, greater attention paid to the marketing mix of price, product, promotion and the introduction of its official website in 2001 have contributed to the growth in numbers. The primacy of the Internet in destination marketing and communications is well established, and destination marketing organizations (DMOs) have had to respond to competition from other destinations and the exponential use of the Internet by consumers in planning their vacations. In 2005, 200 million Americans were Internet users, and of these 84% are travellers. Consumers are now researching, planning and even booking their trips online, and travel blogs are increasingly being used as a source of travel information. This chapter examines and evaluates the official website of the Tourism Division of the Tobago House of Assembly (THA; www.visittobago.gov.tt), the public sector destination management organization charged, *inter alia*, with the marketing of Tobago. The chapter assesses the strengths and weaknesses of the site and provides recommendations for an improved online marketing strategy.

Marketing Island Destinations. DOI: 10.1016/B978-0-12-384909-0.00007-6

Tourism Development in Tobago

The island of Tobago constitutes the smaller of the twin-island state known as Trinidad and Tobago, with a population of about 55000 (www.cso.gov.tt, Central Statistical Office, 2008). Unlike the economy of Trinidad which has buoyant oil and gas and manufacturing sectors, Tobago's economy is services-led, with tourism accounting for 56.8% of the island's employment (WTTC, 2005) and 37% of overall GDP from tourism (www.tobagonews.com, accessed 29 June 2009), and may be even larger if indirect employment in traditional informal sectors is to be added. Nationally, the tourism industry accounts for 5.8% of the labour force and 10.6% of the GDP, with predictions that by 2015 this will increase to 16.7% and 19.2%, respectively (WTTC, 2005). However, 2007 evidenced a decrease in GDP by 3.3% (www.tobagonews.com, accessed 29 June 2009), and this is likely to decline even further given the advent of the global economic crisis in 2008.

It is worth noting that over recent years, the government of Trinidad and Tobago has been paying more attention to the tourism potential in Trinidad, where the focus is on business tourism, cultural tourism, yachting tourism and the MICE (meetings, incentives, conferences and events) market (National Tourism Policy, 2008). This is in contrast to Tobago where the marketing and product development focus has been on upmarket leisure, including eco-tourism and diving. Given the complementary nature of the islands' tourism products, the pair is often unwittingly referred to as 'Terrific TrinidadTranquil Tobago'.

Tobago's tourism potential was recognized from as early as 1957 when the colonial legislature established a Hotel Development Corporation to loan money for the construction and expansion of hotels on the island (Brereton, 1982). From 1956 to 1962, the year that Trinidad and Tobago gained independence, visitor arrivals grew from 28400 to 47600 (*Quarterly Economic Reports, 1957–1963*, cited in Roberts, 1994). The industry was, however, severely set back in 1963 by Hurricane Flora, which devastated the island's nascent tourism industry. Still, the newly elected postcolonial government, the People's National Movement (PNM), endorsed the previously held notion that Tobago should pursue a tourism-led development strategy. Thus, from 1978 to 1996, Tobago's share of accommodation units increased from about one-third of the national total to over one-half (Weaver, 1998), and by 2003 Tobago had a total room stock of 3415 rooms, representing 57.5% of national bed capacity (WTTC, 2005). According to the Advisor to the Chief Secretary for Tourism in Tobago, the island's room stock in 2009 stood at 5000 rooms although only 1002 were what he considered able to meet the needs of the high-end international market.

From the mid-1980s, there was a major thrust in the development of tourism infrastructure and superstructure in Tobago, evidenced by the construction of an international airport, a deepwater harbour, hotels and increased destination marketing, as well as the provision of fiscal incentives to encourage investment in the tourism industry (Budget Speech, 1985, 1988, 1989, 1993, 1998). Additional airlifts in 2001–03 also contributed to the growth in arrivals. For example, there was reinstatement of Condor flights from Germany in November 2001, the inauguration of a

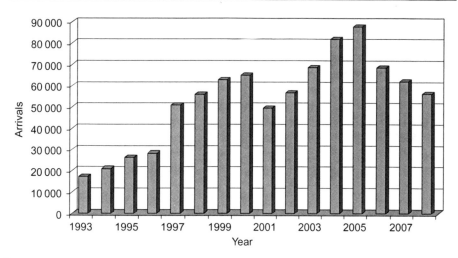

Figure 7.1 Stay-over arrivals to Tobago, 1993–2008.
Source: Tourism Division, THA (2008).

Monarch service from London to Grenada and Tobago in December 2001, the introduction of flights between Washington, DC, and Tobago and between Barbados, Grenada and Tobago in 2002. Further the now-defunct Excel Airways with a seating capacity of 260 had committed to fly three times weekly to the island (WTTC, 2005). In 2004, tourism in Tobago benefited from a Three-Year Tourism Rolling Plan, which provided TT$50 million to the Tourism Division of the THA to enhance promotion and marketing, stimulate airlift, and invest in standards and product development and industry and staff training (*Tobago News*, 1 July 2005, www.tobagonews.com, accessed 29 June 2009).

The result of active government involvement in tourism development (Lickorish, Jefferson & Jenkins, 1991) in Tobago was steady and continuous growth in stay-over arrivals. Figure 7.1 reveals that stay-over arrivals grew from 17 433 in 1993 to 87 896 in 2005. Like many destinations, Tobago's arrivals suffered as a result of the 9/11 terrorist attack in the United States, and from 2006 there is evidence that tourist flows began to decrease, a likely result of a fall-off in scheduled and charter air services and the effects of the onset of the global crisis.

With respect to cruise tourism, Tobago has also experienced modest increases in its arrivals, with the customary November to April being the busiest months for the island. The WTTC (2005: 17) notes that 'while cruise arrivals in Trinidad and Tobago have declined over recent years, Tobago recorded an increase of over 50 per cent in cruise passengers from 2000–2003'. Figure 7.2 shows a steady increase in cruise arrivals up to 2005 and a sharp decline from 2006, which was largely due to the delay by contractors in completing the extension to the pier (*Tobago News*, 20 October 2006a, 9 and 17 November 2006b,c, www.tobagonews.com, accessed 29 June 2009). That cruise ships had to bypass Tobago or be turned back had negative repercussions on Tobago's image and a reduction in income for local taxi drivers, tour companies and other ancillary services. According to one tourism official, the

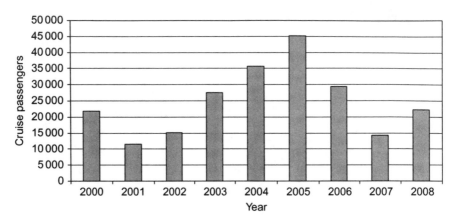

Figure 7.2 Cruise arrivals to Tobago, 2000–2008.
Source: Tourism Division, THA (2008).

THA has now engaged a cruise consultant to help rebuild the credibility of Tobago among international cruise companies.

As was mentioned above, Tobago has positioned itself as an 'upmarket leisure destination' offering a number of niche products such as diving, eco-tourism, weddings and honeymoons, and most recently bird watching (Ali, 2009; O'Donnell & Pefkaros, 2000). Data from 2006 and 2007 (Division of Tourism, 2010) suggest that this target market is bearing some fruit, as 2184 and 4188 tourists, respectively, visited Tobago for a leisure vacation. In the same period, 462 tourists visited for the purpose of weddings and honeymoons, and 707 for business and conventions. Interestingly, the highest number of arrivals in 2006 and 2007 indicated that they were visiting friends and relatives. Overall, the majority of the stay-over visitors came from the United Knigdom and Germany, which are considered Tobago's key source markets. An assessment of the purpose of visit suggests that much more needs to be done in terms of reaching the target market. One suggested strategy is to utilize the medium of the Internet, and in particular the destination's website, as a primary medium for online marketing to its target market and for changing 'lookers' into 'bookers'.

The Changing Role of DMOs

The Internet revolution has changed the way in which businesses around the world conduct sales transactions and provide information to actual and potential customers. While the larger suppliers of tourism services, such as airlines and hotels, have readily embraced this revolution (Krebs, 2004) (e.g. aa.com, hotel.com and travelocity. com), DMOs have been more reticent about coming on board. In fact, as evidenced by a review of many destination websites, even when DMOs launch a website, they take a more conventional approach, acting as a storage mechanism with information on tourism suppliers, visitor attractions and other activities. However, as competition for market share increases among old and newly emerging destinations, DMOs are becoming increasingly sophisticated and innovative, using the Internet and other information and communication technologies (ICTs) as a critical tool for reservations, promotions and distribution of tourism services.

Traditionally DMOs have been charged with the responsibility of optimizing tourism revenues through the development and maintenance of relationships in key international travel markets. According to Rita and Moutinho (1993:5, cited in Seaton & Bennett, 1996:370), other important objectives and primary functions of DMOs are to maintain a wide portfolio of markets, to increase market share, to increase visitor spend and to increase tourism employment. In large part, then, the goals of DMOs are often in harmony with national government development objectives. Middleton and Clarke (2005) suggest that the budgetary constraints of many DMOs inadvertently create binary roles for these organizations, one being facilitation and the other being promotion. In the role of facilitator, the DMO provides assistance to the various sectors of the industry within the related country, such as research, coordination, advice and leadership and marketing opportunities. As promoter, the DMO is primarily responsible for creating destination awareness, communicating the destination brand and positioning through various marketing intermediaries and distribution channel members, providing representation in source markets, building relationships with the travel trade and major suppliers and advising the consumer on the destination, its product and services. In other words, the DMO is critically responsible for creating induced images (Gunn, 1972) of the destination or projecting what the destination offers to travellers in a creative, exciting, appealing and accurate manner.

The highly competitive marketing environment and the changing consumer profile call for DMOs to create destination marketing systems (DMSs) that can effectively meet their facilitation and promotional objectives. To do this, the DMS developed must go beyond being merely a storage mechanism with information on attractions, suppliers and activities and allow for reservations, promotion and distribution, the provision of high-quality data on the region's tourism industry and products, links to other external systems, multimedia kiosks, call centres, interactivity that allows the consumer to build their own itinerary and the availability of the language of online visitors (Buhalis, 2003). Thus 'not only should DMOs attempt to provide information and accept reservations for local enterprises as well as coordinate their facilities, but they [should] also utilize ICTs to promote their tourism policy, coordinate their operational functions, increase the expenditure of tourists and boost the multiplier effects in the local economy' (Cooper, Fletcher, Fyall, Gilbert, & Wanhill, 2005:725). Examples of DMOs with well-developed DMSs are the Australian Tourism Commission, the Singapore Tourist Board, the Canadian Tourism Commission and the Finnish Tourism Board (O'Connor, 2002). Critically, the Internet represents one of the most effective communication media and its utility as a persuasive tool in destination market should not be underestimated (Kim & Fesenmaier, 2008).

The use of ICTs, and in particular the Internet, not only provides benefits to the consumer in terms of personalization but has several other advantages for the DMO, once it is properly integrated into the structure of the organization (Buhalis & Deimezi, 2004). First of all, it can enable the sale of 'last-minute holidays' at a substantial discount so that perishability is reduced; then it has the ability to tangibilize the holiday experience by providing virtual tours of the destination or hotel. Third, the Internet enables retailers to provide up-to-date representations and descriptions of their products. Fourth, it allows for information to be readily available to consumers and businesses and removes barriers of tie zones, increases convenience and global market reach, thereby creating opportunities for businesses (Gretzel, Yuan, & Fesenmaier, 2000; Lehto, Kim, & Morrison, 2006). Fifth, technologies that support the organization can offer cost reduction and increasing efficiency and speed in responding to changing consumer requirements, e.g. in small developing states (Small Island Developing States, SIDS) the Internet offers a big advantage in terms of direct and inexpensive contact with customers, particularly when compared with a standard international phone rates (Hull & Milne, 2001). Finally, and important to competitiveness in islands like Tobago, the Internet represents the potential to overcome some of the inflexibility and dependency inherent in the traditional international tourism system, providing direct access to the consumer and a greater ability for business operators and DMOs to shape their own marketing images (Buhalis & Laws, 2001; Poon, 1993).

In the Caribbean, intermediaries have been solely responsible for developing and disseminating marketing material on behalf of destinations. This has, however, led to issues of control, dependency, homogenization of identity and unnecessary competition among Caribbean DMOs and Ministries of Tourism (MOTs), and to an extent has propelled them to use e-marketing solutions. Tourism organizations therefore cannot overlook the Internet in their marketing mixes, as it can assist destinations in gaining greater comparative advantage. Thus, while traditional distribution and communication channels such as print media, television, radio and brochures cannot be disregarded, the exponential growth of online marketing means that destinations lacking an international online presence could lose a substantial amount of business.

Recognizing the need to improve its strategic marketing and online presence, the THA Tourism Division launched its official destination website Visit Tobago (www .visittobago.gov.tt) in 2001. The rationale behind the website was:

- to widen global market reach;
- to create awareness about Tobago;
- to compete with tourism destinations offering the same product;
- to showcase the unique tourism products of Tobago, e.g. Goat Racing, the Rain Forest and The Tobago Heritage Festival.

Since its inception, the website has been updated twice, in 2004 and 2006, and is currently (July 2009) undergoing another redesign to meet the challenges of the global economic environment and social networking needs of current and potential visitors. It is axiomatic that the Division sees the competitive value in keeping its website fresh and relevant. However, it is unclear what criteria are being used to evaluate the site so that the requisite changes can be made. This chapter therefore seeks to examine the current site using the objectives of the Division and specific criteria borrowed from the general literature on this topic.

Destination Websites as an Online Marketing Tool

Websites are regarded as the 'store front' of organizations as checking online may be the first encounter and first point of information that a would-be consumer has with the business. Fantom (1999) views an effective travel website as the embodiment of a brand linking goods and services to travellers in a global network and acting as a virtual customer service representative. However, having a presence on the Internet does not guarantee success. Like retail businesses, DMOs need to ensure that their website design and content is effectively communicating with customers and primary stakeholders as well as facilitating business transactions in a secure and efficient manner. The fierce competition between destinations also means that DMOs must also focus on designing websites as a tool for influencing travellers' decision-making process (Werther and Klein, 1999, cited in Kim & Fesenmaier, 2008). Cunliffe (2000, cited in Zafiropoulos, Vrana, & Paschaloudis, 2005) argues that poor web design will result in a loss of 50% of potential sales and a loss of 40% of potential repeat visits through negative experiences in accessibility and usability. Other qualities that can undermine the effectiveness of a website include being too wordy but omitting the relevant information, failing to regularly update the information, lacking appeal in terms of colour and layout and having graphics that take too long to load (Zafiropoulos et al., 2005).

What, then, are the elements of a good website? The literature suggests that in order to attract and retain users, a website should exhibit features such as accuracy, relevance, flexible information presentation, customized information presentation, price information and product/service comparability and differentiation, complete product or price descriptions, availability of several languages, sensitivity to cultural differences and word choice and idioms, awareness and the right amount of colour, sounds and images, knowledge of international law and awareness that business transactions can be done in other countries (Kaplanidou & Vogt, 2006; McKillen, 2009; So & Morrison, 2004). Important to a good website also is that there is ease in accepting customers' money, that the text is readable, and that there are well-organized hyperlinks, help functions, interactivity between the customer and the organization and among customers. Table 7.1 condenses the key success factors for website optimization into seven criteria using the AIDA model discussed below.

The Consumer Decision-Making Process

While knowledge of these 'critical success factors' is crucial to the competitive marketing of the destination, equally important is an understanding of the Internet consumer buying or decision-making process. In other words, behind the visible act of making a purchase lies a decision process that must be investigated. This is particularly important to acknowledge for, as Schwartz (1998) notes, individual's behaviour changes when they log on to the Internet. The standard model of consumer buying behaviour processes, where business is transacted in a traditional marketplace, assumes that consumers often implicitly go through a number of stages before making

Table 7.1 Website Evaluation Criteria

AIDA Model	Criteria	Description
A – Attention	Accessibility	Embedded keywords, browser compatibility.
	Usability	Multilingual capabilities, easy-to-read text, ease of navigation including 'back to home' feature, speed of download, fill-in forms or brochures in optional format (PDF or Word).
I – Interest	Informativeness	Strategic application of marketing mix through clear, accurate, comprehensive and concise information and images – customer segmentation, target market, positioning and branding, links to supplier, products, niches, booking options, promotions, etc.
	Creativity in design	Colour, sound, images/photos (still and moving) that are complementary, placement of links/frames on index page, lack of information clutter.
D – Desire	Appeal	Product 'stickiness', calls to action, virtual tours to tangibilize the destination, special offers and package deals, online booking and/or payment option, customization facility.
A – Action	Credibility	Clear identification that the site is official, presence of testimonials/customer reviews, awards from recognized bodies, customer support – contact us hyperlink using phone or email contacts, having FAQs.
	Security	Privacy and security policy, variety of payment options, automatic response mechanisms.

a purchase. The stages are awareness, information search, attitude development, evaluations, purchase and post-purchase. In the virtual marketplace, the decision-making process for consumers (Page & Connell, 2006) is quite similar, and begins with:

Stage 1: an awareness of alternative retail options
Stage 2: attitudes towards using the Internet as a shopping method
Stage 3: evaluation of using the Internet as a shopping tool
Stage 4: the decision to accept/reject the Internet as a shopping medium
Stage 5: post-purchase evaluation.

In stage 1, the consumer recognizes that buying a particular product online is a viable alternative to purchasing it in the traditional marketplace. This awareness may be fuelled by word of mouth, sensitivity to price, promotional efforts, etc. and leads the consumer to explore the specific website to gain more information on the product and the purchasing process. In the next stage, the consumer develops either a positive or negative attitude or user experience towards online shopping. This is often influenced by a number of factors including website accessibility, ease of navigation, relevance of information, language appropriateness and speed, all of which may reinforce or bring about a change in attitude on the part of the would-be buyer. Having formed an attitude towards online shopping, the consumer may then evaluate the specific site in relation to other sites based upon a mix of website 'critical success factors' and other influencers. For example, a consumer may consider a holiday in one of three Caribbean destinations – Grenada, St Lucia and Barbados – but decides on Grenada because of customer reviews of the destination, the images, price, information richness, products, call to action, security and so on.

The fourth stage in the Internet consumer decision-making process is the purchase decision. It is at this point that 'all external and internal variables come together to produce a decision' (Reid & Bojanic, 2010:106) about whether the Internet is a viable shopping medium. It is suggested that this final purchase decision is based upon perceived risk associated with the purchase and its alternatives and the consumer's willingness to take risks. The DMO therefore can only convert 'lookers' to 'bookers' through innovative, creative, informative and secure websites that combine the correct web-design and marketing mix elements at each stage of the process and in such a way that perceived risks to the consumer are reduced. For example, use of customer-to-customer interface (blogs, customer reviews), customer support and a high level of perceived customer relationship management are factors that can help reduce perceived risk.

The final stage in the process is the post-purchase evaluation, which if not facilitated by the destination would be accommodated by www.tripadvisor.com and other similar sites. This stage is one of the most overlooked and underestimated by many destinations and businesses, but represents a very powerful medium for attracting new consumers and retaining repeat patronage. It is at the post-purchase stage that all the elements of the purchase converge – the website information, the actual purchase and the visitor experience at the destination. If there is enough dissonance between the expectation created through online images and information and what was experienced by the visitor, the post-purchase evaluation would be negative. The DMO must therefore be careful that its website portrayals are true to form since managing negative post-purchase evaluation may prove to be quite costly.

As mentioned above, each stage of the consumer decision-making process is influenced by a combination of internal and external factors such as culture, socioeconomic levels, reference groups (external), personal needs and motives, experiences, perceptions and attitudes, and personality (internal) (Kotler, Bowen, & Makens, 2006; Hudson, 2008; Reid & Bojanic, 2010). Role adoption, with its proposed five roles, has also been cited as an influencer of the buyer decision-making process (Engel, Blackwell, & Miniard, 1990). In this model, the consumer may switch roles during each stage of the buying process or the process may in fact have several individuals involved in a single purchase. Accordingly the consumer may be:

Initiator: the individual who starts the purchasing process by gathering the first set of information relevant to the purchase.

Influencer: the individual(s) who endorses or expresses preference in the selection of information.

Decider: the individual who actually makes the decision about whether the purchase should be made – the one with financial authority or control.

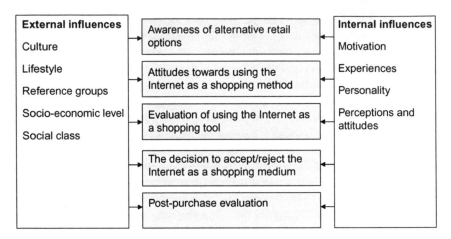

Figure 7.3 The Internet consumer decision-making process.
Source: Adapted and modified from Reid and Bojanic (2010).

Buyer: the individual who actually makes the purchase whether it is through a travel agent, tour operator or online.
User: the individual(s) who consumes the purchase (hotel room, attraction visit, vacation, etc.).

Figure 7.3 illustrates the major steps in the Internet decision-making process and the role external and internal influences play as the consumer makes a purchase decision. Knowledge of these related stages and influences can result in websites that are better designed to optimize marketing communications to the specific target segments, so that ultimately a purchase can be made and a customer retained.

A related model that is also used to assess the consumer buying behaviour process, including Internet buying, is the AIDA model (Figure 7.4). The model assumes that consumers go through four buying stages – attention, interest, desire and action. The first step is where the website gains the attention of the surfer; it then creates interest where the viewer actually navigates within the site; desire for the product is then created by promotions and products, which then results in action where the consumer is actually convinced enough to transact an online purchase (Ferrell & Hartline, 2008; Gebhardt, 2007). In other words, as actual and potential consumers trawl through an organization's website, they are processing the information in sequence: exposure, attention, comprehension, perception, yielding, acceptance and finally retention or action (Gretzel, Yuan, & Fesenmaier, 2000). While consumer decision-making processes are complex (in that they are not as linear as is being suggested), and cannot really fit neatly into any of these models, they continue to be useful in helping us understand how consumers reach decisions.

Marketing successfully on the Internet then involves knowing what makes a good website, being clear about one's target market and understanding how consumers make decisions. Success can be measured in revenue generated, level of enquiries, page views, visits and hits (Buhalis, 2003). However, Tierney (2000) points out that it is difficult to measure the success of a website as the number of hits or visitors to

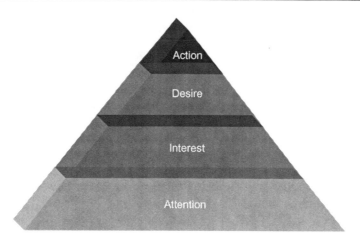

Figure 7.4 The AIDA model.
Source: Gebhardt (2007).

a website only shows volume of traffic, but does not give any insight into the psychographics, demographics or satisfaction of the visitor. Moreover, it is difficult to account for the enquiry conversion rate, meaning how many visitors to the website actually visit the destination (Stergiou & Airey, 2003). Evaluation therefore becomes difficult as there are no standardized methods to account for the complexities of the website. Website evaluation is further exacerbated when DMOs are not familiar with the complexities of the Internet or have insufficient expertise and resources to implement and manage online strategies. The solution is for DMOs to set their evaluation criteria, perhaps based upon best-practice DMSs or other tested mechanisms. Whatever evaluative options are used, the point is that a strategic online presence and concomitant website evaluation can no longer be seen as luxuries but are a sustainability imperative if DMOs are to gain and maintain competitiveness.

Evaluating the Tobago Website

The Visittobago.gov.tt website was evaluated based upon the seven key criteria presented in Table 7.1. The findings are based upon responses from a self-administered questionnaire distributed to visitors in Tobago who used the website prior to getting to Tobago. Most questions were based upon a Likert scale of 1–5, with 1 being poor and 5 being excellent. An online focus group session with potential visitors from various backgrounds was also used to evaluate the site.

Accessibility

Tobago's official tourism website is not easy to locate owing to the number of Internet sites representing Tobago. Using three different search engines or browsers – Yahoo!, Google and Ask Jeeves – search words such as 'Tobago', 'Tobago+tourism',

'Tobago+leisure destination' were typed in to locate the official site, its load time and dead links. Google showed the official website in position 7; Yahoo! in position 8 and Ask Jeeves displayed the site on its second page. In terms of dead links, quite a few were found pertaining to interactive maps and touring Tobago, current news and shopping. In general, once identified the sites took between 3 and 10 seconds to load. Some 80% of the potential visitors found that the site was difficult to locate.

If the Division of Tourism wants to widen its global reach and to raise awareness of Tobago as a destination, more has to be done in making the site accessible to the casual browser, the target market or the person who would have heard about Tobago through word of mouth. If, according to the AIDA model, the website fails to capture the attention of the would-be consumer, then the other stages are hardly likely to materialize.

Usability

Usability refers to the general user-friendliness of a site, which aims at increasing the comfort level of the consumer. The argument is that if a website fails to provide the 'feel-good factor' in terms of ease of navigation, readability and personalization through language relevance, then this can affect the consumer's decision to travel to the destination or to buy online. The Tobago website was not too difficult to navigate given that the hyperlinks to suppliers, attractions, activities, etc. were located at the top of every page. The weakness is that quite a few of these links were dead or broken. This dysfunctionality may have contributed to 33.3% of respondents surveyed at the Crown Point International Airport in Tobago stating that Tobago's website was not very user-friendly. One major deficiency is that there are no multilingual capabilities. This is particularly striking when Germany represents the second largest source market for Tobago.

The Internet buying process suggests that it is at stage 2 that consumers' attitude towards a site is determined. If Tobago's focus is on 'upmarket leisure', then it is imperative that the marketers identify the elements that would create a positive experience from the moment the consumer logs on. Expanding global reach must take into consideration that the globe is educated, technologically savvy and increasingly desirous of speed and convenience.

To the credit of the Tourism Division, the site also hosted information that is of relevance to current and prospective suppliers. To this end a number of application and registration forms are provided for bed and breakfast registration, certification of tour operators, application forms for the use of beach facilities, etc. However, all of these forms require that Adobe Acrobat be installed on the users' computer – a common source of frustration for many users. In addition, the user is unable to type information into the form and quite a few of the forms are presented in landscape rather than profile view, making presentation less than professional. All of these defects undermine the user-friendliness of the site.

Informativeness

Within the context of tourism, providing accurate, current, concise, comprehensive and relevant destination information reduces the perceived risk involved in travel planning (Vogt & Fesenmaier, 1998). Destination information for Tobago was measured by checking website links such as accommodation, shopping, attractions, promotions, events, general information, do's and don'ts. While the site did provide rich information on visiting Tobago, attempts to retrieve specific information were often tedious and time-consuming. For example, the events link does not take the consumer directly to a listing of events including dates and schedules. The consumer has to click on 'calendar of events' then 'what's on in Tobago', which then links to another website, www.whatsoninTobago.com (not the Division's). On this site the consumer then clicks on 'calendar of events' in order to get a full list of monthly events. Also, as was mentioned above, some key links were broken and therefore compromised the richness of the information that was available. The currency of some of the information provided was also questionable as some businesses, e.g. restaurants, had gone out of business. Thus, while respondents rated Tobago highly on richness of information, they were not impressed with the user-friendliness of the site.

If the provision of information is among the most fundamental goals of a destination website and is the key motivation for consumers to visit websites, then the imperative would be to ensure that the information quality is high. Website content is critical in branding and positioning and directly influences the perceived image of the destination (Zafiropoulos, Vrana & Paschloudis, 2005). The quality of information supplied by the DMO is also critical in reducing information asymmetries between the buyer and the seller, thus providing an environment where there is transactional transparency. Moreover, it is the information provided (or lack thereof) that satisfies the interest of the consumer and aids them in making a decision about whether to buy and/or return to a site or to choose an alternative site with which to do business.

Creativity in Design

A great part of arousing the interest of a would-be consumer is the creative design of the website. It must appeal to the sensory nature of humans through colours, sounds, images and layout. In other words, tourism organizations must demonstrate functional aesthetics that would differentiate the destination without compromising its brand elements. Tobago has chosen the tag line 'Green, Clean and Serene', and while the use of the colour green is immediately evident, it is not impactful. For whatever reason, the sense that the consumer is being called to a beautiful space of tranquillity and verdancy is lost. Perhaps this is because the homepage on either side is bordered by 2.5 inches of empty white space rather than colour. This is in contrast to the destination homepages of Grenada, Antigua and Barbuda, US Virgin Islands, Dominica and St Lucia, which are filled with vibrant colours that are appealing to the eye. On the Tobago site, there is also an absence of sound – not even the soothing crash of waves or the whistling of birds. Of the general population surveyed, the majority gave Tobago a 3 rating in terms of creative design and appeal. Barbados and the US Virgin Islands were ranked at 4 and 5, respectively.

The AIDA model suggests that marketers must create a desire for the product or service with the ultimate goal being sealing a purchase. However, creating desire has as much to do with content as with design functions, which motivates, persuades, awakens and invokes specific imagery. Thus 'within the context of destination websites, the emphasis on scenic beauty (using visual, auditory, and/or imagery oriented features) reflects the underlying aim of destination marketing to build a strong and positive associative link or image about the destination and to create seductive experiences, so that positive images encourage potential tourists to visit the destination' (Kim & Fesenmaier, 2008:6).

Appeal

A key component of creating desire for a product is that the product must have a high appeal factor. Appeal refers to the infusion of some idea or purpose into the mind. While the elements of appeal may differ from person to person and may have several influencers, the DMO needs to identify the 'appeal factors' that are critical to its target market and market segments. Some elements of appeal include product 'stickiness', calls to action, virtual tours, special offers and package deals, online booking and customization facility. For the Tobago site, there is little by way interactivity that allows the tourism organization to engage the customers' interest and participation (increasing the likelihood that they will return to the site). There are no virtual tours of the destination (despite a link inviting you to do just that) or the opportunity for the would-be visitor to tour a hotel of their choice. However, in evidence was the use of multimedia, e.g. flash slide shows, which focused on the key niche products of Tobago, including weddings and honeymoons, water sports and leisure. Both actual and potential survey respondents gave interactivity an overall mean score of 2.6, saying that they would have preferred a higher level of interaction and entertainment, including video animations (Scharl, Wober, & Bauer, 2004). Generally the respondents found that the appeal of the website was average (mean of 3.3). The feature that most appealed to actual and potential visitors was the slogan 'Green, Clean and Serene'. The absence of a call to action was regarded as the least appealing for most users.

Credibility

Website credibility is critical in persuading the 'looker' to make a decision to be a 'booker' or moving to the penultimate stage of the Internet consumer decision-making process. After all, the potential visitor cannot be totally confident that what is being showcased on a site actually exists, and therefore they seek out guarantees on the site about the legitimacy of the product or service. These guarantees are often referred to as credibility cues, and include features such as customer reviews/blogs, FAQs section, contact numbers and email addresses, clear signs that the website is the official one and highlighting awards received from recognized bodies; these are all important in building credibility and reducing perceived risk.

The Tobago website provides useful contact telephone and email information, a FAQs section and a feedback form for the visitor. The latter would be helpful in assessing the post-purchase stage of the overall visitor experience. However, there is no blog feature where potential visitors could log in to get reviews on the destination, neither is there an online booking mechanism. The telephone number is not one that is dedicated to visitor information, but is the PBX number to the office. This means that if a potential visitor is calling on weekends or after working hours, they would be unsuccessful in reaching anyone. Interestingly, even though the site was not especially high in providing credibility cues, 60% of actual visitors to Tobago said that they would visit Tobago based upon the website content; 33% were unsure and 7% said they would not. It is suggested that one reason for this is that the other evaluation criteria, when considered en masse, were sufficient to make the visitor decide to book a ticket to Tobago.

Security

For DMOs operating in this contemporary and competitive environment, websites should go beyond creating a positive user experience but be enticing enough to generate revenue through the purchase of a holiday or a service or product within the destination. This is the direction in which many DMOs are going, acting as a one-stop shop for all services offered within a destination. However, the Tobago website, while allowing the consumer to choose, e.g. restaurant and accommodation by type and location, does not provide a purchase option, so that neither a holiday nor products and services can be bought on the Division's website. The 'action' stage of the AIDA model therefore cannot happen, so that the consumer has to resort to buying the holiday from a travel agent, tour operator or perhaps through another online supplier.

Recommendations and Conclusion

The DMO in Tobago understands that it needs to constantly update its website if it is to create awareness of the destination and increase visitor arrivals. This is evidenced by the fact that the official site has undergone two sets of changes since its inception, which according to the findings suggests that some improvements have been made. However, it is unclear what criteria are being used to evaluate and improve the site. If Tobago is to reach its target market more effectively, the overall quality of the site must be enhanced. Some recommendations are:

- Conducting a survey of visitors to determine what search terms they have used to find or confirm information on Tobago. These terms can then be integrated in the text/hypertext/metadata to ensure higher free placement on search engine responses.
- Paying Google and Yahoo! and other better recognized search engines to enhance the search term rankings of Tobago's official website.
- Updating the website regularly so that information is always current.
- Monitoring the links on the site to ensure that all links are working.
- Implementing a robust database management system so that the DMO has some idea of who is visiting the site.
- Renovating the web design and layout (colour, sound, images, multimedia interactivity, language capabilities, call to action, etc.) to increase the appeal and desire to visit the destination.

• Integrating a booking feature with specials and promotions to stimulate interest, so that the potential visitor can book flights, packages, products and services directly.

Website quality is a critical step in driving online business. As the tourism marketplace becomes more competitive, as consumers become more reliant on ICTs, and as global trends exert greater influence on consumer behaviour, there will be an even greater demand for DMOs to be more aggressive, innovative and creative in their efforts to gain and maintain market share. One suggested strategy is the use of online marketing, which uses DMSs to communicate with consumers and suppliers, to persuade would-be consumers and to generate revenue. To accomplish these objectives, DMOs, like the one in Tobago, must be continuously evaluating and monitoring their site using tested criteria to ensure that the potential of the website is optimized.

Discussion Questions and Exercises

1. Identify at least six advantages of a destination having an online presence.
2. Why is it important for a destination marketer to understand role adoption in online purchasing?
3. Discuss the link between role adoption and the Internet consumer buying process.
4. What further recommendations would you suggest for improving the Tobago website?
5. **(i)** Using the evaluation criteria, compare the Tobago website with that of another destination that has a similar destination positioning.
   (ii) What recommendations can you offer the DMO for improving its website?

References

Ali, A. (2009). *Tobago: Clean green and serene*. Forlag: Hansib Publications.

Bowers, R. (2009). Too much violent assaults, *Tobago News*, 9 January 2009.

Brereton, B. (1982). *A history of modern Trinidad*. London: Heinemann.

Budget Speech. (1986). Government of Trinidad and Tobago, 17 December 1985.

Budget Speech. (1989). Government of Trinidad and Tobago, 16 December 1988.

Budget Speech. (1990). Government of Trinidad and Tobago, 22 December 1989.

Budget Speech. (1994). Government of Trinidad and Tobago, 26 November 1993.

Budget Speech. (1997). Government of Trinidad and Tobago, October 1998.

Buhalis, D., & Laws, E. (2001). *Tourism distribution channels: Practices, issues and transformations*. USA: Cengage Learning Business Press.

Buhalis, D. (2003). *E-tourism: Information technology for strategic tourism management*. Harlow: Prentice Hall-Financial Times.

Buhalis, D., & Deimezi, O. (2004). E-tourism developments in Greece: Information communication technologies adoption for the strategic management of the Greek tourism industry. *Tourism and Hospitality Research*, 5(2), 103–130.

Butler, R. (1980). The concept of a tourist area cycle of evolution: Implications for management of resources. *The Canadian Geographer*, 24(1), 5–12.

Central Statistical Office of Trinidad and Tobago. Population Data. (2009). www.cso.gov.tt Accessed 22 June 2009.

Cooper, C., Fletcher, J., Fyall, A., Gilbert, D., & Wanhill, S. (2005). *Tourism principles and practice* (3rd ed.). Harlow: Prentice Hall-Financial Times.

Division of Tourism. (2009). *Tourism statistics for Tobago 1990–2010.* Tobago House of Assembly, Division of Tourism: Tobago.

Editorial. (2005a). THA wants $80.1 million for tourism rolling plan. *The Tobago News.* Friday 1 July 2005, www.tobagonews.com. Accessed 29 June 2009.

Editorial. (2005b). Council upset over cruise liner not being able to dock. 8 April 2005, www .tobagonews.com. Accessed 29 June 2009.

Editorial. (2006a). Cruise arrivals dive by 80%. *The Tobago News,* Friday 20 October, 2006, www.tobagonews.com, Accessed 29 June 2009.

Editorial. (2006b). Dismal cruise ship season ahead. November 9 2006. www.tobagonews .com. Accessed 29 June 2009.

Editorial. (2006c). Taxi drivers angry over drop in cruise ship arrivals, www.tobagonews.com. 17 November 2006. Accessed 29 June 2009.

Engel, J. F., Blackwell, R. D., & Miniard, P. W. (1990). *Consumer behaviour.* Orlando, Florida: Dryden.

Fantom, L. (1999). Creating a travel website that takes your customers where they want to go. *HSMAI Marketing Review, 16*(3), 29–31.

Ferrell, O. C., & Hartline, M. D. (2008). *Marketing strategy* (4th ed.). Ohio: Thomson.

Gebhardt, C. (2007). Celebrity branding: Perils and payoffs. In D. Owens & D. Hausknecht (Eds.), *Marketing in the 21st century: Integrated marketing communication.* Westport: Greenwood Publishing.

Gretzel, U., Yuan, Y., & Fesenmaier, D. R. (2000). Preparing for the new economy: Advertising strategies and change in destination marketing organizations. *Journal of Travel Research, 39*(2), 146–156.

Gunn. (1972). *Vacationscape: Designing tourism regions.* Washington, DC: Taylor and Francis.

Harrison, Mary (2008). Heartbroken for Tobago. *The Tobago News,* 5 December 2008, www .tobagonews.com, Accessed 28 June 2009.

Hudson, S. (2008). *Tourism and hospitality marketing: A global perspective.* London: Sage.

Hull, J., & Milne, S. (2001). From nets to the net: Marketing tourism on Quebec's lower North Shore. In J. O Baerenholdt (Ed.), *Coping strategies in the north.* Copenhagen: Aarsaether Nordic Council of Ministers.

Kaplanidou, K., & Vogt, C. (2006). A structural analysis of destination travel intentions as a function of website features. *Journal of Travel Research, 45*(2), 204–216.

Kim, H., & Fesenmaier, D. (2008). Persuasive design of destination web sites: An analysis of first impression. *Journal of Travel Research, 47*(1), 3–13.

Kotler, P., Bowen, J. T., & Makens, J. (2006). *Marketing for hospitality and 4th edition.* New Jersey: Pearson-Prentice-Hall.

Krebs, L. K. (2004). *The effectiveness of the Internet as a marketing tool in tourism.* Unpublished PhD thesis. Ontario: University of Waterloo.

Lehto, X. Y., Kim, D., & Morrison, A. (2006). The effect of prior destination experience on online information search and behaviour. *Tourism and Hospitality Research, 6*(2), 160–178.

Lickorish, L., Jefferson, A., & Jenkins, C. (1991). *Developing tourism destinations.* Essex: Longman.

Manmohan, E. (2008). Making tobago once again a safe tourist haven, *Tobago News,* 31 October 2008.

McKillen, D. (2009). Web Watch *Medical marketing and media.* www.mmm-online/web-watch.com. Accessed 4 April 2009.

Middleton, V., & Clarke, J. (2005). *Marketing in travel and tourism* (3rd ed.). Oxford: Butterworth-Heinmann.

National Tourism Policy of Trinidad and Tobago. July 24 2008. Trinidad and Tobago: Ministry of Tourism.

O'Connor, P. (2002). The changing face of European destination management systems. *Travel and Tourism Analyst, April.*

O'Donnell, K., & Pefkaros, S. (2000). *Adventure guides to Trinidad and Tobago.* New Jersey: Hunter Publishing.

Page, S., & Connell, J. (2006). *Tourism: A modern synthesis.* London: Thomson.

Poon, A. (1993). *Tourism, technology and competitive strategies.* UK: CABI Publishing.

Population Data. Central Statistical Office of Trinidad and Tobago. www.cso.gov.tt. Accessed 22 June 2009.

Reid, R., & Bojanic, D. (2010). *Hospitality marketing management* (5th ed.). New York: John Wiley and Sons.

Roberts, S. (1994). *Tobago after Hurricane Flora: 1963–1973.* Unpublished Caribbean Study Project. St. Augustine Campus: The University of the West Indies.

Scharl, A., Wober, K. W., & Bauer, C. (2004). An integrated approach to measure web site effectiveness. *Information Technology and Tourism, 6,* 257–271.

Schwartz, C. (1998). Web search engines. *Journal of the American Society for Information Science, 49*(11), 973–982.

Seaton, A. V., & Bennett, M. (1996). *Marketing tourism products: Concepts, issues, cases.* London: Thomson.

So, S., & Morrison, A. (2004). Internet marketing in tourism in Asia: An evaluation of the performance of East Asian National Tourism Websites. *Journal of Hospitality and Leisure Marketing, 11*(4), 93–118.

Stergiou, D., & Airey, D. (2003). Inquiry conversion and tourism website effectiveness: Assumptions, problems and potential. *Tourism and Hospitality Research, 4*(4), 355–366.

Tierney, P. (2000). Internet-based evaluation of tourism website effectiveness: Methodological issues and survey results. *Journal of Travel Research, 39*(2), 212–219.

Twining-Ward, L. (2008). *Tourism carrying-capacity assessment, Tobago.* Tobago: Policy Research and Development Institute, Tobago House of Assembly.

Vogt, C., & Fesenmaier, D. (1998). Expanding the functional information search model. *Annals of Tourism Research, 25,* 551–578.

Weaver, D. B. (1998). Peripheries of the periphery: Tourism in Tobagoand Barbuda. *Annals of Tourism Research, 25*(3), 292–313.

World Travel and Tourism Council. (2005). *Trinidad and Tobago: The impacts of travel and tourism on jobs and the economy.* London: WTTC.

Zafiropoulos, C., Vrana, V., & Paschloudis, D. (2005). An evaluation of the performance of hotel web sites using the managers' views about online information services. *Conference Proceedings of 13th European Conference on Information Systems.* 26–28 May 2005, published by *e-Review of Tourism Research.*

8 Strategic Destination Marketing, Nagigi Style: Olivia's Homestay in Fiji

Anne Campbell

University of Canberra, Canberra, Australia

This stay has had a profound and humbling effect.

Guest comment, Olivia's Homestay visitors' book (2005)

However, among visitors from 'developed' countries, this kind of tourism is not highly favoured and it will probably remain a minority interest – as it must, if it is to survive as an 'alternative' to more organised travel.

Harrison (1992:30)

Introduction

Fiji has long been a popular tourist destination, not only because of its diverse natural and cultural resources, but also because Fiji is marketed as the friendly tourist destination, a culture that is always smiling and inexhaustibly hospitable (Moscardo and Pearce, 2003; Vusoniwailala, 1980). It is an image somewhat marred by political coups in 1987 and 2000, increasing crime rates and continuing political unrest. Despite these events, the Fijian Ministry of Tourism (FMT) and the Fiji Visitors Bureau (FVB) have successfully continued to market Fiji as a tourist-friendly destination, with targeted destination marketing for specific islands and incoming visitor numbers are currently increasing at approximately 9% per annum (Fiji Bureau of Statistics, 2010).

Consistent in the strategic marketing campaign of the FVB is the smiling face of friendly Fijians. It is reinforced in tourist brochures, on tourism websites and the in-flight magazines of Fiji's airline, Air Pacific. The image is predominantly representative of the indigenous Fijian population, although indigenous Fijians are involved in the Fijian tourist industry more as front-of-house labour than as managers or owners of tourist resorts, something that is causing increasing concern (Britton, 1987; FVB, 2006; Hall, 1994; Plange, 1996; Poole, 1991; Salto and Ilaiu, 1980; Samy, 1980).

The high rate of foreign investment in Fiji's tourism industry (Hall, 1994), the estimated 60% leakage to foreign investors (Levett & McNally, 2003), and increasing local discontent over the low level of indigenous participation in the tourism

Marketing Island Destinations. DOI: 10.1016/B978-0-12-384909-0.00008-8

industry – usually in unskilled positions – have led to the consideration of alternative tourism ventures that would bring greater economic benefits to the rural indigenous Fijian community (FMT, 2005). This initiative was village-based tourism, a strategy of the FMT aimed at attracting a wider range of tourists – particularly independent backpackers – and involving village communities in managing tourism ventures. The initiative was supported by the FMT as a means of involving Fijian villagers in income-generating enterprises that would reduce rural unemployment (FVB, 2006).

In 1999, the FMT established an Ecotourism and Village-based Tourism Policy and Strategy (EVTPS) that outlined strategies for sustainable tourism practices and aimed to involve village communities in sustainable tourism ventures. In a country where many members of the rural indigenous community live a subsistence lifestyle, where unemployment is endemic and an estimated 40% of the people live in poverty (*Fiji Times*, 22 February 2010:2), any ventures that provide employment and generate income for rural village communities are welcome.

The strategic marketing initiative for village-based tourism has been extremely successful in the Yasawas, a chain of islands traditionally only available to visitors invited as guests of islanders and with the permission of the *turaga ni koro* (village chief), or for a brief day visit on a local cruise ship. In the last two decades, there has been a rapid and relatively unplanned expansion of village-based resorts in the Yasawas, and by 2007 the Yasawas hosted over 545 000 visitors (Department of Tourism, Fiji, 2007). This is partly the result of the strategic marketing campaign, but also because the Yasawas are now easily accessible by daily catamaran services from Nadi, Fiji's international airport, as well as by air and cruise vessels.

The rapid and uncontrolled development of village-based tourism in the Yasawas was not without problems. Although the development led to employment opportunities and economic growth for indigenous Fijians, most islands in the Yasawas have inadequate supplies of freshwater, only two of the approximately 40 resorts have adequate primary sewage treatment facilities or sustainable disposal systems; there is no coordinated solid waste disposal system; there are a number of unlicensed resorts; there is considerable inconsistency in the quality of services; there is a lack of funding for capital improvements; and social tension between the local community members managing and maintaining the resorts and resort development investors (Department of Tourism, Fiji, 2007).

Compared to the rapid development of village-based tourism in the Yasawas, village-based tourism development elsewhere in Fiji has been negligible, particularly in Vanua Levu, the second largest of the Fiji islands. This is partly because of the high cost of domestic air travel, which discourages budget tourists from travelling to the other islands, but also because existing enclave resorts on Vanua Levu such as the Jacques Cousteau Resort, Namale or Koro Sun were marketed specifically to the high-end tourist wanting to relax and be pampered in an exclusive five-star tropical enclave, or go diving in the footsteps of Cousteau. Most of these resorts are close to Savu Savu, the main port and ferry terminal in Vanua Levu. These enclave resorts are foreign-owned, provide their own transport to and from the airport, have their own restaurants, swimming pools and entertainment and operate in a self-contained environment. They also have access to adequate infrastructure such as sealed roads, electricity, telephone, an adequate freshwater supply and appropriate sewage and waste disposal systems.

This infrastructure is not available in villages in Vanua Levu, which face a similar lack of infrastructure development to that in the Yasawas and indeed in many other less developed countries (Butler, 1992; Harrison, 2003, 2004). Electricity in most villages in Vanua Levu is provided by generator and is only available for a few hours per day. Sealed roads stop at the last high-end enclave resort and are frequently impassable after wet weather. Sanitation is barely adequate for the village, there is no organized solid waste disposal system and the availability of freshwater depends on the season. Cooking facilities in most homes consist of a gas ring or a small open fire in an external cooking shed, and beds, tables and chairs are woven mats on the floor.

These conditions are not conducive to the development of village-based tourism in Vanua Levu. There is also the problem that, like the villages in the Yasawas, any village in Vanua Levu considering similar development faces an ongoing challenge in encouraging development without threatening the fragile natural and cultural resources that attract the tourists. This challenge is not unique to Fiji, but applies to many developing countries in which the biodiversity of the natural environment is a major attraction, where economic development is a major challenge (Ashley & Roe, 2002; Hall & Page, 1996; Howorth, Kami, Gerbeaux, Deo, & Clarke, 2008) and where there is a consistent increase in international visitors (World Tourism Organization, 2008).

The FMT is well aware of the need to spread community involvement in tourism more widely across Fiji, and in 2005 established a Vanua Levu Tourism Development Taskforce as the consultative group for tourism development in Vanua Levu, with the responsibility of driving tourism industry development, and developing, coordinating and implementing tourism policy, initiative and programmes. It was hoped that this initiative would diversify tourism ventures beyond enclave resorts, which in 2004 accounted for most of the 2.5% of total visitor arrivals in Fiji staying in Vanua Levu (Ministry of Tourism, 2005).

To differentiate the Vanua Levu tourist experience, this destination is marketed by the Fiji Tourist Bureau as an 'unspoilt' tropical destination – 'vintage Fiji', where the 'authentic' indigenous Fijian lifestyle can still be experienced. In addition to the high-end enclave resorts, there are now several hotels offering budget accommodation, but there is no explosion of village-based resorts similar to that experienced in the Yasawas. The local Tourism Association would like to encourage the development of village-based tourism, but is aware of the infrastructure constraints, the social challenges and the need to develop sustainable social and environmental tourism practices. They are also aware that the rapid growth of village-based tourism in the Yasawas led to the establishment of unlicensed resorts and would prefer to avoid the problems of poor hygiene and variable quality of service that this can create.

Case Study: Olivia's Homestay

Olivia is in her mid-fifties. She is the sole investor in her homestay venture and supplied the capital through the modest savings she accumulated while providing aged-care in a private home in California over a period of seven years. In 1997, she used these savings to build a basic concrete and galvanized iron, five-bedroom house on her inherited land in Nagigi, a small village set on an idyllic, palm-fringed tropical lagoon about 40 minutes by bus from Savu Savu. Most of the 300 people in the village are related to her in some way, and her extended family already has a productive garden on the family *vanua* (land) where they grow root crops, coconuts and tropical fruit.

The large house was intended to provide accommodation for herself and visiting members of her extended family who were now living in other parts of Fiji. A representative of the local Savu Savu Tourism Association happened to visit her when the house was almost finished and remarked that it would be ideal for homestay tourism, and if Olivia was interested, there was a small amount of support available to install plumbing, electric wiring, paint the house and to complete it to a standard suitable for tourist accommodation. Olivia accepted the offer, and in 2003 the homestay enterprise began.

Apart from this assistance, Olivia received no financial support. Fortunately, her overheads were minimal, as she could grow most of the food needed for the venture on her own land and there was a small village shop that sold canned and dried food. Her main additional expense was providing Western-style beds and bed linen, as she felt that foreigners would probably not be prepared to sleep on woven mats in true Fijian style. She could catch fish in the lagoon, labour to work the farm plot and maintain the extensive grounds was available from the members of her *mataqali* (extended family) already living on the family land and Olivia intended to cook, clean, look after and entertain her guests herself.

Strategic Destination Marketing, Nagigi Style: *Kere Kere*, Intuition and Initiative

Olivia has no background in tourism marketing or tourism management and left school in secondary form three. For someone her age, having a secondary school education at all is unusual as most village children left school at or before the end of primary grade six. When she began her venture, there was no tourism management or tourism marketing workshops available in Vanua Levu to provide her with guidance or advice.

As the village of Nagigi is on the main coastal road of Vanua Levu, and Olivia is a member of the village council, she was aware that the village community had a problem with backpackers who thought they could just get off the bus and pitch their tents in the middle of the village. She convinced the village council that her homestay would be a way of teaching these people the correct protocols of living in a Fijian village, as well as giving them somewhere to stay and bringing additional income and employment to the village community by showing the visitors how to make traditional Fijian craft items.

Although she has no formal education in tourism marketing or management, Olivia has inexhaustible drive, initiative, a passionate belief in sharing her ancestral cultural heritage with outsiders and a strong commitment to her community, and she persuaded the village council that this was a venture worth supporting. She convinced them that the secret to success in tourism ventures is to give the tourists what they want, and that what they want is to understand the Fijian heritage. This belief was generated through a visit to Nagigi by an American couple many years earlier. These visitors told her they were envious of her peaceful life in such a beautiful location and that they wished they could stay there and share her heritage and lifestyle. Olivia took this casual comment seriously, and long before it became fashionable, or a policy of the Ministry of Tourism, dreamed of ways of giving foreigners what they said they wanted: an experience of living in an authentic indigenous Fijian village.

With her house ready for visitors in 2003, her first marketing initiative was to engage tourists visiting Savu Savu in conversation – something that with her outgoing personality, self-confidence and the excellent English gained during her seven years in California was no problem – and then, when they were impressed with the friendliness of the local Fijians, simply ask them if they would like to stay in a real Fijian village with a beautiful beach, not too far from Savu Savu. This low-key, indirect approach worked well, particularly as she sold her vegetables and fruit at the daily markets in Savu Savu where budget tourists and backpackers tended to shop.

With the money from her first homestay guests, Olivia bought some paint and through a *kere kere* arrangement (reciprocal assistance), one of her relatives painted a large sign that she displayed along the road that ran through the village, where it would be seen by any tourist passing through in their hire car or on a local bus. This strategy was also effective, but some time later two young backpackers staying with her said that it would be good for her business to have a listing in *Lonely Planet*.

Olivia had no idea what *Lonely Planet* was, but was ready to listen to new ideas. They showed her their copy of *Lonely Planet* and explained that it was a source of information that many backpackers used to plan their travel around Fiji and that having her contact details in *Lonely Planet* would enable potential visitors to contact her to make a booking before they arrived. She agreed that a listing would be a good idea, but unfortunately had no idea how to do this. The backpackers said that all she needed to do was supply them with her phone and email details and they would contact *Lonely Planet* and do the rest.

This conversation led to two difficulties. One was Olivia had no email address. In fact, no one in the village had a computer or Internet access. The other was that Olivia was adamant that learning how to use a computer and the Internet would be beyond her capabilities, even if she could afford one, which she could not. After some thought, Olivia remembered that her friend in Savu Savu had a computer, and again through a *kere kere* arrangement, her friend agreed to act as an intermediary and provided her own email as a contact point for *Olivia's Homestay* bookings.

Olivia has no idea how this all works. Her life in the village does not include computers, electric appliances, stoves, refrigerators, a television, CD player, mobile phone or any of the things that her visitors seem to take for granted. She knows that there is such a thing as the Internet, but not what or where this thing is. All she really understands is that her friend in Savu Savu sometimes phones her to let her know that some visitors want to make a booking for *Olivia's Homestay*. If Olivia says she has vacancies, she tells her friend and her friend tells the visitors they can come.

Sometimes the visitors themselves phone Olivia when they get to Savu Savu, and in that case Olivia stays home to meet them. But sometimes they just arrive on the bus, or in a hire car or taxi. This can be inconvenient if she happens to be at the market when they arrive (which, in fact, is every day except Sunday). If that happens some visitors go away again, but others just wait until Olivia gets back from the market. It is not possible to know exactly how many visitors have come to Nagigi and gone away again, although usually someone in the village has noticed if a foreigner has gone to her house and left again. But this could have been anyone, not necessarily someone looking for homestay.

It all seems very complicated to Olivia, this Internet booking system. She much prefers people to telephone her. Everyone knows she has a market stall in Savu Savu and is not at home during the day, so if they want to phone her, they should phone in the evening, preferably before 9 p.m., because that is when the generator goes off and she goes to bed. After a day at the market, she is usually tired and the light from the kerosene lamps is not really good enough to sew the rag rugs and *sulus* (sarongs) she makes to sell to the tourists from the boats.

What Olivia really prefers is 'catching' tourists in the market, or at the souvenir stall she now has on the wharf at Savu Savu, ready for the arrival of the inter-island ferries and the huge cruise ships that call there every two months. She soon realized that some tourists do not want to make up their minds about a village homestay immediately, so she used some of her income to get printed business cards that the tourists can keep in case they forget her phone number and want to contact her later on. The business cards still have her friend's email, and Olivia is worried that her friend travels a lot and maybe when she is in another country, her friend will not receive email messages from people who want to stay with Olivia.

Another problem is that *Olivia's Homestay* is expanding and now involves many members of the village community, who provide add-on activities such as rides on the *bilibili* (bamboo raft), snorkelling and fishing trips, visits to the island in the lagoon with the bat colony, lessons in Fijian cooking, massage, *meke* (traditional dancing), music and mat weaving, an activity that encourages the visitors to purchase similar products made by the village women as personalized souvenirs. She can also arrange other attractions such as a *meke* performed by the villagers or *lovo* (traditional feast cooked in underground oven) for larger groups, but Olivia does not know how to let tourists know that these attractions are available as part of her homestay, except by talking to them or giving them a flyer at the wharf or in the market.

International visitors also find it difficult to get to Nagigi. Coming by plane is not so difficult, because there are usually taxis at the airport, and except on Sundays, there are regular buses to Nagigi. But travelling by plane is expensive, and most of the visitors who stay with her are independent backpackers who do not want to spend a lot of money on airfares. There are inter-island ferries to Savu Savu from Suva, but her homestay visitors complain that there is no information on the Internet about the timetable of these ferries, or how much it costs to travel from Suva to Savu Savu. In fact, the ferries arrive at Savu Savu at 4 a.m. and 6 a.m., which is not very convenient for tourists who need to get to Nagigi unless they take a taxi. She knows all this information, but unless the people telephone her and ask about the ferries, how can she tell them?

Olivia is very keen to expand her tourism ventures. She wants to build some traditional-style *bures* (Fijian thatched huts with woven walls) on her land and get a boat so that she can take visitors fishing out beyond the reef. To do this she needs the support of the village council, which supported the homestay venture, but only on the condition that guests must conform to the traditional norms of dress and behavioural protocols while in the village, making Olivia responsible for her guests' conduct. In terms of dress, this means that hats may not be worn in the village and women must wear a long *sulu* (sarong) to cover their legs.

As well as being a member of the village council, Olivia is *turaga ni mataqali* (authorized leader of her extended family) and a member of the local tourism association, and therefore has an excellent relationship with key decision-makers relevant to her tourism ventures. This provides her with access to the support network essential for the sustainability of her tourism venture, but she needs to be careful that her guests obey the village dress code, and she is a little concerned that some foreigners will refuse to do this.

If this happens, the village council may force her to close down her homestay business and lose the independence that she now has, as well as the income that, unlike the enclave resorts, remains entirely in Fiji. She wonders how to market her homestay in a way that will make sure that visitors know how important it is to obey the dress codes and whether having such strict dress codes will mean that visitors, especially the young female backpackers, will stop coming to the village. She has already noticed that although all of them say how much they enjoyed their visit and wished they could stay longer, in all this time there has been only one repeat visitor, and very few people stay for longer than one or two days.

Summary

Olivia's dilemma is both typical of the situation facing village-based tourism in Fiji, in that the infrastructure inadequacies and social issues are similar to those in other indigenous villages, and unique, in that she is a sole female owner and manager of an indigenous village-based tourism venture. Although she is a member of the local tourist association, most of the other representatives are from established enclave tourist resorts with marketing and management issues very different from those of village-based tourism communities. As yet there is insufficient support for village-based tourism in Vanua Levu to give much voice to the needs of this group, which at the moment consists only of Olivia and a few other villages in even more remote locations than Nagigi.

On the positive side, Olivia's homestay initiative has brought many benefits to the village, but she is dependent on the support of the village council for its sustainability, and they do not necessarily share the same concerns. For example, a major concern for the village council is that the young people in the village may be exposed to unacceptable models of behaviour displayed by the foreign tourists staying with Olivia, while for Olivia the concern is that forcing foreign visitors to conform to village codes of dress and behaviour may be seen as an unwarranted imposition and ultimately destroy her homestay business.

Another contentious issue is that it is the authenticity of village life (experiencing the 'real' Fiji) that is the main attraction for the visitors, and this can be threatened by an increase in visitors. That there is a market for an alternative tourist experience in Fiji is demonstrated by the fact that with minimal marketing *Olivia's Homestay* has managed to remain in business for seven years. However, an average of 10 guests per month does not make it a large business venture. Olivia is happy to keep it small, as it is easier to incorporate a small number of guests into the village lifestyle than a larger number, which could easily destroy the very 'authenticity' that attracts this sector of the tourist market.

Despite the unanimously positive comments in Olivia's visitors' book, the fact that there have been almost no repeat visits suggests that one experience of 'authentic' indigenous Fijian life may be enough for most visitors. Even in Nagigi, which is by no means the most remote village in Vanua Levu, the living standard is well below that to which Western tourists are likely to be accustomed. Olivia's house is above the standard of most houses in the village in that guests have beds rather than woven mats to sleep on, and a table and chairs for dining, but there are no insect screens on the windows, or ceiling fans in the rooms, making the bedrooms unpleasantly hot for anyone unaccustomed to tropical temperatures.

Electricity is limited to one fluorescent light in the main living area, with an extension cord to another light on the verandah. The light is insufficient to read by and the power is only on for three hours in the early evening. Two kerosene lamps placed on the floor provide dim light for the rest of the night and are a potential fire hazard should anyone wander around in the semi-darkness. Visiting each other and gossiping is the main form of entertainment in a Fijian village, but unless visitors can speak Fijian, they are unable to participate in this activity.

As there are no cooking facilities for guests, *Olivia's Homestay* rates include three traditional Fijian meals per day. The staple food in Fijian villages is cassava, now supplemented by rice, and as there is no refrigeration in the village, all food is either locally grown, non-perishable or in tins. There is one small village shop, which sells staple commodities such as rice, sugar, flour and tinned foods, but this is still a limited range of produce from which to prepare meals, especially in a kitchen with only a gas cylinder and a double burner for a stove.

Olivia herself compensates for what are very basic living conditions. She has a warm, outgoing personality and takes her task of teaching her visitors about her cultural heritage very seriously. Her visitors' book is full of praise from people from the United Kingdom, Germany, Namibia, the United States and Korea as well as nearby from countries such as New Zealand and Australia, extolling her warm welcomes, her willingness to share her cultural heritage, her home and for the friendliness of the village community:

> An extraordinarily friendly and entertaining visit – lots to learn about Fiji.
>> Finally, we found the true Fiji!
>> Thank you, Olivia. Our stay with you far exceeded our hopes for a real Fijian experience.
>> The place to be! A part of the real Fiji.

There is a strong sense in these comments that it is Olivia herself who is the main attraction of *Olivia's Homestay* and that she manages to make every visitor feel that they are special, a welcome family friend rather than a tourist merely passing through. Marketing this is a little more challenging than marketing an idyllic location on a crystal-clear lagoon fringed by white beaches and gently swaying palm trees. Marketing it in a way that will ensure that the 'authenticity' of the Fijian village experience is retained is even more difficult. Even Olivia's plan to build *bures* to accommodate her guests would change the relationship between herself and her visitors, although Olivia herself probably does not realize this.

Key Issues

The key issues for Olivia and the Nagigi village council are to develop a strategic destination marketing plan that will continue to bring economic benefits to Olivia and the village community while sustaining the traditional lifestyle and cultural values of their indigenous Fijian community. As a number of researchers have demonstrated, village-based tourism can help prevent out-migration from rural communities (Ashley & Roe, 2002; Christie & Simmons, 1999; Colvin, 1996) as well as providing direct and indirect income-generating opportunities such as local tourist activities, the sale of local handicraft products or improved transport (Hall & Page, 1996; Harrison, 1992; Howorth *et al.*, 2008). This is all happening in Nagigi, but for village-based tourism to be sustainable, issues such as a lack of infrastructure, inadequate freshwater, lack of sewage and solid waste disposal also need to be addressed (FVB, 2006; Harrison, 2004; Jafari, 2007). The Nagigi village council is aware of these issues, but there is little they can do about them, and they realize that consideration also needs to be given to negative social and environmental impacts such as overcrowding, littering and sanitation problems and threats to the authenticity of the existing social and cultural environment (Department of Tourism, Fiji, 2007; Salto & Ilaiu, 1980; Tosun, 2007).

Balancing the benefits of village-based tourism with the constraints and possible negative impacts is not easy. Any strategic destination marketing campaign aimed at developing homestay accommodation in indigenous Fijian villages such as Nagigi needs to take this into consideration and to include a 'demarketing' plan (Beeton, 2006:135–138) that could be used if the negative impacts outweigh the positive.

Discussion Questions

1. What do you think are the key constraints in Olivia's current marketing strategies, and how could these constraints be addressed?
2. One of the key issues in this case study is the need to balance village-based tourist development with the conservation of the natural and social village environment. How could strategic destination marketing and the involvement of destination marketing organizations (DMOs) help this tourism venture to maintain this balance?
3. Olivia's visitors' book indicates that it is her personality that is a key part of the attraction of this destination. How would you design a strategic destination marketing campaign that would market Olivia as well as her village?

References

Ashley, C., & Roe, D. (2002). Making tourism work for the poor: Strategies and challenges in Southern Africa. *Development Southern Africa, 19*(1), 61–82.

Beeton, S. (2006). *Community development through tourism*. Collingwood: Landlinks.

Britton, S. G. (1987). Tourism in Pacific Island States: Constraints and opportunities. In S. G. Britton & W. Clarke (Eds.), *Ambiguous alternative: Tourism in small developing countries* (pp. 113–119). Suva: University of the South Pacific.

Butler, R. (1992). Alternative tourism: The thin end of the wedge. In V. S. Smith & W. R. Eadington (Eds.), *Tourism alternatives: Potentials and problems in the development of tourism* (pp. 31–46). Philadelphia: University of Pennsylvania Press.

Christie, L., & Simmons, N. (1999). Wild places: Kapawi lodge in Ecuador's Amazon. *Wildlife Conservation, 102*(6), 56–59.

Colvin, J. (1996). Indigenous ecotourism: The Capirona Programme in Nape Province, Ecuador. *Unasylva, 18*(47), 32–37.

Department of Tourism, Fiji. (2007). *Regional tourism development strategy: Yasawa Islands 2007–2016*. Suva: Department of Tourism, Fiji.

Fiji Bureau of Statistics. (2010). *Visitor arrivals 1999–2009*. Suva: Fiji Bureau of Statistics.

Fiji Times. (2010, February 22). *Foundation reaches out*. Monday, 2.

Fiji Visitors Bureau. (2006). *Realizing the industry's potential through responsible tourism: 2006 Fiji Visitors Bureau marketing plan*. Nadi: Fiji Visitors Bureau.

Hall, C. M. (1994). *Tourism in the Pacific Rim*. Melbourne: Longman Cheshire.

Hall, C. M., & Page, S. J. (1996). Introduction: The context of tourism development in the South Pacific. In *Tourism in the Pacific: Issues and cases* (pp. 1–15). London: International Thomson Business Press.

Harrison, D. (1992). Tourism to less developed countries: The social consequences. In D. Harrison (Ed.), *Tourism and the less developed countries* (pp. 19–34). London: Belhaven Press.

Harrison, D. (2003). Tourism and less developed countries: Key issues. In D. Harrison (Ed.), *Tourism and the less developed world: Issues and case studies* (pp. 23–46). Wallingford: CABI.

Harrison, D. (2004). Tourism in Pacific Islands. *Journal of Pacific Studies, 26*(1&2), 1–28.

Howorth, R., Kami, T., Gerbeaux, P., Deo, S., & Clarke, P. (2008). *Shaping a sustainable future in the Pacific: IUCN strategic priorities for Oceania region 2008–2010*. Suva: International Union for the Conservation of Nature and Natural Resources, Regional Office for Oceania.

Jafari, J. (2007). The socio-economic costs of tourism to developing countries. In T. Huybers (Ed.), *Tourism in developing countries* (pp. 527–546). Cheltenham: Elgar Reference Collection.

Levett, R., & McNally, R. (2003). *A strategic environmental assessment of Fiji's tourism development plan*. Suva: World Wide Fund for Nature.

Ministry of Tourism, Fiji (FMT). (2005). *Tourism development in Fiji – Vanua Levu scope*. Suva: Ministry of Tourism, Fiji.

Moscardo, G., & Pearce, P. (2003). Marketing host communities. In D. J. Singh, T. Dowling, & R. K. Dowling (Eds.), *Tourism in destination communities*. Wallingford: CABI.

Plange, N. (1996). Fiji. In C. M. Hall & S. J. Page (Eds.), *Tourism in the Pacific* (pp. 205–218). London: International Thomson Business Press.

Poole, K. (1991). Small scale secondary tourist accommodation: Appropriate alternatives for Fiji's tourist industry. *Review, 12*(19), 8–17.

Salto, R., & Ilaiu, M. (1980). Tamavua village: For tourists only. In F. Rajotte (Ed.), *Pacific tourism: As Islanders see it* (pp. 89–92). Suva: Institute of Pacific Studies.

Samy, J. (1980). Crumbs from the table: The workers' share of tourism. In F. Rajotte (Ed.), *Pacific tourism: As Islanders see it* (pp. 62–67). Suva: Institute of Pacific Studies.

Tosun, C. (2007). Limits to community participation in the tourism development process in developing countries. In T. Huybers (Ed.), *Tourism in developing countries* (pp. 547–567). Cheltenham: Elgar Reference Collection.

Vusiniwailala, L. (1980). Tourism and Fijian hospitality. In F. Rajotte (Ed.), *Pacific tourism: As islanders see it* (pp. 101–106). Suva: Institute of Pacific Studies.

World Tourism Organization. (2008). Developing countries lead dynamic world tourism growth. *News from the WTO,* 6 March.

9 Tourism, Destination Imaging and the 'New' Paradigm: Rebranding Paradise in the Hawai'ian Islands

Julie Tate-Libby

University of Otago, Dunedin, New Zealand

Introduction

Since its inception as a state in 1959, Hawai'i has been transformed from a 'sleepy island paradise' (Mak, 2008:2) to a popular tourist destination, receiving over 7 million visitors a year (Hawai'i Tourism Authority, 2006). Today, Hawai'i ranks among the top luxury resort destinations in the world, placing third in an annual poll of 6000 luxury travel agencies, as the best destination to view marine life (Honolulu Advertiser, 2004). As Desmond (1999) observes, the average visitor is well informed about Hawai'i before ever touching down on the runway, being inundated with glossy pictures of smiling hula girls, flower leis, sunset beaches and silhouetted couples walking hand-in-hand on the beach. This imaging is disseminated by an enormous media industry that draws on tropes of paradise, honeymooners, romance and the week-long getaway (Costa, 1998).

The touristic image of Hawai'i belies the presence of a strong cultural revitalization movement that began in the 1970s and is known as the Hawai'ian Renaissance. The movement has been manifested largely through language revitalization and the emergence of hundreds of *hula halau* (traditional dance) schools all over the islands (Stillman, 1996). Additionally, the cultural revival has led to the political Sovereignty Movement, which is a demand for restitution from the United States for the illegal takeover of the Hawai'ian monarchy in 1893 and for political autonomy for Native Hawai'ians (Manicas, 2004). For many scholars and community activists, destination resort tourism is seen as having stripped Hawai'i of its identity and culture and turned it into a non-place (Auge, 1995; Relph, 1976). As travel-writer, Lawrence Lawrence Osbourne (2006:4) notes in the *Naked Tourist*,

> The entire world is a tourist-installation, and the awful taste of simulacrum is continually in his mouth. ... I thought for a while of simply checking into a hotel in Hawai'i and sitting there for two weeks in front of a television. Somewhere like the

Marketing Island Destinations. DOI: 10.1016/B978-0-12-384909-0.00009-x

Hilton Waikoloa, perhaps, where I could laze on an artificial beach and take a monorail to the hotel nightclubs.

Tourism studies in Hawai'i (Buck, 1993; Costa, 1998; Desmond, 1999; Hammond, 2001) have largely replicated this theme, arguing that mass tourism has eroded Hawai'ian culture and identity and rendered the islands inauthentic and artificial. This chapter suggests, however, that recent trends towards sustainability and diversified agriculture among scholars and Native Hawai'ian activists are being appropriated within the tourism industry to create a 'greener' Hawai'i. This chapter begins with the history of tourism development in Hawai'i and the imaging of Hawai'i by the Hawai'i Visitors Bureau (HVB), and later the State of Hawai'i's Tourism Authority (HTA). Today, an emerging grassroots effort to reclaim a Hawai'ian identity through diversified agriculture and traditional Hawai'ian practices is reflected in recent media campaigns and studies produced by the HTA. Based on qualitative fieldwork from 2007/2008, this research suggests that significant tensions exist between corporate media campaigns, a state-run tourism agency and lay persons involved in cultural preservation and economic sustainability.

Tourism Development in Hawai'i

Historically, the development of tourism in Hawai'i was linked to the plantation era and monopoly by a few individuals. As long-time Hawai'i tourism executive Robert C. Allen recalls in his memoirs, 'No other resort complex in the world ever came together under similar circumstances, created as it was by individuals of considerable skill who gathered together the elements of a sleepy exotic resort and created the booming Hawai'i visitor Mecca' (Allen, 2004:x). By the late 1800s, descendants of missionary and merchant families known as *kama'aina*[1] began leasing large tracts of land for planting sugar. Throughout the early twentieth century these wealthy families, eventually known as the Big Five, broadened their control over the sugarcane industry by incorporating other industries on the islands, including banks, insurance companies, shipping lines, railroads and wholesale and retail outlets (Kent, 1983; Greaney, 1976). In 1903, Honolulu businessmen and *kama'aina* families who had recently formed the Honolulu Chamber of Commerce began advertising Hawai'i in mainland publications, printed guides, pamphlets and other literature on Hawai'i through the inception of the Hawai'i Promotion Committee (HPC), which eventually became the HVB, and finally the Hawai'i Visitors and Convention Bureau (HVCB) (Crampon, 1976). A private organization, the HVCB was originally funded by donation from *kama'aina* families who lobbied annually for subsidies from the state treasury. For almost a century, the HVCB-dominated tourism marketing in Hawai'i until the passage of Act 156 in 1998, which established the HTA as a

---

[1] Literally, *kama'aina* translates as 'child of the land', but in this context it refers to the white plantation families who established themselves in Hawai'i in the 1800s (Kirkpatrick, 1989).

state agency to oversee tourism marketing and planning. Funding for the HTA was allocated from the newly established hotel room tax (Mak, 2008).

Post-War Tourism and the Kama'aina Elite

Infrastructure in the form of roads, shipping and airports received a massive boost during the Second World War (Hitch, 1992), paving the way for future tourism development. By the 1940s, faced with a failing sugar industry, the plantation families began a series of internal reorganizations that included selling off unprofitable enterprises and disentangling themselves from each other to gain the flexibility needed to liquidate commercial agricultural land on the islands while still retaining thousands of acres for tourist development (Kelly, 2004). Land-rich and cash-poor, the Big Five companies now began to make deals with larger multinational corporations such as Bank of America, Prudential Life Insurance or Signal Oil, supplying land in exchange for capital to develop resorts like the Mauna Kea Beach Hotel on the Big Island (Greaney, 1976; Kelly, 2004). The end result was that Hawai'i became almost totally dependent on tourism and land development in the form of destination resorts, condominiums and vacation home complexes (Aoudé, 1994, 2004; Kelly, 2004; Stauffer, 2004).

After Hawai'i became a state in 1959, more development projects took place using government funds to build a tourist infrastructure. Overall, US$260 million was spent over a six-year period to turn Hawai'i into a major Pacific tourist centre (Hitch, 1992). To help fund infrastructure (e.g. water and sewer systems), Hawai'i's taxes became the fifth highest in the United States (Mak, 2008). Tourism boomed, increasing by over 41% in 1959 and 22% in 1960 (Mak, 2008). Land became a contested issue, with fewer than a hundred people owning half of the island's lands (Kelly, 2004). Today, according to the Office of Hawai'ian Affairs, the Government (federal, state, county) owns approximately 38% of the land, while six private landowners own 36% of the remaining land in the state (Young, 2006).

After 1959, Japanese investment began to play a crucial role in tourism development during the late 1960s and early 1970s. In the 1960s, Japanese investor Kenji Osano purchased three prominent Waikiki hotels – the Princess Kaiulani, the Moana and the Surfrider (Kim, 1994). Osano founded Kokusai Kogyo Co., which became the owner of the three hotels, totalling 1070 hotel rooms and several other prime Waikiki properties. Other Japanese investment firms also brought Japanese ownership of the tourism sector in Honolulu up to well over 50%. The rising value of the yen over the dollar, cheap interest rates in Japan and the high cost of real estate in Tokyo prompted a rush of foreign investment in Hawai'i, which peaked during the early and late 1980s (Kelly, 2004). By 1997, Japanese tourists comprised three out of every ten visitors, including domestic visitors (Mak, 2008). The rise in Japanese visitor numbers to Hawai'i was enhanced by the introduction of the jumbo jet in 1970 and prompted tour companies to sell convenient prepaid group packages to foreign destinations, which became extremely popular in Hawai'i during the 1980s and 1990s (Kim, 1994).

Tourism in Hawai'i Today

Currently, Hawai'i's tourism industry is characterized by the mega-resort/hotel complex owned by multinational corporations (Kelly, 2004). The location of these resorts, far from airports or town centres, has rendered Hawai'i's tourism industry almost entirely automobile-dependent (Kim, 1994), resulting in congestion of many highways and a workforce that must commute long distances for work. Additionally, the tourism industry is controlled by outside interests, with little to no community involvement (Rohter, 1994). For these reasons some scholars (Kelly, 2004; Osorio, 2001; Minerbi, 1999; Trask, 1993) see tourism as an extension of the colonial project, controlled by multinationals and benefiting foreign investment. As Kim (1994:4) notes,

> The vestiges of Hawai'i's colonial past are still expressed through large landholdings concentrated in the hands of a few. While other states have preserved their colonial architecture, Hawai'i has gone even further in terms of conjuring new images of a colonial past in the form of new resorts and visitor plantations.

Foreign investment, which controls over half the industry, remains beyond state control as under the US constitution, only the Federal Government can mandate foreign trade policy (Kim, 1994). The United States' long-standing commitment to free trade paved the way for Japanese-owned tourist enterprises. Like its predecessor, sugar, tourism's labour demands have resulted in massive in-migration to the state, causing an influx of labour that keeps real wages from rising (Hitch, 1992; Young, 2006). Concurrently, land speculation throughout the last two decades has caused the average cost of living to escalate. As Kim (1994:47) postulates, 'Real estate speculation has become a favored local activity in a state whose residents seem to display uncanny disposition towards gambling and trips to Las Vegas.' The median cost of a home in Hawai'i in 2006 was $625 000, with selling prices averaging $700 000 (www.to-hawai'i.com/real-estate). Land speculation and foreign investment have significantly driven up the prices in desirable areas as foreign investors have the means to pay over and above the market value (Kelly, 2004).

Marketing Hawai'i: The HVCB and the HTA

In terms of attracting tourists, tourism marketing in Hawai'i has been hugely successful. James Mak, professor of economics at the University of Hawai'i, has argued that 'Hawai'i's success in developing tourism is much envied by other tourist destinations' (Mak, 2008:2). In 1999, the HTA claimed that 'Hawai'i is the strongest brand in the world, with global recognition and far less negatives than other destinations' (Hawai'i Tourism Authority, 1999). Tourism's rapid growth in Hawai'i can be seen in annual visitor numbers, which rose from 296 000 in 1960 to 1.7 million in 1970, 3.0 million in 1980, 6.7 million in 1990 and 6.9 million in 2000 (Mak, 2008). Key generating markets were couples, honeymooners and families from theUS mainland, particularly the West Coast. Japanese visitor arrivals also grew exponentially between 1960 and 2000, peaking in 1997 at 2152 million arrivals per year.

Tourism marketing in Hawai'i has long relied on Hawai'i as a honeymooner's paradise (Costa, 1998; Desmond, 1999), and as keeper and disseminator of Hawai'i's brand for over a century, the HVCB has been largely responsible for this imaging. In an analysis of advertisements from the mid-1990s, for example, Costa (1998) notes the use of the word 'paradise' in nearly every publication. Tag lines include '... Discover Romance and Adventure in the Exotic Beauty of this Tropical Paradise' or 'Come Share the Dream of My Tropical Paradise' (Costa, 1998:327). Other features that make Hawai'i marketable include its amenable weather, its natural beauty, its location between the US mainland and Japan, its perceived safety and its famous 'Aloha Spirit' (Mak, 2008).

With the establishment of the HTA in 1998, however, the HVCB became one of several contractors hired to market Hawai'i's tourism. By 2004, while the HVCB was still contracted to promote leisure travel to North America (worth US$24.2 million), the HTA distributed the rest of its former marketing responsibilities between four other firms. These firms were in charge of advertising Hawai'i tourism to Asia, Japan, Europe and the rest of Oceania (Mak, 2008). Hawai'i's long-term brand emerged as a contentious issue, prompting Governor Lingle to comment, 'We worked for 100 years to create the image of Hawai'i that we want, that conjures up certain images in people's minds. How do you maintain that consistency of image now that you've broken this up into five contracts?' (Yamanouchi, 2003:A1–A5). At stake was the consistency and quality of a brand that had been previously cultivated by a single agency.

A New Paradigm and the State of Hawai'i

In the mid-1990s, Hawai'i's tourism declined for the first time since 1959, in face of competition from other island destinations like Fiji, Tahiti or Samoa where the scenery was just as spectacular, the prices cheaper and the destination more exotic (Mak, 2008). This decline sparked a concern within the industry as a whole, prompting a number of studies commissioned by the HTA and the State of Hawai'i on tourism and its long-term sustainability. These studies included *Sustainable Tourism in Hawai'i* (Department of Business, Economic Development & Tourism, 2003), *Socio-Cultural Impacts of Tourism in Hawai'i* (Knox & Associates, 2003), Hawai'i Island Tourism Strategic Plan 2006–2015 (Hawai'i Tourism Authority, 2006), the *Hawai'i 2050 Sustainability Plan* (State of Hawai'i, 2008), the Huki Like 'Ana: A Call to Action (Native Hawai'ian Hospitality Association, 2007a) and the *Hawai'i Culture Initiative Action Plan*, also produced by NaHHA (Native Hawai'ian Hospitality Association, 2007b). These reports represent a shift from the consumer-oriented tourism of the past to a new tourism based on maintaining a sense of place and building respect. The reports suggest that attitudes towards tourism are changing and that most residents feel the need for more government intervention in policy planning and protection for Hawai'i s natural and cultural resources.

For example, The Hawai'i Island Tourism Strategic Plan (Hawai'i Tourism Authority, 2006) emphasizes finding a sustainable balance between tourism and keeping Hawai'i 'a good place to live' (Hawai'i Tourism Authority, 2006:2). Based on a recent survey of resident attitudes towards tourism (Market Trends Pacific Inc. and John M. Knox & Associates Inc., 2008), the report indicates that attitudes had worsened, particularly in West Hawai'i, which includes the tourist centre Kailua-Kona. Between 2002 and 2005, the percentage of residents who strongly agreed with the statement 'Overall, tourism has brought more benefits than problems to this island' decreased 16 percentage points to 33% in West Hawai'i (Market Trends Pacific Inc. and John M. Knox & Associates Inc., 2008). Likewise, the percentage of residents who reported strongly believing that 'This island is being run for tourists at the expense of local people' increased 21 percentage points to 42% in West Hawai'i (Market Trends Pacific Inc. and John M. Knox & Associates Inc., 2008:3). The toursim strategic plan also points out several challenges facing tourism in Hawai'i such as maintaining affordable airfares with rising fuel costs (particularly with tickets to and from Japan), providing visitor satisfaction as hotel room prices rose 20% in two years, and finding ways to keep Hawai'i's tourism product 'fresh and unique' (Hawai'i Tourism Authority, 2006:10).

The effect of these reports has been a marked change in the way Hawai'i is being marketed. In 2009, the HTA started an online blog called 'So Much More Hawai'i' (Hawai'i Tourism Authority, 2010). The blog features topics like 'Kauai Share Your Table, Local Food, Pono Media, Aloha in Your Cup and the Conscious Traveller' (Hawai'i Tourism Authority, 2010). The shift from a honeymooner's paradise to a sustainable eco-destination can be seen on Hawai'i.gov, the Official Site of the State of Hawai'i, which lists 'most popular' links, including, among other things, 'heiau, hiking, mountain biking, farm tours, kayaking, whale watching and weddings' (ehawai'i.gov., 2010).

On the Big Island, the shift towards sustainability, diversified agriculture and community-based tourism can be seen in regional events throughout Hawai'i Island that emphasize local, organic produce, the proliferation of farmers' markets and small-scale tourism venues. Many of these productions are funded by the HTA via their County Product Enrichment Program, a programme that gives money to individual counties for tourist events. This on-the-ground activity has generated much media interest. A recent issue of *Hawai'i Island Journal* (Conrow, 2007) features such articles as 'What's in Your Backyard?', 'Stylishly Green', 'Endangered Reefs', 'Is God Green?', 'Less Theatre, More Farming', 'The Limits of Tourism', 'The Green Bride', 'The Eco-Clodhopper' and 'Green Cleaning Supplies' (Conrow, 2007:3). The issue's cover story included an interview with Ramsey Taum, Head of the University of Hawai'i, School of Travel Industry Management, on sustainable tourism and Native Hawai'ian culture. Taum notes, 'Aloha really acknowledges sustainability because it's about reciprocity – giving and receiving' (Conrow, 2007:7). In this case the values of *aloha* (Native Hawai'ian ethos of right living and generalized reciprocity) are reworked to emphasize sustainable living. Taum goes on to emphasize that *aloha'aina* (love of the land) and *malama'aina* (care of the land) are contemporary values of stewardship. Taum remarks, 'One common misconception however, is that adopting culturally-based traditional systems entails the need to go back someplace'

(Conrow, 2007:7). Instead Taum sees the old practices as a way of bridging the old with the new to create a new kind of society.

Local Voices: A New Kind of Tourism

The shift from a paradise destination to a sustainable Hawai'i can also be seen in local attitudes towards tourism on Hawai'i Island. One respondent who does *lu'aus* (feasts) for small tourist groups in her backyard explained that by establishing a relationship with tourists as equals and friends first, she and her husband were then able to share Hawai'ian culture in a way that deconstructed the power relationship between tourist and host. 'The tourist is not up here, you know? They are here...' – and she gestured with her hand to show two equal participants. At their backyard *lu'au*, guests are invited to help bury the pig in the *imu* pit and place *ti* leaves over the top. They are instructed in lei making and flower garlands while listening to 'Aunty' tell stories about her childhood. While sceptics might conclude that this is simply another marketing niche, the Johnsons[2] feel strongly that their kind of inter-action with tourists is not exploitive, but helps to re-establish a basis of commonality between themselves and tourists. In the typical tourist *lu'au*, the *imu* pit, music and hula dancing are all performed to provide entertainment for the tourist (Desmond, 1999). At the Johnson's, however, the tourist becomes an invited guest who is encouraged to participate, thereby becoming part of the culture itself.

Other residents in the Ka'ū District of Hawai'i Island talked about creating a 'living *ahupua'a*' in lieu of another resort development that had been recently proposed for Punalu'u Black Sands Beach. The 'living *ahupua'a*' model was seen as both a revitalization of pre-contact Hawai'i and also a more cutting-edge kind of development than a mega-resort and golf course complex. One resident named Craig said,

> I'd like to see the whole Punalu'u area preserved as an *ahupua'a* system, a living classroom to re-create the ancient practices of trade from mountain to the sea. You could have educational centers, foot trails, biking paths, kalo paddies, and agricultural plots that reflect ancient Hawai'i.

In this case, the vision for Punalu'u included a re-creation of ancient Hawai'ian subsistence practices for the purpose of educating visitors and locals alike. Correspondingly, such practices were perceived as being more ecologically sound, based on ancient wisdom and indigenous knowledge, and therefore a 'green' alternative. Another resident couple, one Native Hawai'ian and one a long-time resident, emphasized respect in the living *ahupua'a* model by putting the *kupunas* (Hawai'ian elders) in control of education:

> I think we'd like to see something more cutting edge, something that gives owner-ship in what is going on there. A culturally appropriate ... a living ahupua'a with

[2]All personal names have been changed.

cultural experts living there to share what they know, like weaving or whatever. There would be a community, a living village and yes, there would be visitors to that village. The visitors would give people a role to play, an opportunity to have a ground-up management instead of the top-down approach. It's about giving respect to the culture. So you would have kupunas at the top of the pyramid and at that point you start to honour the culture and then you can have a win/win experience for everyone.

One young man, Dave, who worked as a cultural practitioner for the Amy Greenwell Botanical Gardens, noted that he was seeing a shift from the resistance-oriented engagement of Native Hawai'ian activists to a more proactive engagement of Native Hawai'ians within a younger generation:

> I would say there's more of a global perspective shift, not just the Hawai'ian Renaissance, but later than that, like mid-1990s where First Nations people are becoming politically active, making their own decisions and getting education. That's translated into a shift from resort tourism to community-based tourism...

He cited the example of Kaho'olawe, the Hawai'ian island occupied by the US military until Native Hawai'ian activists persuaded the government to give it back to them. Kaho'olawe has become, over the years, an icon of the renaissance movement. 'After we got the US military out, now it's become this issue of what do we do with it? And native practitioners are trying to start cultural tourism initiatives, to educate our own people and also tourists.'

Conclusions

Historically, Hawai'i's tourism industry was tied to the plantation era, controlled by economic elites. Eventually, multinational corporations monopolized the industry, creating the booming visitor Mecca of Hawai'i today. As with the rest of the industry, the dissemination and marketing of Hawai'i's paradisal image remained beyond local control. This may be changing. At a state level, Hawai'i's tourism policy appears to be shifting from accommodation of the resort industry towards efforts for building a more sustainable tourism. Resident opinion surveys feature prominently in the state and HTA reports, as do concerns over land zoning, environmental impacts and cultural preservation. These policy shifts look promising for Hawai'i's future where sustainability and indigenous cultural practices are becoming the focus of tourism planning and marketing.

On the one hand, this trend may reflect, as scholars have noted elsewhere, local and national efforts at cultural 'branding' (AlSayyad, 2001; Fakeye & Crompton, 1991; Morgan, Pritchard, & Pride, 2002). On the other hand, it also signifies local efforts to take more control over an industry that has historically marginalized Native Hawai'ians and remained beyond local control. Either way, it appears that Native Hawai'ian culture and a more sustainable Hawai'i is becoming a key feature of tourist promotion. How these trends will impact the Hawai'ian struggle for political autonomy remain to be seen. Laypersons' visions for a living *ahupua'a* and educational tourism by culture-sharing may be so qualitatively different that efforts to promote or brand it, as such, could be detrimental. The new paradigm in Hawai'i reveals that while tourism has been responsible for much of Hawai'i's cultural and physical decline, it is also tourism that is seen as the panacea for correcting it.

Discussion Questions

1. Do recent trends towards Native Hawai'ian hospitality models and sustainability signify that the state is responding to local concerns, or are tourism planners simply in search of more lucrative niche markets?
2. How will recent marketing trends by the HTA for a more sustainable Hawai'i affect the Hawai'ian Sovereignty movement? Will Native scholars continue to take a critical stance towards tourism or will they embrace the new models as a vehicle for Native autonomy and cultural revitalization?

References

Allen, R. C. (2004). *Creating Hawai'i tourism*. Honolulu: Bess Press.
AlSayyad, N. (Ed.). (2001). *Consuming tradition, manufacturing heritage: Global norms and urban forms in the age of tourism*. New York: Routledge.
Aoudé, I. G. (1994). Hawai'i: The housing crisis and the state's development strategy. *Social process in Hawai'i: The political economy of Hawai'i, 35*.
Aoudé, I. G. (2004). Tourist attraction: Hawai'i's locked in economy. In P. Manicus (Ed.), *Social process in Hawai'i: A reader* (3rd rev. ed.). Honolulu: University of Hawai'i Press.
Auge, M. (1995). *Non-places*. London: Verso.
Buck, E. (1993). *Paradise remade: The politics of culture and history in Hawai'i*. Philadelphia: Temple University Press.
Conrow, J. (2007). Sustainable Hawai'i: Traditional Hawai'ian practices for the twenty-first century. *Hawai'i Island Journal, 21*(April), 1–10.
Costa, J. A. (1998). Paradisal discourse: A critical analysis of marketing and consuming Hawai'i. *Consumption, Markets, and Culture, 1*, 303–346.
Crampon, J. (1976). *Hawai'i's visitor industry: Its growth and development*. Honolulu: University of Hawai'i School of Travel Industry Management.
Department of Business, Economic Development & Tourism (2003). *Sustainable tourism in Hawai'i, progress on the study, planning for sustainable tourism in Hawai'i: A study on the carrying capacity of tourism*. Report to the 2003 Legislature.
Desmond, J. C. (1999). *Staging tourism: Bodies on display from Waikiki to sea world*. Chicago: University of Chicago Press.
eHawai'i.gov. (2010). *Official site of the state of Hawai'i* [online]. http://www.eHawai'i.gov. Accessed 18 March 2010.
Fakeye, P., & Crompton, J. (1991). Image difference between prospective, first-time and repeat visitors to the Lower Rio Grande Valley. *Journal of Travel Research, 30*(2), 10–16.
Greaney, E. (1976). Hawai'i's Big Six: A Cyclical Saga', the encyclopedia of Hawai'i, a 1976 bicentennial project. University of Hawai'i, 1–37.

Hammond, J. (2001). Photography, tourism, and the Kodak Hula Show. *Visual Anthropology*, *14*(1), 1–32.

Hawai'i Named Best Destination. (2004). *Honolulu Advertiser, April 13*, C1.

Hawai'i Tourism Authority. (2006). *Hawai'i island tourism strategic plan* [online]. http://www.Hawai'i tourismauthority.org/pdf/tsp2005_2015_final.pdf. Accessed 15 January 2008.

Hawai'i Tourism Authority. (2010). *So much more Hawai'i: A blogger's view of paradise* [online]. http://www.somuchmoreHawai'i.com. Accessed 18 March 2010.

Hitch, T. K. (1992). *Islands in transition: The past, present, and future of Hawai'i's economy.* Honolulu: First Hawai'ian Bank.

Hiyashi, A. (2006). *Hawai'ian databook. Office of Hawai'ian Affairs.* http://www.oha.org/index. php?option=com_content&task=view&id=102&Itemid=178. Accessed 11 November 2009.

John M. Knox & Associates, Inc. (2003). *Socio-cultural impacts of tourism in Hawai'i: Impacts on the general population.* Prepared for the project *Planning for Sustainable Tourism in Hawai'i* for the Knox & Associates, Department of Business, Economic Development and Tourism.

Kelly, M. (2004). Foreign investment in Hawai'i. In P. Manicus (Ed.), *Social process in Hawai'i: A reader* (3rd rev. ed.). Honolulu: University of Hawai'i Press.

Kent, N. J. (1983). *Hawai'i: Islands under the influence.* Honolulu: University of Hawai'i Press.

Kim, K. (1994). The political economy of foreign investment in Hawai'i. *Social Process in Hawai'i: The Political Economy of Hawai'i*, 35.

Kirkpatrick, J. (1989). Trials of identity in America. *Cultural Anthropology*, *4*(3), 301–311.

Mak, J. (2008). *Developing a dream destination.* Honolulu: University of Hawai'i Press.

Market Trends Pacific Inc. and John M. Knox & Associates Inc. (2008). *2007 Survey of resident sentiments on tourism in Hawai'i.* Honolulu: Hawai'i Tourism Authority.

Manicus, P. (Ed.). (2004). *Social processes in Hawai'i: A reader* (3rd ed.). Hightstown, NJ: McGraw-Hill Custom Publishing.

Minerbi, L. (1999). Tourism and native Hawai'ians. *Cultural Survival Quarterly*, *23*, 2.

Morgan, N., Pritchard, A., & Pride, R. (2002). *Destination branding: Creating the unique destination proposition.* Burlington, MA: Elsevier-Butterworth-Heinemann.

Native Hawai'ian Hospitality Association. (2007a). *Huki Like 'Ana: A call to action: Recommendations from members of the Hawai'ian community regarding Hawai'i, host culture and tourism.* Honolulu: Hawai'i.

Native Hawai'ian Hospitality Association. (2007b). *Hawai'i culture initiative action plan.* Honolulu, Hawai'i. http://www.nahha.com/docs/Final-Action-Plan-012508KW.pdf.

Osbourne, L. (2006). *The naked tourist: In search of adventure and beauty in the age of the airport mall.* New York: North Point Press.

Osorio, J. K. K. (2001). What kine Hawai'ian are you?' A mo'olelo about nationhood, race, history, and the contemporary sovereignty movement in Hawai'i. *The Contemporary Pacific*, *13*(2), 359–379.

Relph, E. (1976). *Place and placelessness.* London: Pion.

Rohter, I. (1994). A green economy for Hawai'i. *Social Process in Hawai'i: The Political Economy of Hawai'i*, 35.

State of Hawai'i. (2008). *Hawai'i 2050 sustainability plan: Charting a course for Hawai'i's sustainable future.* Honolulu: State of Hawai'i.

State of Hawaii, Hawaii Tourism Authority. Ke Kumu: Strategic Directions for Hawaii's Visitor Industry. (June 1999). http://www.hawaiitourismauthority.org/documents_upload_path/ reports/HTALEG-Report-12-31-1999.pdf.

Stauffer, R. H. (2004). The tragic maturing of Hawai'i's economy. In P. Manicus (Ed.), *Social process in Hawai'i: A reader* (3rd rev. ed.). Honolulu: University of Hawai'i Press.

Stillman, A. K. (1996). Hawai'ian hula competition: Event, repertoire, performance, tradition. *The Journal of American Folklore, 109*(434), 357–380.

Trask, H. K. (1993). *From a native daughter: Colonialism and sovereignty in Hawai'i.* Honolulu: University of Hawai'i Press.

Yamanouchi, K. (2003). HTA rebuts critics' concerns. *Honolulu Advertiser, June, 8,* F1 & F2.

Young, L. K. (2006). *Native Hawaiian databook: An office of Hawaiian affairs publication.* http://www.oha.org/pdf/databook/2006.

10 St Kitts and Nevis Marketing Strategies

Novelette Morton*, Devon Liburd$ and Carolyn James*

*St Kitts Tourism Authority, Toronto, Canada; $Nevis Tourism Authority, Nevis, West Indies

Introduction

St Kitts is part of the twin-island Federation of St Kitts and Nevis (SKN) and belongs to the Leeward Islands of the West Indies archipelago. St Kitts is 68 square miles in area and is located two miles northwest of its sister island Nevis (36 square miles), and 200 miles southeast of Puerto Rico. The total population of the Federation is 45 000 – approximately 34 000 persons inhabiting St Kitts and approximately 11 000 living in Nevis. This volcanic and lush country has been blessed with natural beauty, steady northeasterly winds, moderate rainfall and almost year-round sunshine.

Like most of the Caribbean countries, SKN focuses on tourism as the main driver of socio-economic growth and development. The many benefits of tourism have been researched and well documented: tourism generates jobs, provides foreign exchange, generates taxes and other direct and indirect revenues for governments, fosters linkages with other sectors such as agriculture and fishing, attracts local and foreign investment, and encourages entrepreneurial activity (Teaching Tourism in the Caribbean, 2007).

This chapter considers the strategies that SKN employs in order to achieve competitiveness. It begins by providing an overview of the tourism industry in SKN, and examines the various policy initiatives that are being undertaken by the governments to stimulate the economy through tourism development. The chapter also explores the marketing strategies, niche markets and products and partnerships that the islands of SKN, respectively, engage in in an effort to achieve sustainable competitive advantage. The challenges that are faced in marketing the destination are also examined, including the effect of the global economic crisis. The chapter ends by offering recommendations for a well-managed tourism sector, and suggests a blueprint for closer collaboration between the public and private sectors to facilitate a robust tourism economy.

Tourism Development and Marketing in SKN

The focus on tourism as a development strategy began since the 1960s when the sugar industry began to decline. With the official declaration in 2005 that sugar will

Marketing Island Destinations. DOI: 10.1016/B978-0-12-384909-0.00010-6

no longer lead the economy of SKN, the Government has intensified its efforts to develop SKN as a preferred tourism destination. In fact, some recent upscale developments, such as Christophe Harbour, Kittitian Hill and the Ocean's Edge Resort, have signalled a significant step in tourism development, and once well managed can deliver on the promise of expanded economic opportunities for the residents of SKN.

The Federation of SKN is confident that with an effective destination marketing strategy and plan in place, the country will be able to achieve its objectives and ultimately increase its market share. In 2002 and 2006, the Government of SKN commissioned consultants to design a strategic plan for tourism development for the Federation. The 2002 Strategic Report was based on extensive market research and interviews with more than 100 industry stakeholders. In addition, a Strategic Planning Retreat was organized to define the core challenges facing the industry, and to outline the development priorities of the wider community. One of the strategic issues that emerged was marketing and promotion, and consequently a taskforce was created to plan the marketing strategy that would be adopted by the islands (TDI Corporation, 2002). In particular the strategy noted that given the limited financial resources available for destination marketing, alternative approaches clearly defined and measurable through targeted pilot projects should be adopted. The competition from bigger countries in the Caribbean by virtue of larger budgets has influenced St Kitts' decision to move away from the general interest market, which promotes sun, sea and sand, and to focus more on the specific niches of romance, diving and sports and events. Another critical proposal that recognized the limited financial resources was that the Department of Tourism and overseas promotion offices work with travel partners to establish a public/private marketing fund to support efforts to promote development of these special interest travel markets.

The absence of visitor demographic research data had to some extent undermined the marketing efforts of SKN in that planners did not have a good sense of who the customers were, their purpose of travel, how they heard about SKN and their motivation for visiting SKN. To address this shortcoming, there has been the redesign and distribution of a new immigration card in 2007, technical training in market research for employees and the introduction and implementation of exit surveys at the airport and cruise ship terminal.

All indications are that the tourism sector has strengthened considerably in St Kitts. There is therefore a need for the various stakeholders to meld their efforts to ensure global competitiveness. A sustainable and quality tourism product is based on St Kitts' unique combination of a healthy natural island environment, a rich cultural heritage and hospitable and trainable citizens. According to the Minister of State, this desirable destination product must be communicated to St Kitts' target audiences with messages that are clear, consistent and compatible with the vision of the country.

Over the years, the statistics indicate that there has been significant growth in the cruise sector. Stay-over tourism remains a challenge, although the presence of the St Kitts Marriott Resort, opened in 2003, has ushered in notable increases in the number of visitors overall. Table 10.1 provides statistics on visitor arrivals over the period 2000–2006, and highlights the decline experienced in 2001–2002, part of a global fall-off in travel and tourism in the wake of the September 11 terrorist attack.

Table 10.1 Visitor Arrivals to SKN, 2000–2006

Year	Air and sea arrivals				Total arrivals	Tourism expenditure EC$ million
	Stay-overs	Excursionists	Total air arrivals	Yacht and cruise ship		
2000	73 149	3201	76 350	170 887	247 237	158
2001	70 565	3662	74 227	259 134	333 361	168
2002	68 998	3336	72 334	167 054	239 388	152
2003	90 599	3457	94 056	150 429	244 485	203
2004	117 531	3746	121 277	254 535	375 812	277
2005	127 728	3671	131 399	215 351	346 750	297
2006	135 792	3893	139 685	203 075	342 760	310

Source: Ministry of Sustainable Development (2008).

Although Table 10.1 presents aggregates as opposed to arrivals by generating markets, it is well known that the United States is the main tourism market for SKN, followed by the Caribbean, Canada and the United Kingdom. Much effort is being made to increase arrivals from the United Kingdom and Europe, and it is expected that Canada will continue to grow given the strengthening of the Canadian dollar and its economy in general.

SKN, like many other countries in the Caribbean, has been affected by the effects of the global economic crisis in the United Kingdom and North America. During 2009, visitor arrivals, specifically the number of stay-over tourists, dropped. Some hotels, such as the St Kitts Marriott Resort and the Ocean Terrace Inn, had to lay off some of their workers in 2009 owing to increasing costs, low occupancies and financial constraints. The cruise sector, however, has shown considerable resilience and continues to make great strides, with over 450 000 passengers estimated to call between the period October 2009 and May 2010. This is an area that the Government is focusing on to help maximize benefits for allied businesses such as taxi operators, boutiques, souvenir shops and craft vendors. Despite the fall in overall arrivals, there is growing optimism evidenced in the increase in the number of flights by Delta Airlines, British Airways and American Airlines as a result of increased demand in source markets in December 2009.

In addition, a report issued by the Fiscal Division of the Ministry of Finance in January 2010 concerning the outcomes of the Government's financial programmes indicated that for the period January–November 2009, fiscal surpluses were recorded for the recurrent account (EC$10.3 million) as recurrent revenue of EC$395.7 million exceeded recurrent expenditure of EC$385.4 million. This suggests that SKN has been relatively successful in confronting the challenges posed by the economic crisis. In light of this positive trend, SKN continues to make prudent fiscal decisions and adopt innovative marketing strategies to survive the global economic downturn facing the region. Cost-effective marketing strategies employing the use of the Internet and special promotional packages are just two of several methods the tourism sector has been using to reach its target markets. A more sustained and creative approach will have to be developed to ensure that the Federation continues to thrive.

The Federal system that governs SKN means that there are two separate destination management organizations (DMOs) in each island and the islands are marketed independently of each other, utilizing separate budgets. However, on occasions as in the case of World Travel Market in 2007 and *The Visitor Magazine*, the destination is marketed as 'Two Islands, One Paradise'. In St Kitts, the St Kitts Tourism Authority plays the lead role with respect to promoting and marketing the island (Tourism Authority Act, 2002). Its functions include formulating and instituting measures designed to enhance the role and image of St Kitts as a tourist destination, as well as designing, encouraging and implementing suitable marketing strategies for the effective promotion of the tourism industry (Draft Policies & Procedures Manual, 2003:11). In Nevis, the DMO is the Nevis Tourism Authority. While marketing strategies may differ because of the product, there is a shared vision based upon enhancing destination competitiveness and achieving maximum customer satisfaction by providing value (Nykiel, 1997).

The Tourism Authority maintains a presence in its key markets of United States, Canada and Europe via its overseas offices based in the respective countries. The role of these offices includes *inter alia* serving as point of information and distribution for the destination's range of tourism products, maintaining close contact with the travel trade industry, and working closely with airlines such as American Airlines (AA) and US Airways to gain market information. The overseas directors also plan and manage familiarization trips (FAM trips) with the travel trade through its active membership in Caribbean Tourism Organization (CTO) United States Chapters, and through trade shows, sales calls and mailings, negotiate co-op marketing plans with tour operators, and in general partner with travel writers, photo-journalists, public relations agencies, travel agents and tour operators to further promote the destination.

Marketing and Promotional Strategies for St Kitts

E-marketing, including online social media such as Facebook and Twitter, plays a key role in informing prospective visitors about the destination. The St Kitts website www.stkitts-tourism.com provides a comprehensive overview of the tourism product, addressing aspects such as the history and culture of the people, and gives a broad perspective of country life. It also provides information on hotels, restaurants and activities tourists can engage in while in St Kitts. The Tourism Sector Strategy (2006) states that results from the International Perceptions Survey indicated that 52% of respondents booked their vacation over the Internet and that 18.3% first learned of St Kitts on the Internet. The destination's presence on the Internet has to be further strengthened to extend the reach to surfers exploring holiday possibilities. A number of recommendations will be explored later to upgrade the website and generate more business.

Advertising is another important component of the overall marketing strategy. The Tourism Authority advertises in a number of magazines that relate to the destination's niche markets such as *Islands Magazine, Dive Training* and *Destination Honeymoons and Weddings*. Given financial constraints, St Kitts does not invest much money in television advertisements although those may have wide-reaching impact. A number of DVDs have been produced to highlight the Music Festival, a major event on the country's calendar of tourism activities, as well as the culture and history of the country. These are shown at trade shows, and distributed to the travel trade. *The Visitor Magazine*, a comprehensive tool highlighting the tourism product, is produced locally and is often disseminated at overseas trade shows, as part of press kits and in local hotel rooms.

Press and public relations are critical to the destination's marketing strategy. The country has employed the services of a public relations agency to address its public relations needs. The company has been primarily responsible for organizing press trips to the destination so that travel writers and photo-journalists can obtain a close-up view of what the destination has to offer. Consequently, St Kitts has received wide coverage in a number of leading newspapers where there is extensive readership and possibly great impact. Interviews and press conferences with the Minister and other key officials at major events have been staged to 'get the word out' about the destination. Public relations is a very inexpensive medium for generating interest in the tourism product as the monetary value of every article that is published can be ascertained. The positive publicity is also viewed as more credible than an advertisement, because an article/editorial is written by an independent third party.

Although the government is mainly responsible for destination marketing, there is greater need for public and private sector partnerships if the destination is to expand its marketing thrust in traditional and non-traditional markets. The private sector is therefore being encouraged to invest more dollars to fuel marketing efforts and to stimulate the sector.

Branding St Kitts

Since St Kitts' marketing resources are limited, it is crucial to its success that its branding as a tourist destination is effective. A new logo has also been introduced as a graphic depiction of the island's brand promise. It seeks to provide an exclusive and recognizable visual style that is unique to the island. This reinforces the strength of its tourism product. The logo comprises three discrete components: a symbol, the logo type and the tag line. The introduction of this new brand identity has been very effective in helping to cement and maintain the destination's image. The symbol, the national flower of St Kitts, the Poinciana or Flamboyant, is used to create an image that is distinctive to the island. The logotype is an elegant script typeface used to reflect the grace and beauty of the island and its people. The tag line 'Explore ... Feel ... Love ... Remember' is an implied invitation to experience the island in its entirety. It is also a promise that the destination will deliver an enriching, emotional and memorable encounter with the island and its people.

The effective application of this recently introduced brand has been consistent throughout all of the vehicles used to market St Kitts. This has resulted in maximum reach and impact of its very limited promotional dollars.

Marketing Niche Products in St Kitts

The marketing of St. Kitts as a tourist destination has become much more focused in recent years, as a result of the decision to reposition the destination in the market-place. Prior to this policy, the destination sought to reach all market segments. Now marketing efforts are concentrated in three primary areas:

1. Destination Weddings and Honeymoons
2. Dive Tourism
3. Sports and Events Tourism.

Attention to these niches allows the destination to focus on attracting the more mature, sophisticated, affluent and demanding travellers of the baby-boomer generation, who seek a more varied experience, and are willing to travel outside of their hotel boundaries in an effort to interact with the destination. These segments also explore opportunities to learn about the island's history, nature and culture, and to interact with its people as part of this process. There is much evidence to prove that this segment has provided the greatest benefits to St Kitts, both economically and socially, and many of these visitors have embraced the destination to the point of purchasing residential properties on the island.

The catalyst for this new approach or vision stems from the Tourism Marketing Policy (2008), which is underpinned by notions of sustainable tourism development and is therefore based on marketing a:

> unique combination of a healthy natural island environment; a rich cultural heritage; intelligent, trainable and genuine local people; and a high level of innovativeness and commitment from the widest variety of stakeholders cooperating for the mutual benefits of customers and suppliers.
>
> The Tourism Marketing Policy, Procedures and Brand
> Guidelines for St Kitts, (2008:1)

Salient to this approach to marketing has been attempts by the St Kitts Tourism Authority to communicate this vision to its target markets in a clear, consistent, focused and compatible manner. The destination has identified several 'specialist shows' that provide opportunities to meet the relevant market segments, e.g. DEMA (US) Dive Market, Outdoor Adventure Show & Sportsman Show (Canada), Incentive Works (ITME) and Meetings & Convention Business.

Marketing the Events Segment in St Kitts

Events tourism has increased in significance in the overall marketing strategy of St Kitts. It has helped tremendously in generating traffic to the destination during the summer/fall period when hotel occupancy tends to be low. St Kitts has successfully hosted one of the top Caribbean music festivals, the St Kitts Music Festival, held in June since 1996. In October 2008, St Kitts hosted the International Soca Awards Competition, which built on the momentum created by the country's music festival and drew on performing artistes from the wider Caribbean and soca music lovers all over the world.

The destination is also becoming a Caribbean favourite for hosting sporting activities since the upgrading of its facilities to host World Cup Cricket in 2007, and the construction of the Silver Jubilee Stadium, which was the venue for the Carifta Games in 2008. St Kitts now hosts cricket teams and clubs from the United Kingdom, Canada, India, Australia, South Africa and the West Indies. In addition, its Thomas McBroom 18-hole Championship Golf Course allows for the hosting of Caribbean golf tournaments.

In October 2006, St. Kitts added another facet to its efforts at garnering more business through events tourism. It hosted its first International Fashion Show with participants from North America, Europe and the Caribbean, and fashion writers from around the world. This has become an annual event.

The country's own diaspora plays an integral part in its marketing efforts. The island's Annual National Carnival is a major attraction for its people at home and abroad. Carnival officially takes place from the middle of December to 2 January, and attracts nationals from all over the world. More and more of the diaspora segment are choosing to seek accommodation in the island's many hotels, and are accountable for a big part of the sector's annual revenue. As such, deliberate planning goes into working with the various national associations in the target markets, including providing support by the overseas representatives of the St Kitts Tourism Office in the areas of joint marketing and promotions.

Strategic Partnerships in Destination Marketing for St Kitts

The relevance of partnerships in the overall marketing strategy is enormous in view of the increasing demands being placed on the annual budget of the St Kitts Tourism Authority. Activities executed with industry partners lend themselves to the policy of selective marketing in an effort to reach the 'right' clientele. In the United States, American Airlines, Delta Airlines and US Airways are all party to special promotions hosted by the destination. This may take the form of an educational evening for travel agents, a direct mail campaign to particular geographic segments, a familiarization visit to the destination or a media trip.

St Kitts also capitalizes on its partnership as a member of the CTO. This partnership allows for the enhancement of destination marketing through participation in joint activities like its annual Caribbean Week in Canada or the Tourism and Investment Forum held in June in Washington, DC. There are other collaborative efforts built on a relationship with other destinations that provide exposure to consumers and the travel trade through the pooling of resources. This approach to marketing is very common in Canada and the United Kingdom. In Canada, the relationship operates under the Team Caribe banner. It aims to provide education, create awareness and to market the Caribbean region. Marketing and promotional activities include joint consumer and trade evenings, and cost sharing for advertisements and attendance at trade and consumer shows.

One of the success stories that relate to partnership and marketing in St Kitts and the sister island of Nevis is the Annual Campaign to generate travel to the destination during the autumn months. The campaign is called 'Fall in Love with St Kitts and Nevis'. It involves stakeholders from the sector on both islands providing incentives and discounted prices for accommodation, meals, site and side trips and souvenirs – all of these components creating the perfect holiday experience. It is promoted in the marketplace by the airlines, tour operators, wholesalers and specialist agents in an effort to generate tourist traffic to the destination.

The spirit of partnership in marketing is also visible in the destination's budget spend with its industry partners. A substantial portion of its budget is dedicated to advertising with tour operators and wholesalers in the marketplace. This also includes participation in annual road shows, purchase of in-flight advertising for audiovisual presentations on charter aircraft, website promotions and other 'special' exercises. As much as 50% of the budget of the Canadian Office of the St Kitts Tourism Authority is used for this purpose.

Tourism Development in Nevis

This section presents an overview of the promotional strategy Nevis adopts to promote tourism internationally. Generally marketed as an upscale destination, Nevis appeals to the 'well-seasoned' traveller, who is willing to pay a 'little extra' to get away from it all. The island is blessed with natural beauty and a wealth of history. Because of its unique features, Nevis does not support a large tourism capacity, but has been able to attract very small high-quality tourism and related developments.

This small island, Nevis, has positioned itself as a growing tourism destination by investing in infrastructure and geothermal research to support the industry. Special emphasis has been placed on road networks, transportation via air and sea, and utilities development.

The accommodation sector ranges from intimate family-run guest houses, located on or in close proximity to the beach, to five-star destinations, the Four Seasons Resorts and the Plantation Inns being the most well known. Built on old sugar plantations, these two properties embody the themes and concept of the plantation era of a major great house with guest cottages scattered around the estate. The grounds of these inns are beautifully landscaped and most are located on the slopes of Nevis Peak amid lush greenery.

The wealth of history that Nevis possesses is brought alive in its many heritage sites and attractions. Once visitors land on Nevis, they feel as if they are 'taking a step back in time'. In the midst of its natural beauty, tranquil and peaceful nature, Nevis provides a range of activities that visitors can enjoy at their own leisure and pace.

Target Market for Nevis

With just over 400 hotel rooms on the island, Nevis markets itself as an upscale destination, targeting experienced travellers who are in the mid- to upper-income bracket levels. The target market is over the age of 35 and is interested in nature, relaxation and getting away from the everyday hassle. Emphasis is also placed on the wedding and honeymoon market. The Nevis Tourism Authority's main generating market is North America, with the most emphasis being placed on the East Coast. The reasons for this are twofold. First, statistics show that traditionally arrivals from the United States average 55% of annual tourist arrivals to Nevis, with most of those people coming from the East Coast. Second, the ease of travel and air access make this market a rational choice.

The Branding Strategy of Nevis

The Nevis Tourism Authority Act in 2001 allowed for the establishment of the Nevis Tourism Authority and consequently a Nevis tourism brand. The brand placed emphasis on communicating an 'upscale image', peace and tranquillity and the naturalness of the island and its people. The brand logo 'Nevis … Naturally' was meant to embody the brand elements to the consumer in a clear and consistent manner. The logo is therefore used in all activities employed by the authority. This includes the destination brochure, printed advertisements, controlled journalist reports and other collateral materials, such as banner-stands, table-top and booth displays. The distribution channels chosen are also consistent with Nevis' brand image and include the use of the Internet, targeted consumer and trade expositions and use of specialist tour operators and travel agents.

Nevis' Communication and Distribution Tools

Advertisements

Advertisements are meant to arrest attention, hold interest, arouse desire and obtain action (Kotler, Bowen & Makens, 2002). They also have rational, emotional and moral appeal, for example Figure 10.1. This is in alignment with the brand strategy and the targeted audience developed by the Nevis Tourism Authority. There is an appeal to the upscale traveller interested in natural beauty and some measure of relaxation. The brand is easily identifiable through the choice of pictures and the use of the logo. The tag line 'It's not easy to get here, but it's harder to leave' creates interest; the descriptive words used arouse desire, and the contact information is a prompt to take action. 'Come! Let Nevis cast its spell on you. Then leave if you must' is an appeal to the emotion.

The Internet

The website www.nevisisland.com is filled with tourist information, historic and other general information about the island. There is information and links to accommodation and activities visitors can participate in while on the island. This information is both useful for the individual traveller sourcing the Web for the right destination and also very important as a sales support for the specialist tour operators and travel agents.

It's not easy to get here,
but it's harder to leave.

Lush hillsides where the only sounds are the whisper of
breezes and the chirping of birds. Golden sand beaches
fringed with clear, blue water. Gracious people who greet and treat
you as friends. All these await you on Nevis, along with fine food,
accommodations from luxury villas to enchanting Plantation Inns at
the Caribbean's top-rated resort, and activities to suit every taste.
Come let Nevis cast its spell on you. Then, leave if you must.

Nevis Tourism Authority
Main Street, Charlestown Nevis, WI
869.469.7550 • 866.55.NEVIS Toll Free
869.469.7551 Fax
nta2001@caribsurf.com
www.nevisisland.com

Figure 10.1 Nevis Tourism Authority Advertising.

Trade and Consumer Travel Expositions

Nevis participates in top trade and consumer travel expositions that specialize in different interest areas, e.g. the Luxury Travel Show held every January in New York and other luxury shows throughout the year. At these shows emphasis is placed on portraying Nevis as an upscale destination. The same theme is used in all the collateral material highlighted at these shows. Exhibits are simple and are cleared of the clutter that may confuse the consumer as to the message being communicated.

Travel Agents and Tour Operators

The Nevis Tourism Authority works with travel agents and tour operators who specialize in luxury travel. This is done through sales calls to these agents, familiarization visits and participation in trade show expositions.

Destination Brochure

The destination brochure also seeks to communicate an upscale image to the potential traveller. It is a simply designed, neat brochure that fits into a legal-size envelope. Though simple, it is filled with all the information necessary to assist someone making a choice. The emphasis is placed on accommodation, and each hotel is given a page to communicate general information. The design of each page is consistent from one property to the other, communicating the upscale image. There is a pull-out sheet with hotel contact information and current rack rates. This is changed every year. Other pages of the brochure include information on guest houses, villas and activities. The brochure is enclosed in a shell jacket with a slot available for inserts with general information about Nevis. The inserts include:

- Calendar of Events
- General Information
- Nevis Heritage
- Land Based Activities
- Water Based Activities
- Getting Married on Nevis
- Getting to Nevis.

The life of the brochure is 18–24 months, but the inserts can be updated and printed as new information becomes available. The brochure is printed on high-quality paper chosen to communicate the branded image of Nevis. Distribution of this brochure is done by mail from requests received through airmail, email and telephone. In addition, brochures are distributed at all promotional activities participated in by the Tourism Board.

Marketing Impact

Internet World Statistics (2005) show that 68% of North Americans use the Internet. An increase of 107% usage was recorded from 2000 to 2005 (Internet World Statistics, 2005). Dimanche, Havitz, and Howard (1993) suggest that destination management organizations (DMOs) should take advantage of the unique capabilities afforded by the Internet to customize the provision of information for effective targeting strategies. Studies by Cai, Feng, and Breiter (2004) show that people with high levels of income were found to be more likely to use the Internet than those of medium and low levels. The design of the website and the importance of the Internet as a distribution channel play a key role in Nevis' strategy.

Challenges Facing the Twin-Island Destination

One of the challenges facing tourism development in SKN prior to the construction and opening of the St Kitts Marriott Resort and the Four Seasons Resort in Nevis was the stay-over sector, which during the period 2000–2002 saw a decline in tourist arrivals (*Air & Sea Arrivals, 1978–2006*). In the following period, 2003–2006, the projected arrivals moved from over 90 000 to over 135 000. This growth in the stay-over sector is attributable to the presence of the Marriott and Four Seasons Resort, which have hosted major meetings and conventions in their large conference facilities. It is expected that the stay-over sector will grow even further as a number of upscale hotels and villas are being constructed. By 2010, the South East Peninsula, which is the area earmarked for upscale developments, will no doubt be transformed. A strong and visible private sector bodes well for stronger destination marketing both in terms of attracting investors and visitors to the destination.

As mentioned earlier, stakeholder partnerships are a logical outflow of expanded tourism development. As outlined in an earlier section, the Government is the chief financier of destination marketing and its activities. With the anticipated growth in the tourism private sector, it is incumbent upon all parties to join forces and work together to grow the destination. The Hotel and Tourism Association is well poised to foster this partnership and to engage its members in collaborating with government. Major trade shows should be jointly attended and sponsorship secured for some of the collateral material. Attention must be paid to the issue of airlift, especially in light of the huge sums of money paid to major airlines to guarantee flights.

The Way Forward

The future looks bright for tourism development in SKN. However, careful planning and engagement with the private sector in the area of destination marketing should assist in enhancing the destination's image in target markets. Greater focus also needs to be placed on attracting the diaspora and ethnic markets. Finally, the countries of the Organization of Eastern Caribbean States (OECS) have committed to joining forces in terms of regional marketing, an issue that has been on the agenda of the CTO for many years. Undoubtedly, amalgamating one's resources to market in specific target markets gives individual countries more scope to stretch their limited dollars, and can only redound to the benefit of member countries.

Discussion Questions

1. Tourism is the engine of growth for SKN. When compared with other Caribbean countries, St Kitts has a limited marketing budget of US$3.5 million to cover the main source markets of the United States, Canada and the United Kingdom. However, the Government has set a target to increase tourist arrivals by 3% in 2010. Tourism statistics for 2008 revealed

that there were 123 603 stay-over visitors and 400 883 cruise passengers. What are the most strategic ways that SKN can utilize this budget to achieve government objectives?

2. What options can the country pursue to ensure that it remains competitive in the tourism industry?

3. Of the three main source markets – the United States, Canada and the United Kingdom – the United Kingdom was the fastest-growing market for 2008–2009. Identify the factors responsible for this growth, and point out what other strategies the destination can employ to vigorously promote the destination in the United Kingdom, given its financial constraints and the downturn in the British economy.

References

Cai, L. A., Feng, R., & Breiter, D. (2004). Tourist purchase decision involvement and information preferences. *Journal of Vacation Marketing*, *10*(2), 138–148.

Caribbean Tourism Human Resource Council. (2007). *Teaching tourism in the Caribbean: A resource manual for teachers of tourism at the secondary level*. Caribbean Tourism Human Resource Council, Barbados.

Dimanche, F., Havitz, M. E., & Howard, D. R. (1993). Consumer involvement profiles as a tourism segmentation tool. *Journal of Travel and Tourism Marketing*, *1*(4), 33–52.

Draft Policies and Procedures Manual. (2009) for the St Kitts Tourism Authority.

Internet World Statistics. http://www.internetworldstats.com. Accessed November 2005.

Kotler, P., Bowen, J. T., & Makens, J. C. (2002). *Marketing for hospitality and tourism* (3rd ed.). New Jersey (NJ): Pearson/Prentice Hall.

Ministry of Sustainable Development. (2008). *Tourism statistics*.

Nevis Tourism Authority. http://www.nevisisland.com. Accessed November 2005.

Nykiel, R. A. (1997). *Marketing in the hospitality industry* (3rd ed.). Michigan: Educational Institute of the American Hotel & Motel Association.

OTF Group. (2006). *St. Kitts and Nevis tourism sector strategy*.

Ministry of Toursim. (2008). *Tourism marketing policy and procedures and brand guidelines for St. Kitts*.

TDI Corporation. (2002). *St. Kitts and Nevis strategic plan for tourism development*.

The St. Christopher Tourism Authority (Amendment) Act, No. 11 of 1999.

11 Port-of-Spain: The Meetings and Conventions Capital of the Southern Caribbean

Acolla Lewis-Cameron

The University of the West Indies, St Augustine, Trinidad and Tobago, West Indies

Introduction

Trinidad lies within one of the world's most tourism-intensive regions, the Caribbean. Yet, unlike its neighbours, it has not relied heavily on income from travel and tourism since its economy is dominated by the energy sector, which contributes approximately 45% to the country's gross domestic product (GDP) (WTTC, 2005). However, within recent times, tourism has been identified as one of five sectors that should be developed to contribute to the country's economic development. One of the key elements of the Government's Vision 2020 goals is the positioning of Port-of-Spain as the 'Meetings and Conventions Capital of the Southern Caribbean'. The successful establishment of a Conventions Bureau is an important step towards achieving this goal.

The purpose of this chapter is to assess Trinidad's potential for developing and strategically marketing the conventions product. It is with this in mind that the chapter begins with an overview of the global meetings and conventions industry. It continues with an examination of the tourism environment in Trinidad. This is followed by a critical assessment of the Tourism Development Company's (TDC) marketing strategy of positioning Port-of-Spain as the Meetings and Conventions Capital of the Southern Caribbean. The chapter then concludes with an analysis of the extent to which Trinidad can effectively develop and market the conventions product.

The Meetings and Conventions Industry

The meetings and conventions sector of the tourism industry is one of the most competitive and lucrative of market segments, and is becoming one of the fastest-growing sectors in the industry. In recent decades, the amount of convention space has exploded worldwide, with convention space in North America alone doubling from 42.8 million square feet in 1986 to an anticipated 85.5 million square feet in 2007 (Detlefsen, 2005). The reality in this increasingly connected marketplace is that meetings, events and conventions can be hosted anywhere in the world, resulting in keen competition

Marketing Island Destinations. DOI: 10.1016/B978-0-12-384909-0.00011-8

among potential host destination sites. Countries that were not previously major players in the conventions market, e.g. China and India, now house some of the world's most modern convention and event facilities. For other countries, like Trinidad, the conventions industry is now viewed as an alternative market to support other tourism offerings and to gain a competitive edge in the globally competitive marketplace.

Meetings and conventions tourism is now a truly global industry, with developed and developing countries having increasing opportunities to participate as hosts. Although the industry has significant global reach, the top 25 convention destinations over the last 20 years have been located in the developed North, with the United States, the United Kingdom and Germany maintaining the top three positions between 1999 and 2001 (International Congress and Convention Association, 2009). According to Rogers (2003:7), 'while competition is increasing from countries seeking to act as suppliers to the conference industry, the markets from which to win business still remain relatively few in number'. He cites two noteworthy reasons for this. First, the headquarters of many international associations, where those organizing events on behalf of those bodies are based, are located in Western Europe and North America. Second, market intelligence is much better developed in respect of the conference organizers in the most experienced conventioneering countries. Notwithstanding this, the possible benefits to be accrued from participating in this industry are significant enough to continue to attract new players. Thus, competition is likely to intensify, with new destinations challenging the position of mature conventioneering countries.

Research conducted in the United Kingdom, a mature convention destination, has highlighted some noteworthy trends that will affect the convention industry in the United Kingdom, with implications for the global conventions industry. Notably, the business environment is expected to experience an increase in competition, higher expectations of customers and faster communications. The industry will witness changing use of technology and technological advancements. Socially, the research noted that the continued growth in international travel will facilitate conference attendance. From a political perspective, it was suggested that the political stability of the host nation will become increasingly important as a site selection criterion for international organizers (Weber & Ladkin, 2004).

Benefits of the Industry

Meetings and conventions are considered a notably lucrative source of income for destinations, and for cities in particular, as they cater to the high-yield end of the market. Convention participants spend much more than the average traveller, thus creating substantial economic impact for the host city's economy. It is noted that on average a conventioneer stays in a city from 3.8 to 4.5 days and spends from US$525 to US$970 (Priporas, 2005). In 2001, conference visitors to the United Kingdom spent an average of €146 per day, compared with an average of just €56 per day for all categories of visitors (Rogers, 2003). On a national level, the industry generated roughly 8% of the overall US$1.3 trillion US travel and tourism industry (Kapoor, Powell, Abbott, 2006). Most important, the economic impact of meetings and conventions is spread throughout the economy of the host city, since conventions influence a spectrum of businesses including hotels, restaurants and entertainment organizations (Astroff & Abbey, 1995; Kapoor *et al.*, 2006).

Another notable benefit is that meetings and conventions take place throughout the year, which stabilizes the seasonal pressures of tourism. This can constitute a major source of shoulder and off-season demand, since most associations and corporate meetings are held during the spring and autumn, which are traditionally low-demand periods for most tourist destinations (Oppermann & Chon, 1997; Priporas, 2005). By extension, Rogers (2003) highlighted the fact that the all-year-round nature of the industry leads to the creation and sustenance of permanent jobs, which is atypical of the leisure sector. Meetings and conventions also facilitate 'green' tourism as this type of tourism has fewer negative impacts on the environment. Conference delegates are fewer in number and they move as a group for the most part, thereby minimizing traffic congestion and environmental pollution (Rogers, 2003).

Success Factors for the Conventions Business

For managers in the public sector and companies interested in local tourism development, the challenge is how to identify the conditions and dynamics that lead to creating successful convention destinations (Bernini, 2009). Researchers have approached this challenge by examining the dynamics of the site selection process from two perspectives – the delegates/attendees (Oppermann & Chon, 1997) and the conference planners/associations (Chacko & Fenich, 2000; Crouch & Ritchie, 2004). Oppermann and Chon's (1997) framework for delegate decision-making included factors such as the health, financial and family status of the delegate, time availability, career aspirations and location factors such as climate and destination image. In terms of the desired conference benefits, delegates are interested in being educated, gaining new skills and developing new business/professional relationships.

The Crouch and Ritchie conceptual model of the dynamics of the site selection process highlights nine selection factors along with other antecedent conditions and competing site influences. These include accessibility, local support, extra-conference opportunities, accommodation facilities, meeting facilities, information, site environment and other criteria. Based on this model, Crouch and Ritchie (2004) studied the Australian domestic conventions industry to determine which of these factors were significant in that context. The results indicated that site attractiveness is strongly related to the proximity of sites to convention participants, the degree to which convention attendees needed to or could be accommodated on-site, accommodation room rates, cost of the convention venue, perceived food quality at the site and extra-conference opportunities.

Chacko and Fenich (2000) utilized Crouch and Ritchie's conceptual model in a US context and examined the selection factors in seven known convention cities. In this study, promotional appeal was the most significant attribute in all seven cities. The argument is that it makes it easier for planners to market the convention site to potential attendees. The other three attributes that were significant in three cities included hotel room availability, site environment and extra-conference opportunities and destination services. The latter refers to local support received from the city's

Convention Visitors' Bureau (CVB), convention centre and destination management companies. Interestingly, the one commonality between the US and Australia was the availability of extra-conference opportunities.

Based on research conducted in Italy, Bernini (2009) noted five key factors that were significant contributors to becoming a successful convention destination. These factors were:

- concentration of local resources necessary to perform convention business;
- quality convention products and services;
- development of a skilled and specialized labour force;
- the presence of an associated agency such as a CVB;
- government policies that organize service delivery, target investments and develop human resources.

The results of these studies indicate that there is no clear pattern of attributes that can be universally applied to all destinations. Context plays a critical role in decision-making. What is made clear is that 'destinations need to create unique combinations of attributes to develop strong competitive positions, and they must do so using an intimate knowledge of the factors that associations value most in their site choice decisions' (Crouch & Ritchie, 2004:128). Moreover, Jago and Deery (2005) further note that the relationship between the convention agency, the convention planner and the delegate in the site selection process is also integral to the process.

Marketing Environment for Convention Destinations

Destinations competing for convention business operate in a very dynamic and highly competitive global environment. Over the last decade, there has been a flood of new entrants to the market, particularly among Asian countries, including Vietnam, Cambodia and China. Among the more established conference destinations, North America has shown the most growth. Farmer (2005) states that the building of new meetings space in that region is reaching unprecedented levels, and that where there is no room for new construction, existing facilities are renovating and adding amenities and technology. The rapid expansion of the supply of convention venues in a growing number of destinations warrants the development of a balanced convention product, high-quality support services and a strategic approach to developing and marketing the destination's convention product.

Continuous advances in communications technology further define the operating environment for convention destinations and provide a welcome opportunity for these destinations to gain/maintain a competitive edge. Davidson and Rogers (2006:62) note that 'communications technology solutions are now helping venues attract more business by providing the infrastructure needed to make all types of meetings more engaging and more effective for those who attend them'. For example, RF (radio frequency) and RFID (radio frequency identification) are already in use at some conference destinations, and this allows for access control and the collection of registration materials can be more easily tracked. Moreover, the ability to develop increasingly sophisticated websites gives destinations a powerful tool to market themselves.

In addition to communications technology, the design of convention venues is increasingly being used as a marketing tool for destinations. 'For planners, it's not what meetings they can bring to convention centres, but what those centres can bring to their meetings' (Minton, 2005:65). Appearance, design and functionality are critical features of a successful convention venue. 'It has been said that conference centres have the potential to be regarded as the 'castles of the future' – iconic buildings that, if well designed, can become the symbol of the city in which they stand' (Davidson & Rogers, 2006:64). In terms of functionality, the trend is towards venues that are flexible and customizable in their design and layout. Thus, the focus for convention venues is not solely on accommodating events but also on enhancing events. In this way, the appearance, design and functionality of the venue become a unique selling proposition for the destination.

Trinidad: The Tourism Environment

Trinidad is one of two islands that form the Republic of Trinidad and Tobago. These islands are located at the southernmost end of the chain of Caribbean islands at the crossroads of North, Central and South America. Trinidad, the larger of the two islands, is home to the centre of government, and its capital city, Port-of-Spain, is a major financial centre in the Caribbean. Trinidad stands in stark contrast to the sister isle of Tobago as the island is rich in natural resources such as oil and gas, whereas Tobago is more serene with sandy beaches and coral reefs. For this reason, Tobago is seen as the centre of leisure tourism activity.

In Trinidad, the energy sector has assumed the dominant role of income earner and has been the engine of growth over the last four decades, contributing approximately 45% to the country's GDP. As a result, the country's travel and tourism growth has been slow-moving as compared to the other islands in the Caribbean. Government policies have historically sought to limit and control tourism activity, and the concentration on the energy sector in the 1970s diverted attention away from tourism as a source of foreign exchange revenues.

The Government of Trinidad and Tobago (GOTT), in pursuit of its aim of developed nation status by 2020, recognizes that the energy sector is unable to fully sustain the economy in order to achieve this goal. Therefore, tourism has been identified as one of the economic development tools that the Government can use to reduce the country's reliance on the energy sector. According to the Vision 2020 Tourism Strategic Development Plan (GOTT, 2004:v),

> By the year 2020, the Trinidad and Tobago tourism product will be a significant economic sector contributing significantly to the nation's GDP, through job creation and increased revenues, driven by a uniquely differentiated, internationally competitive product, complemented by comprehensive, fully functional physical infrastructure, modern, competitive institutional framework and supported by the people of Trinidad and Tobago.

Trinidad and Tobago's tourism industry is currently in its growth stage, and it directly contributes approximately 10.6% to the country's GDP (WTTC, 2005:10).

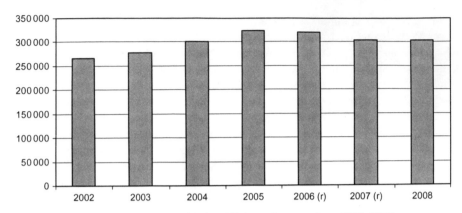

Figure 11.1 Stopover visitors to Trinidad and Tobago, January–June 2002–2008.
Source: TDC (2009).

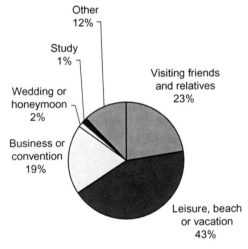

Figure 11.2 Stopover visitors to Trinidad and Tobago by purpose of visit, 2008.
Source: TDC (2009).

This is in comparison to the manufacturing sector, which contributes 5.5% to GDP, and the energy sector, which accounts for approximately 45% of GDP (CSO, 2008). According to the (WTTC, 2005), travel and tourism's direct and indirect contribution to GDP is expected to increase from 13.8% to 16.5% by 2015. International arrivals to Trinidad and Tobago, as seen in Figure 11.1, have shown consistent growth by over 40% since the mid-1990s, equalling or exceeding the growth recorded by other Caribbean islands over a six-year period. Tourism in Trinidad is set on a growth path, which is expected to continue for some time.

Analysis of the stopover visitors to Trinidad and Tobago by purpose of visit reveals that the market can be divided into three main categories, namely leisure travellers, visiting friends and relatives (VFR) and business travellers. This has been the pattern of stopover visitors throughout this decade. Figure 11.2 shows the most recent breakdown of these markets in terms of percentages. It is against this background that one of the goals noted in the Vision 2020 Tourism Strategic Development Plan is 'through the establishment of a Tourism Industrial Park and rehabilitation of the Port-of-Spain Waterfront, position Port-of-Spain as the Meetings and Conventions Capital of the Southern Caribbean in support of its existing status as the business center of the sub region' (GOTT, 2004:v).

The Meetings and Conventions Industry in Trinidad

As highlighted earlier in the discussion, the meetings and conventions business is a highly sought-after market in a very volatile global tourism industry. Trinidad finds itself in a position where it is seeking to penetrate an already well-established industry. The capital city of Port-of-Spain is earmarked as the hub for the conventions product. In terms of accommodation, Port-of-Spain houses two of the larger conference facilities in the English-speaking Caribbean in the form of the Hyatt Regency Trinidad (43 000 square feet of meeting space) and the Hilton Trinidad Conference Centre (40 000 square feet). Other options for large events include the Cascadia Hotel and Conference Centre, the Crowne Plaza and the theatre of the new National Academy of the Performing Arts. The city also offers a diverse shopping experience, and exciting nightlife including various clubs, bars, comedy shows and live theatre, thereby providing a vast variety of post-business entertainment and attractions for our business visitors.

In order to assess Trinidad's potential to both develop and effectively market the conventions product, a number of interviews were held with several stakeholders from the TDC, the Ministry of Tourism and the Trinidad Hotels, Restaurants and Tourism Association. The assessment was twofold – an overall SWOT analysis of the industry and an analysis of the marketing strategy employed by the TDC (see Table 11.1).

Based on the findings from the stakeholders who will play a critical role in the organizing and execution of meetings, Trinidad is fairly well positioned to aggressively pursue the conventions market. Using Crouch and Ritchie's (2004) nine selection factors, Trinidad is in a favourable position in terms of accessibility (good air access to and from main markets), local support (sufficient buy-in from the private sector at this initial stage) and extra-conference opportunities (good variety of post-conference activities available in both Trinidad and Tobago). These are some of the key success factors noted in both the Australian and the US contexts.

The challenges lie in the areas of accommodation facilities where there is a shortage of room stock in the capital to attract large meetings. Concomitantly, meeting facilities are also inadequate. The issue with the site environment is twofold. First, the traffic congestion within and around Port-of-Spain is a major deterrent for delegates desirous of engaging in extra-conference activities. Second, the service quality levels across the tourism sector are low in comparison to international standards. In order to address some of these shortcomings, the Investment Unit of the TDC is aggressively pursuing international investors to invest in quality accommodation

Table 11.1 SWOT Analysis of Trinidad's Potential for the Conventions Product

Strengths	Weaknesses
• Trinidad already has a very vibrant business community as a result of a strong energy sector and a growing manufacturing sector. • The destination has experience in hosting conferences and large meetings, e.g. Summit of the Americas and Commonwealth Heads of Government Meeting both in 2009. • Good airlift, particularly coming out of North America. There is now a connection to Central America with flights via COPA Airlines. • There is sufficient buy-in and commitment from the private sector. • Trinidad has a diverse range of extra-conference activities. One of the strengths of the destination is its ability to offer a dual experience. The participant will be able to have a very strong constructive meeting in a commercial thriving hub and still be able to experience the warmth and tranquillity of Tobago, which is a 15-minute flight away.	• The destination is unable to accommodate large meetings in excess of 700 delegates because of limited-quality accommodation available in Port-of-Spain. • More training and development required for destination managers. • There is a need for service quality improvement throughout the tourism industry. • There remains a challenge with the packaging of the product for the meetings market. • The cost of interregional travel is very high, which can be a deterrent for attracting meetings from the region. • Major traffic congestion in and around Port-of-Spain.
Opportunities	**Threats**
• The meeting market is stable in the midst of a crisis. Leisure travel is by choice. In the meetings business the decision-making is different and a little bit more stable. • There is a higher spend among business travellers as opposed to the leisure traveller. • The TDC has a good relationship with the two local universities, University of the West Indies and University of Trinidad and Tobago, which allows for the development of a partnership to attract and host conferences.	• The existence of more experienced and well-known convention destinations in the source markets. • There is intense competition in the region for the meetings business and several destinations have some advantages over Trinidad, e.g. Bahamas has a greater room stock; Puerto Rico has a more focused approach in going after the market; Puerto Rico, the main competitor, also has an exhibition centre and is in the process of building hotels around the centre to support that infrastructure.

stock in the capital. Furthermore, the Ministry of Tourism has secured the services of an international consultant to engage in a National Service Improvement Programme to be rolled out over a three-year period. This is an attempt to improve the service levels across the destination.

The Marketing Strategy

Conventions Bureau

One of the consistent success factors for conventions destinations noted in the literature is the establishment of a Conventions Bureau. The launching of the bureau by the Ministry of Tourism in September 2009 was certainly a step in the right direction. The bureau was established as a department within the TDC. With a mandate to position Port-of-Spain as the meetings, conferences, incentives and events capital of the Southern Caribbean, the main focus of the Trinidad and Tobago Conventions Bureau will be the effective marketing of Trinidad and Tobago as the destination of choice for regional and international meeting planners.

In the establishment of the bureau, the services of a consultant were employed for a period of six months in order to provide a structure for operations and to seek buy-in from industry stakeholders to support this initiative. The staffing structure for the bureau includes the head of the bureau, sales and marketing coordinator, research officer, conventions coordinator and an administrative assistant. The services offered by the Conventions Bureau include:

- introductions to local service providers including hotels, meeting facilities, event/meeting planners, social venues, transportation suppliers, tour operators and destination management companies;
- professional assistance including liaising with local suppliers, collecting bids and proposals, coordinating site visits and providing information on social programmes and pre- and post-conference tours and activities;
- promotion and publicity inclusive of providing destination brochures, presentations and DVDs and publicizing events on the website, events calendar and newsletters (TDC, 2010).

It must be reiterated that the development and marketing of the conventions product in Trinidad is still in its embryonic stage. Therefore, many of the marketing efforts are plans as opposed to actual activities engaged in. Nevertheless, it is necessary to assess the strategic marketing approach being adopted by the Conventions Bureau.

Target Market

The two main geographical markets targeted at the outset are North America and the Caribbean. According to the literature and the research conducted by the bureau, North America accounts for a large percentage of conventions business and is therefore one of the more lucrative markets to pursue. At present Trinidad has good access between Port-of-Spain and some of the main hubs in the US, including Miami,

Atlanta and New York. The Caribbean market is identified as a stable potential source of conventions business as Caribbean organizations have a history of organizing many meetings. Although high regional airfares were noted as a challenge, the region is fairly well served by the regional carriers.

In pursuing these two markets, the Conventions Bureau is cognizant of the fact that the main competition in the region is Puerto Rico and Jamaica. The former has put forward a very aggressive plan; they have built a state-of-the-art exhibition centre; they have a number of hotels with convention facilities and other properties are under construction; and US citizens do not need passports to visit the destination. Jamaica's marketing budget is relatively sizeable in comparison to Trinidad, which gives it greater leverage in its marketing efforts. This destination also has the advantage of its proximity to the North American market and a range of extra-conference activities.

Specific sectors have been identified as potential markets for conventions business, including the energy sector, multicultural associations and groups, trade/business associations and various corporations. Notably, there will be a strong outreach towards the association meetings, especially the local universities – University of the West Indies and the University of Trinidad and Tobago. The intention is to engage in dialogue with lecturers at the local universities to find out what associations they are members of so that the bureau can utilize these networks to expand its business reach. Given the current limitation of meeting space, the maximum size of any targeted meeting will be 1200 participants.

Communications Strategy

The Conventions Bureau has identified four main components in its plan to communicate the destination's message to the target market. The first is that of advertising in specific publications. *Successful Meetings* magazine and *Meetings and Conventions* magazine are two industry-specific publications earmarked as outlets for advertising the destination's conventions services. A second component highlighted is the development of a website primarily as an information portal for destination planners in the target market. The intention is that this site is a link accessible from the destination's general website. A third aspect of the communication strategy is sales missions to the target market, North America in the first instance. Fourth, attendance at relevant trade shows will form an integral part of the agenda. The International Congress and Convention Association annual events have been earmarked as major events on the bureau's calendar.

Assessment of the Marketing Strategy

With reference to Butler's tourist area life cycle model, Trinidad can be considered to be in the exploration stage with respect to its conventions product. At this stage, the strategic focus of the bureau needs to be expansion. With this in mind, the marketing response should be one of increasing awareness in target markets. A greater breadth of marketing efforts is required as opposed to depth at this stage. The competitive nature of the conventions business demands that Trinidad explores further options in terms of exposing the market to the destination's product. An expansion focus requires diverse and creative exposure techniques, and the Conventions Bureau has only just begun to tap into the range of options available in terms of an appropriate marketing response.

One of the more widely used and effective options is that of a website. The TDC is in the process of streamlining its websites so as to avoid duplication and to develop one main portal. According to the bureau, the intention is to develop a site for the conventions business as a link from TDC's main site. The website will not be used as a strategic marketing tool *per se*, but rather as a point of information dissemination for convention planners in the target markets. As highlighted above, 'sophisticated websites give destinations a powerful tool to market themselves'. Clearly, no longer are websites seen as information rooms but are now instrumental strategic tools in a destination's marketing armoury. In light of this, the bureau has to be more strategic in its development and use of the proposed website, with a focus on expansion, exposure and the eventual purchase of the destination's conventions product.

In addition to an effective website, the development of conventions centres provides a competitive edge for destinations pursuing the conventions business. According to Davidson and Rogers (2006), the focus for these venues is not only on accommodating events but also on enhancing events. The successful convention destinations pride themselves on their state-of-the-art convention facilities, which are used as a key marketing tool to win conventions business. At present, Trinidad has to use the various meeting facilities available at the hotels in the capital, including the Hyatt as the main meetings venue, and the Hilton and Crowne Plaza. However, if the destination is to compete with the major players in the industry, the development of a conventions venue is critical to its success.

Conclusion

The meetings and conventions sector of the tourism industry continues to grow at an unprecedented rate, with no immediate signs of abating as more and more destinations in both the developed and developing world seize the opportunity to diversify their tourism product. The sector is lucrative and provides a stable source of income for a destination throughout the year, thus engaging with the perennial challenge of seasonality in the industry. Penetration of and survival in this sector demand a unified effort between both the private and public sectors, along with a number of critical success factors that need to be in place.

Without a doubt, Trinidad is well positioned geographically and otherwise to maximize the benefits to be derived from the development of this sector. Although several weaknesses and threats have been highlighted, the destination has the relevant resources to address the identified issues. Importantly, the Conventions Bureau is established and is well on its way to executing the mandate given by the Ministry of Tourism. This is a critical first step in placing the destination on the conventions map. However, an analysis of the findings from interviews reveals that the bureau has to take a more strategic approach to its marketing agenda. According to Farmer (2005), the rapid expansion of the supply of convention venues in the growing number of destinations warrants the development of a balanced convention product, high-quality support services and a strategic approach to developing and marketing the destination's convention product.

Discussion Questions

1. Compare and contrast Trinidad as a conventions destination to another destination of your choice.
2. To what extent do you think Trinidad can compete with the established conventions destinations in North America and South-East Asia?
3. In your view, how can Trinidad be more strategic in its approach to developing and marketing the destination's conventions product?

References

Astroff, M. T., & Abbey, J. R. (1995). *Convention sales and services*. Las Vegas, Nevada: Waterbury Press.

Bernini, C. (2009). Convention industry and destination clusters: Evidence from Italy. *Tourism Management*, *30*(6), 878–889.

Central Statistical Office. (2008) *National account*. http://www.cso.gov.tt/cso/statistics/accounts.aspx. Accessed March 2008.

Chacko, H., & Fenich, G. (2000). Determining the importance of US convention destination attributes. *Journal of Vacation Marketing*, *6*(3), 211–220.

Crouch, G., & Ritchie, B. (2004). The determinants of convention site selection: A logistic choice model from experimental data. *Journal of Travel Research*, *43*, 118–130.

Davidson, R., & Rogers, T. (2006). *Marketing destinations and venues for conferences, conventions and business events*. London: Butterworth-Heinemann.

Detlefsen, H. (2005). *HVS journal 2005: convention centers: is the industry overbuilt?* New York: HVS International.

Farmer, R. P. (2005). The meeting industry's growth fuels a surge in renovations, expansions and new constructions. *The Meeting Professional*, *25*(8), 17–20.

Government of Trinidad and Tobago (GOTT). (2004). *2020 Tourism development strategic plan*. Trinidad and Tobago: GOTT.

International Congress and Convention Association. (2009). http://www.iccaworld.com. Accessed 2 July 2009.

Jago, L. K., & Deery, M. (2005). Relationships and factors influencing convention decision-making. *Journal of Convention and Event Tourism*, *7*(1), 23–35.

Kapoor, P., Powell, P., & Abbott, J. (2006). Conventional disputes, unconventional resolutions: An analysis of dispute resolution in the meetings, conventions, and exhibition industry. *Journal of Convention and Event Tourism*, *8*(3), 45–70.

Minton, E. (2005). What planners really want. *The Meeting Professional*, June.

Oppermann., & Chon, K. (1997). Convention participation decision-making process. *Annals of Tourism Research*, *24*, 178–191.

Priporas, C. V. (2005). Is it difficult to market a city as a convention destination? The case of Thessaloniki. *Journal of Convention and Event Tourism*, 7(2), 87–99.

Rogers, T. (2003). *Conferences and conventions: A global industry*. London: Butterworth-Heinemann.

Tourism Development Company. (2009). Facts and figures: Visitor arrivals data, stopover statistics 2002–2008. *Tourism Development Company*, Trinidad and Tobago.

Tourism Development Company. (2010). *Trinidad and Tobago convention bureau*. http://www.tdc.co.tt/convention_bureau.htm. Accessed 28 January 2010.

Weber, K., & Ladkin, A. (2004). Trends affecting the convention industry in the 21st century. *Journal of Convention and Event Tourism*, 6(4), 47–63.

World Travel and Tourism Council (2005). *Trinidad and Tobago: The impact of travel and tourism on jobs and the economy*. London: WTTC.

12 Weathering the Storm – Crisis Marketing for Small Island Tourist Destinations

Barney G. Pacheco and Acolla Lewis-Cameron

The University of the West Indies, St Augustine, Trinidad and Tobago, West Indies

Introduction

The tourism industry, by virtue of its character, is one that is especially exposed to crisis situations. For the majority of Small Island Developing States (SIDS), tourism is their main or sole earner of foreign exchange, and the industry thrives on a fragile resource base, the natural environment. The components of the tourism system of these islands therefore exhibit greater internal sensitivity than those of developed mainland destinations, and natural or man-made disasters can transform the reputation, desirability and marketability of these destinations overnight. For these reasons, the tourism industry is highly vulnerable to internal and external crises such as outbreaks of disease, crime and natural disasters. Global tourism crises are evidence that destination crisis marketing can no longer be treated as a problem confined to a few specific destinations; it is now a global issue. Since 11 September, destination crisis marketing has been moved beyond the cloisters of academia to become a critical economic, political and social priority for many nations in which tourism is a significant industry.

Given the economic significance of tourism to these island economies, any crisis invariably results in negative ramifications for the destination that ripple through the economy. Grenada is cited as an example where in 2004 hurricane Ivan completely destroyed the tourism industry, the very foundation of the economy. The volcanic eruption in Monsterrat in 1995 left the island destitute, while spiralling crime in the tourist centres of Ocho Rios and Montego Bay in Jamaica continue to negatively impact on the tourism industry. Every year, mainly during the hurricane season, the Caribbean region in particular is compelled to rally its forces to respond to a crisis. For island destinations, the unspoken question is 'who will it be next?' The fundamental challenge for island destinations at a time of crisis is maintaining a positive image of the destination and regaining the visitor's confidence in the destination.

At a time of crisis, marketing and promotion must become a higher priority as well as the leveraging of relationships with external agencies such as tour operators and aid agencies. Indeed, much of the previous literature on crisis management has been devoted to outlining strategies that can be used to counter emergent threats.

Marketing Island Destinations. DOI: 10.1016/B978-0-12-384909-0.00012-X

This chapter is not, however, simply another 'how-to' guide in dealing with a crisis but rather outlines a theoretical framework to assess the impact of crises on the brand equity of destinations and the speed with which these affected destinations will be able to overcome the threat to their long-term attractiveness. In so doing, the proposed conceptual model distinguishes between endogenous and exogenous crises, and addresses the ability of destinations that vary in 'destination equity' to cope with the crises. An important assertion of the present chapter is that while crises often evoke negative connotations, they also provide an opportunity for smaller destinations to strengthen their brand equity and establish their niche.

The Caribbean Tourism Environment

Small island states in the Caribbean have found it comparatively easy to attract tourists, and thus, the tourism industry has become the cornerstone of the majority of these island economies. Since the initial rush to develop tourism in the islands, tourism in the Caribbean has experienced exponential growth, and this trend is set to continue. In terms of international tourist arrivals, the Caribbean's share of world tourist arrivals is less than 2%, but this is triple that of South Asia's, more than double that of Oceania and bigger than that of South America or West Asia (Pattullo, 1996). Tourist (stay-over) arrivals in the Caribbean have grown by 70.5% over the past decade or at an average annual rate of 5.5%, which has been somewhat faster than the growth in international tourist movement worldwide (Caribbean Tourism Organization, 2001).

The tourism industry in the Caribbean depends on a delicate mix of a fragile natural environment and the hospitality of the locals. The natural attractions of these islands form the heart of the tourism resource base. They include year-round pleasant climates, relatively unspoiled beaches and reefs, and undisturbed and preserved natural environments such as wildlife, flora and fauna and mountains. These features and more are evident in the Caribbean islands ranging from the lush mountains of Jamaica to the tropical rainforests of Dominica and the historic plantation houses of Nevis. From a human resource perspective, the attitude of the locals towards tourism is crucial to the region's industry. The impact of tourism on these resources in the Caribbean has far greater implications than in the more developed mainland destinations. As Baum and Conlin (1995) observed, in small island states

> the influx of large numbers of tourists to an island destination is likely to have a more profound effect on the destination in cultural, social and environmental terms because of the destination's small scale.

Clearly, given the nature of tourism in the Caribbean, a crisis can damage the destination's infrastructure, jeopardize its image as a safe place to visit and have a devastating effect on tourism demand and consumer confidence. A mismanaged disaster can easily evolve into a long-term crisis for the local tourism industry. Through a domino effect, a tarnished image can threaten tourism sustainability, which, in turn, can threaten the area's long-term economic viability. With the notable exception of the Bahamas, however, Caribbean countries suffer from inadequate funding for destination marketing, and the majority of the monies dedicated to tourism are spent on promotion, not on research. A deep understanding of the nature of crises and the strategic options available to affected destinations are thus woefully lacking. In the next section, we provide a conceptual framework that facilitates a better appreciation of crisis events and offers guidance on the choice of a strategic response.

Crises and Tourist Destinations

Terrorism, natural disasters and political instability have come to dominate the discourse of contemporary media and international affairs. More importantly, their impact on tourism demand has become increasingly apparent, as has the importance of crisis management in tourism destinations. In fact, it has been global crises such as the 9/11 terrorist attacks on the United States and the Asian financial crisis that have caused much controversy and growing interest in crisis management theories and their application to tourism destinations (Aktas & Gunlu, 2005).

There are varying approaches to defining a crisis. For the purpose of this chapter, Beirman's (2003:4) definition is most appropriate. He defines a crisis as

> a situation requiring radical management action in response to events beyond the internal control of the organisation, necessitating urgent adaptation of marketing and operational practices to restore the confidence of employees, associated enterprises and consumers in the viability of the destination.

Aktas and Gunlu (2005) further indicate that there are different types of crises in tourist destinations. They suggest that one way of determining the type of crisis would be to look into its origin, scope, duration and motive. Table 12.1 depicts crisis types in tourist destinations with a focus on the damaging effect of the crisis.

As implied in the table, all crises have a detrimental impact on tourist destinations and deter tourists from visiting the affected destination. However, a noteworthy aspect of the Aktas and Gunlu (2005) framework is the recognition that not all crisis types lead to similar consequences, but differ from each other in terms of the scope and the extent of the damage caused. To better understand the issue, we can refine the model by distinguishing between endogenous and exogenous crises. *Endogenous* crises arise from within a specific destination and have an impact primarily on visitors to that destination. *Exogenous* crises, however, are triggered by events outside the destination and are beyond a destination's control. Examples of the repercussions that such exogenous crises can have include the impact of 9/11 on Caribbean economies and SARS on travel to affected Asian countries.

A limitation of this framework, however, is that it does not take into account the nature of the tourist destination when evaluating the impact of the crisis and seems to implicitly assume that the effects are ubiquitous across destination types. The focus of this chapter therefore is on the origin and scope of the crisis and their impact on Caribbean destinations that vary in 'destination brand equity'.

Table 12.1 Crisis Types in Tourist Destinations

	Damaging effect of the crisis			
	'Minimal'			**'Maximum'**
Origin of the crisis	Crisis in competitors		Crises in generating markets	Crisis in the destination
Scope of the crisis	Local	Regional	National	International
Duration of the crisis	One-time		Repetitive with intervals	Consecutive and ongoing
Motive of the crisis	Technological/environmental/sociocultural/economic/political			

Source: Aktas and Gunlu (2005).

Destination Brand Equity and Crises Impacts

The literature has clearly revealed that tourism is the lifeblood of the majority of islands in the Caribbean. Notwithstanding this, Caribbean destinations are at different stages in their tourism development. Butler's (1980) tourist area life cycle (TALC) can be used to illustrate this. The TALC asserts that the product is the destination and that destinations experience life cycles that are analogous to product life cycles. Thus, Butler (1980) argues that a destination goes through seven stages of development from exploration to eventual rejuvenation (see Figure 12.1). Based on the TALC, it is not difficult to view these destination 'products' as unique brands, which vary along a continuum of desirability and net worth. Further, it can be asserted that a brand's value (a destination's brand equity) changes as it moves from one stage of the TALC to the next.

Although the concept of branding has been applied extensively to products and services, tourism destination branding is a relatively recent phenomenon. There is general agreement among academics and practitioners, however, that places can be branded in much the same way as consumer goods (Olins, 2002). A destination brand can thus be considered as the sum of what potential visitors think when they hear the name of the destination. This, in turn, influences what travellers expect when they select one place over another and may be a key determinant when choosing between competing locations. In other words, a destination brand is the totality of perceptions that a customer holds about the experiences associated with a specific destination.

In addition to the utilitarian aspects of destinations – sun, beaches, etc. – a key dimension that travellers rely on to evaluate the attractiveness of specific destination brands is the overall image associated with the destination. Because of the intangible nature of the travel experience, destination image has been identified as a crucial factor in travel choice and tourism marketing (Dann, 1996). Because tourism centres are, by definition, places with high visibility, it is therefore not surprising that crises that affect popular destinations receive wide publicity. A negative image caused by a

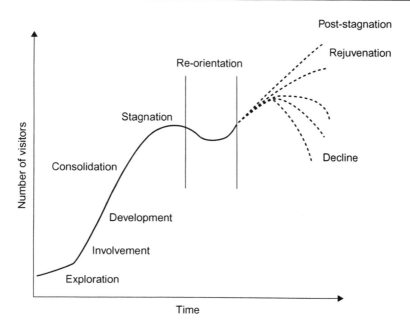

Figure 12.1 Modification of the Butler tourist cycle of evolution model.

tourism crisis may thus outlive physical damage and erode the positive associations that exist for that destination. This erosion of destination brand equity may actually cause more harm to a destination's tourism sustainability than the initial disaster itself.

Just as in the product domain, destination brands vary in their strength or general attractiveness. In this context, we use the term *destination brand equity* to refer to the extent to which a prospective tourist believes or perceives a destination is capable of providing a satisfying experience. The more favourable the image of a destination, the higher its equity and the greater its likelihood of being chosen as a preferred destination. It is important to note, however, that while high brand equity implies a favourable predisposition towards the destination, it is not an absolute guarantee that travellers will choose to visit the destination.

From a cognitive psychology perspective, brand equity is based on brand knowledge that consists of a variety of associations linked to a brand node in memory. Hence, brands with high equity are characterized by having a greater number of net positive and unique associations (Palazón-Vidal & Delgado-Ballester, 2005). In general, high-equity brands have perhaps been most often conceptualized via familiarity (e.g. prior knowledge or exposure to the brand), the favourability of associations (e.g. brand attitudes and brand desirability) or through outcome-oriented measures (e.g. market share leader), while low-equity brands have often been operationalized as the polar opposites of high-equity brands (Hoeffler & Keller, 2003). Destination brand equity is therefore fragile because it is reflective of travellers' perceptions and beliefs and can be prone to large and sudden shifts beyond the destination's control because of visitors' exposure to a crisis.

Although the repercussions of a tourism crisis are likely to negatively affect all destinations, the long-term damage can vary for each. A crisis, very often, generates substantial brand awareness and may succeed in creating negative perceptions about the affected destinations. This may be particularly problematic for high-equity destinations since, as Kent and Allen (1994) note, consumers may selectively pay more attention to information about well-known brands.

From the perspective of protecting brand equity, it may be judicious to focus on limiting damage to brand associations (Smith, Thomas, & Quelch, 1996). An identical response to a crisis can, however, have dramatically different effects on brand equity, depending on visitors' prior expectations about the destination. Researchers suggest that prior positive expectations create a ceiling effect, in the sense that new positive information cannot improve an already high positive evaluation. In similar fashion, a crisis setting, which provides negative information, may create a floor effect, whereby negative expectations for a low-equity brand means that a crisis will not significantly lower evaluations of the destination.

Ahluwalia, Burnkrant, and Unnava (2000) demonstrated that consumers who have a high level of commitment to a brand are more likely to counter-argue with negative information. Additionally, there is evidence that a strong positive brand image can mitigate the potential negative impact of a negative trial experience (Smith, 1993). With prior positive evaluations, cognitive evaluations should be more receptive and less critical for brands with which people have more experience (Chattopadhyay & Basu, 1990). This suggests that high-equity destination brands should be more resistant to crises. The expectancy disconfirmation framework (Yi, 1990) would suggest, however, that it is precisely these brands that would be most vulnerable to crises since the greater the expectation the more severe the dissonance created by performance failure. Visitors may come to expect more from a destination with high brand equity and be more disappointed or alarmed than if a similar crisis were to occur in a destination where expectations were lower.

In sum, visitors' existing positive expectations may provide destinations with a form of insurance against the potentially devastating impact of crises. For these destinations, brand equity may prove to be less fragile than initially expected. Conversely, destinations where expectations are more modest may have to undertake aggressive support for their brands simply to preserve brand equity.

Crisis Mitigation and Recovery

While it is important to observe and measure the impact of a crisis on Caribbean destinations, it may be myopic not to expect that the ability of these destinations to recover from the crisis may also be moderated by their brand equity prior to the event. While most destinations would respond to a crisis by implementing some form of damage control, visitor perceptions and prior experience with the brand may determine whether travellers perceive such actions as a credible signal that the problem is being effectively handled. In turn, this may impact on their willingness to continue to support the brand and consequently the speed with which the destination can recover from the effects of the crisis.

As Dawar (1998) suggests, crises may actually provide an opportunity for firms to enhance their brand equity by investing large sums in crisis management efforts and thus signalling their commitment to the brand. Further evidence to support this view is provided by Cleeren, Dekimpe, and Helsen (2008), who show that pre-crisis loyalty and familiarity offer protection against the ravages of a product-harm crisis. In similar fashion, destinations that have been ravaged by a crisis have an opportunity, through aggressive marketing campaigns, to successfully rehabilitate and even strengthen their brand image. The speed of this recovery depends to a large extent, however, on the destination's image prior to the crisis event.

A key challenge for destinations when faced with a crisis is the loss in trust in the ability of the destination to provide an enjoyable experience. Visiting a destination after a crisis has occurred may be viewed as an inherently risky decision by tourists, and differences in the perceived strength of the destination's brand equity may influence the speed with which that trust is regained. As such, we expect a positive impact of the destination's pre-crisis brand equity on the post-crisis willingness of consumers to visit that destination. We wish to argue, however, that the locus of responsibility for the crisis is likely to emerge as an important moderator of this effect. Specifically, while destinations with high brand equity may be most vulnerable to exogenous crises, they are also likely to recover the fastest from the effects of such crises. The interplay between brand equity and the speed of recovery in the aftermath of a crisis is thus more complex than a cursory analysis might suggest.

In the case where an external crisis affects all Caribbean destinations, as happened with the terrorist attacks of 9/11 in the United States, we expect that not only will the destinations with stronger brand equity be less affected by the crisis but that their speedier recovery may actually impede the recovery of destinations with lower brand equity. This cross-purchase effect is thus likely to further impede the speed with which those low-equity destinations are able to recover from the crisis, while it is unlikely that the reverse impact will be observed. These destinations also face an additional disadvantage in that they may need to invest the most resources to counter the effects of the crisis but typically have the fewest resources to do so, further slowing their rate of recovery. Moreover, we must be sensitive to the fact that not all destinations make a rapid recovery from crises. Oaxaca, Mexico, for example, is still struggling to recover from the impact of political turmoil that occurred in 2006.

Table 12.2 outlines the theoretical framework that underpins the previous discussion. We argue that although the repercussions of a tourism crisis are likely to damage all destinations, the extent to which specific destinations are harmed by a crisis is likely to vary depending on the locus of the crisis and the inherent brand equity of the destination. As prior research has established, however, brand perceptions are fluid and can change dramatically over time (Andrews & Kim, 2007). Destinations that have been negatively affected by a crisis thus have the ability to effectively manage the crisis and protect their brand image. Our model therefore suggests that a destination's resiliency in the face of a crisis and the speed of recovery in the aftermath of such threats will also depend on its brand equity. To the extent that the crisis is

Table 12.2 Impact of Crises on Destination Brand Equity

		Destination brand equity	
		High	**Low**
Origin of the crisis	Exogenous	Q1 – Negligible to minimal impact (very quick recovery)	Q2 – Minimal to moderate impact (slow recovery)
	Endogenous	Q3 – Moderate to severe impact (quick recovery)	Q4 – Moderate to severe impact (very slow recovery)

seen as temporary and unlikely to occur, the damage to visitor perceptions of high-equity brands is likely to be minimized.

Quadrant 1: High Destination Brand Equity/Exogenous Crisis

The impact of the crisis is likely to be minimal. The fact that the crisis is external to the destination suggests that visitors will attribute problems to forces operating outside the control of the destination and be tolerant of a negative experience. Additionally, since tourists already perceive the destination in a positive light, they are more likely to discount negative information about the destination. The net effect is that the destination's brand equity is only slightly tarnished and can be refreshed with minimal marketing efforts, leading to very rapid recovery.

Bahamas – 11 September Terrorist Attack

The Bahamian economy is very similar to that of Aruba in that tourism drives the economy. The main difference between the two islands is that the Bahamas is also dependent on the financial services sector. Travel and tourism contributes 50% to the Bahamian economy, and this proportion is expected to rise to 51.7% by 2019. The industry accounts for 1 in every 1.7 jobs or 62.7% of total employment (WTTC, 2009a). The Bahamas lies between 25 and 45 minutes away from the major south Florida markets by air, and 2.5 hours away from its primary New York/New Jersey markets. This proximity to the United States has resulted in a dependency on the US market as over 80% of the international arrivals to the island are from the United States. The challenge with this is that any major shift in the US market that affects US travel has direct repercussions for the Bahamian tourism industry.

The terrorist attack in the United States on 11 September sent a shock wave throughout the tourism industry in the Caribbean, but the Bahamas was among the most adversely affected Caribbean destinations – an estimated 33% decline in arrivals was recorded during the last four months of 2001.

Table 12.3 Tourist Arrivals in the Bahamas, 2001–2004

Year	2001	2002	2003	2004
Stay-over arrivals	1537780	1513151	1510169	1561312
Cruise arrivals	2551673	2802112	2970174	3360012

Source: Caribbean Tourism Organization (2004).

> The complete cessation of flights between the USA and the Bahamas occurred for the first time in history, in the days following this event. Hotels in the Bahamas emptied as soon as their US-bound guests arranged their return transportation home. Conventions, business meetings and pleasure travel were cancelled *en masse*, as paranoia about the security of air travel set in.
>
> Pratt (2003)

In order to avert a possible economic crisis in the Bahamas, the then Director of Tourism, Vanderpool-Wallace, coalesced the industry partners from the hotels, promotion boards, the government and non-government organizations to participate in an emergency action plan to address urgent issues. The immediate issue was not the restoration of faith in the Bahamas brand, but rather the boosting of arrivals to the destination as a result of the fear of flying. Some of the strategies employed by the Bahamas included placing sympathetic messages on behalf of the Bahamas in major media markets, use of new media tools and the pulling of advertisements in major markets, especially in geographic areas close to Ground Zero (Pratt, 2003).

The report for the Bahamas showed total recovery in visitor arrivals in under two years. Between 2001 and 2002, there was a 1.6% decrease in stay-over arrivals, followed by a further 0.19% decrease in 2003. Important to note in Table 12.3 is the continued increase in cruise arrivals during and after the crisis. This suggests that the more significant impact was with the stay-over passengers who were affected by the airborne terrorist attack. By 2003, there was a 3.3% increase in stay-over arrivals over 2002. The quick turnaround of the Bahamian tourism industry can be partially attributed to the swift and comprehensive response by the Director of Tourism. One can also argue that there was no long-term negativity attached to the Bahamian brand by potential visitors but rather a concern with the more global issue of the threat of terrorism.

Quadrant 2: Low Destination Brand Equity/Exogenous Crisis

The impact of the crisis is likely to be moderate but greater than in equivalent high-equity destinations. While all destinations may be affected by an exogenous crisis, we propose that lower-equity destinations will find it more difficult to enter consumer's evoked set since they will be perceived as not having the capacity to offer sufficient value-added to compensate for their greater risk. In the same way that a rising tide lifts all boats, the reverse is also true. In this case, less attractive destinations are less resilient and affected more by a crisis than high-equity destinations that have a buffer of positive associations to rely on. Recovery is likely to be slow.

Grenada – Hurricane Ivan, 2004

The Grenadian government developed a greater dependence on the tourism sector in recent years, with the decline of its agricultural sector that once dominated the economy. In 2009, the contribution of travel and tourism to gross domestic product (GDP) was 25% and employment in the sector accounted for 23.7% of total employment or 1 in every 4.2 jobs to 13 000 jobs (WTTC, 2009a). The island witnesses an influx of visitors mainly from the United States, United Kingdom and Canada. In 2004, 'Increases were recorded in arrivals from the major markets – Canada (92.5%), Europe (85.7%) and the United States (24.1%)' (Grenade, 2008: 197). Despite these figures, many argue that Grenada's tourism industry has remained on a small scale (Nelson, 2005) and has not risen to the heights of popularity enjoyed by many of its Caribbean counterparts.

Hurricane Ivan severely damaged the entire island of Grenada in 2004, with brutal winds in excess of 135 mph. Although there was no major loss of life, tremendous damage was done to the island's infrastructure, including homes, schools and hotels, the electrical distribution network and communications grid and the airport and seaport. Reports state that the southern portion of the island suffered the most damage. The Preliminary Assessment of Damages Report done by the World Bank in 2004 states:

> The tourism industry was particularly hard hit during Hurricane Ivan. … While beaches and shore areas remain intact, 70% of the supporting infrastructure has been damaged. Aside from the loss of infrastructure, the damages to the island's inland natural resources have diminished the appeal of the island.

Visitor statistics for Grenada from 2000 to 2003 show an exponential increase with an all-time high of 142 400 in tourist arrivals for 2003 (Central Bureau of Statistics, 2009). However, in 2004, there was a decline in tourist arrivals to 133 900. The destination felt the effects of the hurricane with a 26.6% decrease in the following year, with arrivals averaging at 98 000. The following years report a slow recovery for the tourism industry in Grenada, ranging from a 20% increase in 2006 and 8.84% in 2007. The destination has not been able to return to the exponential increase in visitor arrivals prior to Hurricane Ivan. Table 12.4 shows the arrivals before and after Ivan.

Varied efforts on the part of the Board of Tourism in Grenada have helped the tourism sector to stay afloat at the destination. The introduction of new activities at the destination and a focus on other markets, such as the diving and yachting markets, are some post-Ivan initiatives that have been used. However, the WTTC Tourism Impact Data and Forecasting Tool (2009c) reveals that tourist arrivals for this destination will not return to consistent growth until 2012 with an all-time high of 143 000 predicted for 2015.

Table 12.4 Tourist Arrivals in Grenada, 2002–2008

Year	2002	2003	2004	2005	2006	2007	2008
Stay-over arrivals	132 400	142 400	133 900	98 244	118 654	129 147	104 907

Source: Caribbean Tourism Organization (2004).

Quadrant 3: High Destination Brand Equity/Endogenous Crisis

The impact of the crisis is likely to be moderate to severe. Under this scenario, tourists view the destination very favourably and are likely to attribute blame to the destination when the crisis is 'home grown' rather than externally driven. Here, individuals are likely to question the validity of their previously held positive brand associations. The heightened media attention for these high-equity destinations is likely to further exacerbate the situation. One can also argue that for a destination with high brand equity, tourists are likely to have exceedingly high expectations about the experience they are likely to receive, and the disconfirmation of these expectations can exacerbate the image problem faced by the destination. While the short-term damage to the destination brand is likely to be higher than in a low-equity destination where expectations are lower, the prior positive associations enjoyed by the destination may provide a context that is used to assess the effects of the crisis. The speed of recovery is thus likely to be faster than in a low-equity destination as visitor evaluations gravitate towards their prior positive associations.

Aruba – Natalie Holloway's Murder

Tourism is the mainstay of the Aruban economy, contributing 67.1% to GDP. In employment terms, 1 in every 1.3 jobs is in the travel and tourism industry, which represents 78.6% of total employment, and 16.7% of total government spending is in travel and tourism (WTTC, 2009b). Without a doubt, there is a heavy dependency on the tourism industry to sustain the livelihoods of the locals. The United States is the main source market for Aruba, accounting for 75% of stay-over visitors to the island, with the remaining 25% divided between Europe, Canada, Venezuela and the rest of the world. Aruba's brand equity is notably high in the American market.

In 2005, Aruba's tourism industry was tainted by the alleged murder of a young American tourist. Natalee Holloway, an 18-year-old graduate of Mountain Brook High School in Birmingham, Alabama, travelled to the island with 125 members of her senior class. On Monday, 30 May 2005, she did not show up for her flight back to the United States. Without a crime scene, a body or a confession, the case of the missing schoolgirl was closed in 2007. From 2005 to early 2006, Aruba was badly hit by this incident, with the negative publicity leading to a 5.2% drop in visitor arrivals

Table 12.5 Tourist Arrivals in Aruba, 2004–2008

Year	2004	2005	2006	2007	2008
Stay-over arrivals	728 157	732 514	694 372	772 073	825 137 (est.)

Source: Central Bureau of Statistics (2009).

as compared to the steady increase in stay-over arrivals in previous years. According to Aruba's Minister of Tourism and Transportation, Edison Briesen,

> This incident has kept us 'hostage' for more than a year. In 2006, we even launched an ad campaign worth $5 million in the United States to counter the negative broadcast.
>
> Heyer (2008)

According to the WTTC (2009b), despite this highly sensationalized case, Aruba's travel and tourism sector is expected to report 3.3% per annum growth, in real terms, between 2008 and 2017. The year August 2005 to August 2006, as we have seen, saw a 5.2% decline in the number of visitors to the island, but from mid-2006 there has been a continuous increase in visitor numbers in line with what obtained pre-Natalee Holloway. Table 12.5 illustrates the arrivals over the period.

Minister Briesen was confident that Aruba had turned the corner in just over a year after the tragedy, and the United States remains the number one market for the island. Since 2007 the island has benefited from a massive refurbishment drive of hotels and transportation facilities, and the low-cost carrier Jet Blue now operates a direct service from Boston. However, although the arrivals figures are promising, Briesen is well aware that it will take some years before Aruba is once again seen as one of the safest places to visit in the Caribbean. In agreement, Rob Smith of the Aruba Hospitality and Security Foundation surmised, 'it's obviously affected our worldwide integrity, or at least our perceived integrity. ... I believe that long-term the world will know the truth about our destination.'

Quadrant 4: Low Destination Brand Equity/Endogenous Crisis

The impact of the crisis in this case is likely to be moderate to severe. In this context, tourists have low expectations about the destination's ability to provide an appealing experience. The endogenous crisis may therefore be perceived as consistent with these lowered expectations, and can act as confirmatory evidence supporting an unfavourable evaluation of the destination, thereby negatively affecting visitor arrivals. Moreover, the crisis event is likely to draw attention to the destination among an audience that may have previously been unaware of the destination's existence. Unfortunately, the associations that accompany this new-found familiarity in the wake of the crisis are likely to be negative, further eroding the attractiveness of the

Table 12.6 Tourist Arrivals in Montserrat, 1995–1999

Year	1995	1996	1997	1998	1999
Stay-over arrivals	18 000	9000	5000	8000	10 000

Source: Caribbean Community Secretariat (2003).
Air arrivals only – CTO estimate.

destination. Additionally, the lower brand equity of the destination makes it more likely that visitors will be sceptical about its recovery claims, and they are also less apt to respond favourably to marketing communications emanating from the destination after the crisis. This will serve to further slow the pace of recovery and may lead to long-term damage to the destination's brand equity unless aggressive recovery strategies are quickly implemented and sustained over time.

Montserrat – Volcanic Eruption

Montserrat had a thriving tourism industry prior to 1995, with earnings from tourism representing approximately 25% of the island's GDP (Caribbean Community Secretariat, 2009). In 1995, the Soufrière Hills Volcano in the southern part of the island began erupting following a three-year period of seismic activity that began in 1992. This eruption resulted in the first evacuation of southern Montserrat followed by the abandonment of Plymouth the following year. In 1997, a further eruption led to the closure of the island's main airport, the W. H. Bramble airport, the evacuation of more than half of the island's inhabitants and significant damage to the tourism industry's infrastructure.

The impact of the volcanic eruption had a significant effect on the tourist arrivals to the island, as shown in Table 12.6. There was a 50% decrease in stay-over arrivals between 1995 and 1996, while arrivals were at an all-time low in 1997, a 44% decrease from 1996, when the devastating impact of the volcanic activity was felt throughout the island. The stabilization of the volcano in 1998 exhibited a 50% increase in tourist arrivals when compared with 1997. Subsequently, there has been a slow but steady restoration of confidence in this sector as witnessed by an increase in tourist arrival figures by 1999 to 10 000, compared to 5000 visitors in 1997.

According to the Montserrat Tourist Board, the industry is now undergoing a revival, with the volcano representing one of the island's unique draws. The main objective of the Montserrat Tourist Board is the diversification of the tourism product in order to appeal to a wider market and to revitalize tourism as a significant contributor to the economy. An Exclusion Zone encompassing the Soufrière Hills Volcano has been in place and life has refocused to the north.

It should be noted, however, that the volcanic eruption in Montserrat destroyed much of the physical capacity of the island to accommodate tourists, and the effects of this event may thus be more extreme than in other low-equity destinations facing an endogenous crisis. In such places, the crisis may have a more moderate effect on arrivals than the current example indicates.

Conclusion

A major contribution of the current chapter is that, unlike previous studies, we focus attention on a critical contextual factor, destination brand equity, which can influence the impact and rehabilitation of a destination's image. In addition to creating a theoretical framework outlining the interplay between the locus of the crisis and a destination's brand equity, we also provide a broad cross-section of real-world examples to buttress our conceptual arguments. This serves to not only increase the external validity of our model but also provides a deeper understanding of the challenges facing destination marketers across the Caribbean. As part of crisis management planning within the various Caribbean destinations, destination marketers might reflect on the following questions about their destination brand:

1. What is the image of our destination brand among tourists, the travel industry and other key stakeholders?
2. What level of brand equity do we currently enjoy?
3. What type of crisis could our brand undergo?
4. How seriously would our brand equity be diluted by these crises, and how quickly could we recover?

By differentiating those crises that may inflict minimal damage from those that threaten the very viability of the tourism industry in a destination, destination marketers in the various Caribbean territories will be better positioned to determine the resources that may be needed to counter crises that develop as well as design marketing strategies that are appropriate for the level of threat posed by these events.

Discussion Questions

1. With reference to specific destinations, examine the ways in which a destination's brand equity can be impacted by a crisis.
2. Do destinations with the same level of brand equity get affected differently by a crisis depending on their stage in the TALC?
3. How helpful is the model in understanding both the shorter- and longer-term impacts of a crisis on tourist destinations?
4. How can the model be used to develop an appropriate marketing strategy for destinations in crisis?

References

Ahluwalia, R., Burnkrant, R. E., & Unnava, H. R. (2000). Consumer response to negative publicity: The moderating role of commitment. *Journal of Marketing Research*, *37*(May), 203–214.

Aktas, G., & Gunlu, E. (2005). Crisis management in tourist destinations. In W. F. Theobald (Ed.), *Global tourism*. London: Elsevier Butterworth Heinemann.

Andrews, M., & Kim, D. (2007). Revitalising suffering multinational brands: An empirical study. *International Marketing Review*, 24(3), 350–372.

Baum, T., & Conlin, M. V. (Eds.), (1995). *Island tourism: Management principles and practice*. Chichester: John Wiley.

Beirman, D. (2003). *Restoring tourism destinations in crisis: A strategic marketing approach.* London: CABI Publishing.

Butler, R. W. (1980). The concept of the tourist area life cycle evolution: Implications for the management of resources. *Canadian Geographer*, 14, 5–12.

Caribbean Community Secretariat. (2003). *CARICOM environment in figures 2002.* United Nations, New York: Caribbean Community Secretariat.

Caribbean Community Secretariat. (2009). *Montserrat: A profile.* http://www.caricom.org/jsp/ community/regional_issues/montserrat_profile_c1.jsp?menu=community. Accessed 8 February 2010.

Caribbean Tourism Organization. (2001). *Working document for the regional summit on tourism.* http://www.caricom.org/tourismdocuments.htm. Accessed 3 April 2006.

Caribbean Tourism Organization. (2004). *Latest tourism statistics.* www.onecaribbean.org/ content/files/2004Bahamasstats. Accessed 17 July 2009.

Central Bureau of Statistics. (2009). *General visitors statistics.* http://www.cbs.aw/cbs/ manageDocument.do?dispatch=view&id=1271. Accessed 16 July 2009.

Chattopadhyay, A., & Basu, K. (1990). Humor in advertising: The moderating role of prior brand evaluation. *Journal of Marketing Research*, 27(November), 466–476.

Cleeren, K., Dekimpe, M. G., & Helsen, K. (2008). Weathering product-harm crises. *Journal of the Academy of Marketing Science*, 36(2), 262–270.

Dann, G. (1996). Tourist's images of a destination: An alternative analysis. *Journal of Travel and Tourism Marketing*, 5(1 and 2), 41–55.

Dawar, N. (1998). Product-harm crises and the signaling ability of brands. *International Studies of Management and Organization*, 28(3), 109–119.

Grenade, W. (2008). An unwelcome guest – unpacking the tourism and HIV/AIDS dilemma in the Caribbean: A case study of Grenada. In M. Daye, D. Chambers, & S. Roberts (Eds.), *New perspectives in Caribbean tourism*. London: Routledge.

Heyer, H. (2008). US still drives business to Aruba after Holloway case closed, eTurbo news: Global travel industry news. http://www.eturbonews.com. Accessed 16 July 2009.

Hoeffler, S., & Keller, K. L. (2003). The marketing advantages of strong brands. *The Journal of Brand Management*, 10(6), 421–445.

Jenkins, C. L. (1997). Impacts of the development of international tourism in the Asian region. In F. M. Go & C. L. Jenkins (Eds.), *Tourism and economic development in Asia and Australasia* (pp. 48–64). London: Cassell.

Keller, K. L. (1993). Conceptualizing, measuring, and managing customer-based brand equity. *Journal of Marketing*, 57(January), 1–22.

Kent, R. J., & Allen, C. T. (1994). Competitive interference effects in consumer memory for advertising: The role of brand familiarity. *Journal of Marketing*, 58(July), 97–105.

Mather, S., & Todd, G. (1993). *Tourism in the Caribbean (special report no. 455).* London: Economist Intelligence Unit.

Mathieson, A., & Wall, G. (1992). *Tourism: Economic, physical and social impacts.* England: Longman Group Limited.

Montserrat Tourist Board (2010). *Volcano adventures.* http://www.visitmontserrat.com/index. php?categoryid=11. Accessed 8 February 2010.

Nelson, V. (2005). Representation and images of people, place, and nature in Grenada tourism. *Geografiska Annaler: Series B, Human Geography*, 87(2), 131–143.

Olins, W. (2002). Branding the nation – The historical context. *Journal of Brand Management*, *9*(4–5), 241–248.

Palazón-vidal, M., & Delgado-Ballester, E. (2005). Sales promotions effects on consumer-based brand equity. *International Journal of Market Research, Quarter 2, 47*(2), 179–204.

Pattullo, P. (1996). *Last resorts: The cost of tourism in the Caribbean*. London: Cassell.

Pratt, G. (2003). Terrorism and tourism: Bahamas and Jamaica fight back. *International Journal of Contemporary Hospitality Management, 15*(3), 192–194.

Sausmarez, N. (2004). Crisis management for the tourism sector: Preliminary considerations in policy development. *Tourism and Hospitality Planning and Development, August 2004, 1*(2), 157–172.

Smith, R. E. (1993). Integrating information from advertising and trial. *Journal of Marketing Research, 30*(May), 204–219.

Smith, N. C., Thomas, R. J., & Quelch, J. A. (1996). A strategic approach to managing product recalls. *Harvard Business Review, 74*(September/October), 102–112.

Weaver, D. B. (1998). *Ecotourism in the less developed world*. UK: CAB International.

World Bank. (2004). *Grenada-Hurricane Ivan preliminary assessment of damages*. http://siteresources.worldbank.org/INTDISMGMT/Resources/grenada_assessment.pdf. Accessed 8 February 2010.

World Travel and Tourism Council. (2005). *Trinidad and Tobago: The impact of travel and tourism on jobs and the economy*. London: WTTC.

World Travel and Tourism Council. (2009a). *Travel and tourism economic impact: Aruba*. London: WTTC.

World Travel and Tourism Council. (2009b). *Travel and tourism economic impact: The Bahamas*. London: WTTC.

World Travel and Tourism Council. (2009c). *Tourism impact data and forecasting tool*. London: WTTC.

Yi, Y. (1990). A critical review of consumer satisfaction. In V. A. Zeithaml (Ed.), *Review of marketing* (pp. 68–123). Chicago, IL: American Marketing Association.

13 The Competitive Island Destination

Acolla Lewis-Cameron * *and Sherma Roberts*§

*The University of the West Indies, St Augustine, Trinidad and Tobago, West Indies; §The University of the West Indies, Cave Hill, Barbados, West Indies

Introduction

The competitive destination is one that has the 'ability to increase tourism expenditure, to increasingly attract visitors while providing them with satisfying, memorable experiences, and to do so in a profitable way, while enhancing the well-being of destination residents and preserving the natural capital of the destination for future generations' (Ritchie & Crouch, 2003:2). Strategic marketing is an integral component to a destination achieving this status. Each chapter in this text has addressed a different aspect of destination marketing, and together they have presented a holistic understanding of the critical issues and challenges involved in marketing island states. Key strategies were also highlighted and provide a roadmap for marketers as island states seek to become or remain competitive in this volatile global marketplace. In this concluding chapter, emphasis is placed on delineating those proposed strategies that can be utilized by island states to assist them in further asserting their position in the global tourism environment.

SIDS Realities

The opening chapter of this book provided an overall context for the case discussions as it highlighted the unique environment within which island states operate. Small Island Developing States (SIDS) share features and experiences that set them apart from more developed mainland destinations. The distinct context of SIDS is captured in the differences in the role of tourism in the economy and the resources upon which the industry is dependent. In terms of the former, the tourism industry in many SIDS is the mainstay of the local economies, with a significant degree of foreign ownership. With respect to the physical and human resources, the industry thrives on a fragile natural environment, and because of the smallness of these islands the environmental impacts are more severe than on mainland destinations. These island economies are significantly affected by changes in the global environment.

In contrast to the vulnerabilities of SIDS, these islands possess significant strengths in the areas of democracy and improved standard of living and quality of

Marketing Island Destinations. DOI: 10.1016/B978-0-12-384909-0.00013-1

life that are vital conditions for the development of a competitive and sustainable tourism industry. For the twenty-first century and beyond, some SIDS may find that their peripheral geography may compromise their market share. This is particularly significant against the backdrop of increasing environmentalism. What is required here is that SIDS across the various regions engage in collaborative competition where critical resources are shared to gain market advantage. In the same way that the concept of twinning of cities across regions has evolved, SIDS can also look to twinning of destinations at a competitive price and value-added experience.

Strategic Marketing Response

Against a backdrop of a changing global marketplace and the specific context within which SIDS operate, it is incumbent on destinations to be proactive, resilient and strategic in their approach to marketing their destinations. Each case study has addressed pertinent issues and provided useful suggestions on appropriate strategic marketing options available to SIDS. Based on the case studies, three core strategic responses have been advanced. First is that destinations must have a clear understanding of their respective identity in order to navigate this changing environment. Second, destinations must engage in the effective use of marketing tools that are available in order to remain competitive. Third, a volatile environment demands that SIDS be prepared to respond strategically to any type of crisis. Each of these responses will be discussed in turn.

A Clear Identity

Many destinations are aiming to shape how the world imagines and perceives them by using seductive images and consistent marketing campaigns. For SIDS, the core issue is the potential tourist's ability to differentiate between islands given the similarity in the product offerings. Therefore, a competitive small island is one that understands who they are, who is their target market, and can effectively differentiate itself from its competitors and effectively communicate its message to the 2020 tourist. Central to achieving this goal is the development of an effective branding and positioning strategy.

The recognition that destination image is a major factor in destination success has led some tourist boards and resort marketers to consider applying branding to destination marketing. Marketing agencies at all levels have a vested interest in building strong and positive images for their destinations. However, the extent to which image-building benefits their targets can be greater if it takes place in the context of branding. The importance of destination branding is made clear by Morgan, Pritchard, and Pride (2004) when they stated that 'the battle for customers in the tourism industry will be fought not over price but over the hearts and minds – in essence, branding ... will be the key to success'.

The discussion on the islands of Norfolk, Barbados, Mauritius and North Cyprus underscores the importance of image development and destination branding in their respective contexts. In the face of an unanticipated decline in the market from the Builders' generation and an increase in market share among baby-boomers seniors, the Norfolk Tourism Authority recognized that change was inevitable for survival. At the core of the island's strategic response was a refreshing of its image and the rebranding of its product. There was a brand shift from 'Norfolk Island' to 'The World of Norfolk'. Aspects of the image that were previously seen as limitations were transformed into strengths to achieve very strong points of differentiation from competitors in the South Pacific.

In a similar vein, the island of Mauritius also experienced a decline in visitor numbers over a period of time, which prompted the tourism authorities to embark on a branding initiative in 2006, which, among others, had the goal of diversifying the image and repositioning the destination in its various target markets. The result of this rebranding process was the brand 'Mauritius' with the tag line 'C'est un plaisir', which was launched in October 2009. The findings from the Mauritius study revealed a key element in the image and branding process. The author noted that underlying motives play a significant role in influencing the decision process in comparison to cognitive images. Hence, destination marketers should have a thorough understanding of visitors' motives, and these should feature prominently in marketing and advertising campaigns.

In the Barbados context, the destination has benefited tremendously from a favourable image in its target market and a strong brand among its Caribbean neighbours. The destination's common reference as 'Little England' and the 'wintering ground of the rich and the famous' has been a catalyst for growth in tourist arrivals from the main source market of the United Kingdom. Unlike the need for rebranding in Norfolk and Mauritius, the Barbados Tourism Authority's mission is to strengthen the position of its brand in its key markets. While maintaining its upmarket image, Barbados shifted its promotional tag line from a global view of 'Just Beyond Your Imagination' to 'Experience the Authentic Caribbean'. Some of the key areas that contributed to the market position strengthening included variables such as customers' perception and satisfaction linked to the sun, sea and sand image and friendliness of the people.

Of the four cases, the island of North Cyprus presents the strongest case for the need for a clear identity. The island has not been able to maximize tourism's contribution to the economy owing to its international political and economic isolation alongside other challenges such as scarcity of resources, a comparatively small domestic market, difficulties in forming and running businesses and accessibility to markets to promote the destination and its products. Based on the North Cyprus experience, the case authors have come to the realization that 'only those destinations that have a clear market position and appealing attractions will remain at the top of consumers' minds when they book their holidays. In the highly competitive and dynamic global tourism environment, there is a need to develop a clear identity, or 'brand' based on reality, while also reflecting the core strengths and 'personality of its product'. With this in mind, the island is now seeking to carve a niche in specific target markets, notably nature–adventure trips, ecotourism, culture, education and health so as to gain some competitive advantage in its sphere of operations.

Underlying the three case discussions is the recognition that effective image development, destination branding and positioning of the destination are critical components in communicating the destination's message to its target audience. These components establish and reinforce in the mind of the target market the distinct identity of the destination. In all cases, these components were instrumental in differentiating the destination from its competitors. The Barbados case suggests that, 'for a truly strong market position it is necessary for a destination to differentiate itself from its competitors on meaningful attributes for the customer which offer a competitive edge'. Secondly, the components allow the destination to better align its destination offerings to the changing needs of the target market. In the Norfolk case, the author succinctly captures this idea when he states that 'in the normal course of events a brand that is based on an image that offers value to its intended target audience should succeed provided that the product is able to match the expectations that have been created by the brand'. Understanding the motives for destination choice is critical in this alignment process as highlighted in the case of Mauritius. Thirdly, as highlighted in all case studies, a destination's image and brand are not static elements and should be reviewed over time to ensure that there is always that alignment that is at the heart of a destination's competitiveness.

Effective Use of Marketing Tools

'If you are not online, you are not on sale.' This statement was noted on a World Tourism Organization site in 1999. In the 1990s, the strategic focus for destinations was ensuring that the destination was visible on the World Wide Web as the Internet in particular was revolutionizing the tourism industry as a whole. Ten years later, findings from the research conducted in Tobago reveal that just being visible on the Internet is insufficient to remain competitive. There has been a marked shift from ubiquity to presence. According to Gobe (2001), ubiquity is seen, but presence is felt. Successful e-marketing involves more than just dissemination of information, but rather embraces an emotional connection with the consumer. The role of the destination management organization (DMO) must be therefore redefined if it is to be a strong competitor.

Two noteworthy issues came to the fore in the Tobago case that are of significance to destination marketers. First, 'website quality is a critical step in driving online business'. Based on the case, an effective quality website must be easily accessible, usable, informative, attractive, credible and secure. As the most powerful communication tool in destination marketing, a paradigm shift is required on the part of island marketers to ensure that their websites meet and exceed these criteria in order to attract the 'new' consumer and to remain competitive.

Second, the role of the DMO is instrumental in this process. As noted in the chapter, 'the destination marketing system (DMS) developed must go beyond being merely a storage mechanism with information on attractions, suppliers and activities and allow for reservations, promotion and distribution, the provision of high-quality data on the region's tourism industry and products, links to other external systems, multimedia kiosks, call centres, interactivity that allows the consumer to build their own itinerary and the availability of the language of online visitors'. The message is clear: DMOs need to be more strategic, aggressive and targeted in the development of DMS at the destination.

Niche Product Marketing

Over the last two decades, many SIDS have turned to mass tourism as an economic panacea to either support or replace other industries, namely agriculture. As noted in the discussion on SIDS realities, destinations are challenged to develop in a more sustainable manner and to compete with emerging destinations that offer similar products. These two challenges, among others, have forced many SIDS to consider alternative tourism products. In order to remain competitive, the shift that is required on the part of SIDS is the effective development, management and marketing of niche tourism products to supplement any existing mass tourism activities. The four cases on Fiji, Hawai'i, St Kitts and Nevis, and Trinidad provide a useful insight into this shift and its related challenges.

In the Fijian case study, the high rate of foreign investment in Fiji's tourism indus- try, the high leakage to foreign investors and increasing local discontent over the low level of indigenous participation in the tourism industry led to the consideration of an alternative tourism venture in the form of village-based tourism, which would bring greater economic benefits to the rural indigenous Fijian community. Evidence from the case suggests that village-based tourism as an example of niche tourism has been successful in some communities, notably Yasawas, but not without concomitant chal- lenges. The examination of Olivia's homestay, the case under study, reveals that for SIDS the marketing of a niche product requires some level of training in destination marketing, access to the Internet as a key communication tool and training in the area of product packaging.

The Hawai'ian Islands have become known for a superior mass tourism 3S prod- uct since 1959. In fact, it has been argued that 'Hawai'i's success in developing tour- ism is much envied by other tourist destinations'. However, by the mid-1990s many scholars and community activists saw destination resort tourism as having stripped Hawai'i of its identity and culture and turned it into a non-place. Similar to the Fijian experience, the residents' attitude towards tourism was deteriorating as residents felt that not enough was being done to protect the cultural and natural resources of the islands. The destination marketers' response to this was a shift from marketing Hawai'i as a honeymooner's paradise to a sustainable eco-destination. The challenge for the Hawai'ian tourism authorities is striking that balance between consumer- oriented tourism and a new tourism based on maintaining a sense of place and build- ing respect.

The Caribbean islands of St Kitts and Nevis mirror the 3S product focus of Fiji and the Hawai'ian Islands. The competition from their Caribbean counterparts who possessed larger marketing budgets influenced St Kitts' decision to move away from the general interest market that promotes sun, sea and sand and to focus more on the specific niches of romance, diving and sports and events. The marketing of St Kitts as a tourist destination has become much more focused over recent years, as a result of the decision to reposition the destination in the marketplace.

Unlike Fiji and the Hawai'ian Islands, Trinidad's development and marketing of its niche product was not in response to the challenges of mass tourism. Trinidad finds itself in a unique position, whereby the destination is a newcomer to the tourism industry, although its sister island Tobago has been promoting mass tourism for several years. After more than 30 years of an almost exclusive reliance on the petroleum industry, the country is seeking to diversify into the tourism industry. Given the level of infrastructural development and the activities available in the destination's capital city of Port-of-Spain, the destination's marketers are of the view that the meetings and conventions product is an appropriate niche product that can be explored.

In the four cases discussed, the identified niche products are seen as a viable addition to the tourism offerings at the different destinations. The development of niche products gives destination marketers the opportunity to further differentiate their product offerings, expand their market share and develop in a more sustainable manner. The challenge for marketers remains the development of a consistent message that effectively captures the varied offerings of the destination without resulting in confusion in the minds of the potential target market on the identity of the destination.

Armed for Crisis

The tourism industry, by its very nature as described in the opening chapter, is highly susceptible to both endogenous and exogenous crises. The fragile nature of SIDS makes them more vulnerable to natural disasters. For these very tourism-dependent islands, crisis preparedness and recovery are critical to the survival of the industry. Much attention has been given in the literature to the development of comprehensive crisis management plans because for island destinations the unspoken question is 'who will it be next?' The recent global financial crisis in particular has forced destinations to engage more aggressively in strategic destination marketing to survive.

Although not delineating a list of strategies to treat with a crisis, the final case study points to the importance of being armed to respond accurately to a crisis. The thesis of the case authors is that although the repercussions of a crisis are likely to damage all destinations, the extent to which specific destinations are harmed by a crisis is likely to vary depending on the locus of the crisis and the inherent brand equity of the destination. By differentiating those crises that may inflict minimal damage from those that threaten the very viability of the tourism industry in a destination, destination marketers in the various Caribbean territories will be better positioned to determine the resources that may be needed to counter crises that develop as well as design marketing strategies that are appropriate for the level of threat posed by these events.

Conclusion

The survival of SIDS in the tourism industry rests heavily on their ability to be pro-active, aggressive and strategic in their planning, development and marketing initiatives. There has been no other time in history where the level of competition between emerging and long-standing destinations has been as fierce as what is being experienced currently. As a result, the issue of strategic destination marketing has taken centre stage in the battle for the tourist dollar. For SIDS with their relative strengths and inherent vulnerabilities, the issue is how to remain relevant, cutting-edge and sustainable in the midst of increasing competition.

The case studies discussed in this book provide useful insights into the peculiar challenges faced by SIDS in a constantly changing global marketplace. In terms of a strategic response, three areas have been highlighted as critical to an island's competitiveness, namely a clear definition of the destination's identity, the effective use of marketing tools and being prepared for a crisis. It is important to note that these identified areas are not exhaustive and their relative importance will vary from destination to destination. Notwithstanding this, the evidence from the case studies suggests that a competitive island destination is one that understands its context and strategically responds to the challenges of the global tourism environment by taking into consideration, albeit not exclusively, the core priority areas that emerged from the case discussions.

References

Gobe, M. (2001). *Emotional branding: The new paradigm for connecting brands to people.* New York: Allworth Press.

Morgan, N., Pritchard, A., & Pride, R. (2004). *Destination branding: Creating the unique destination proposition.* London: Butterworth-Heinemann.

Ritchie, J. R. B., & Crouch, G. I. (2003). *The competitive destination: A sustainable tourism perspective.* London: CABI.

Lightning Source UK Ltd.
Milton Keynes UK
28 January 2011

166543UK00001B/33/P